QASR IBRIM

THE CATHEDRAL CHURCH

97 EXCAVATION MEMOIR
Edited by J R Anderson

QASR IBRIM

THE CATHEDRAL CHURCH

BY

FRED ALDSWORTH

WITH CONTRIBUTIONS FROM
HANS BARNARD, PAUL DRURY

AND THE LATE
PRZEMYSLAW GARTKIEWICZ

EGYPT EXPLORATION SOCIETY
3 Doughty Mews, London WC1N 2PG
2010

LONDON

Sold at the offices of

The Egypt Exploration Society
3 Doughty Mews
London WC1N 2PG
www.ees-shop.com

A catalogue entry for this book is available from the British Library

ISBN 978-0-85698-190-6

Typeset by Fred Aldsworth
Printed by Commercial Colour Press Ltd,
Angard House, 185 Forest Road, Hainault, Essex, IG6 3HX

CONTENTS

List of Figures vii

List of Plates ix

Preface xiii

Introduction 1

PART ONE: THE EVIDENCE

Chapter 1: 1963 Season 9

Chapter 2: 1964 Season 21

Chapter 3: Excavations and investigations by P M Gartkiewicz 40

Chapter 4: The Standing Building 55

Chapter 5: The Architectural components 91

Chapter 6: The Bishop Miel or Mielkuda inscriptions 115

PART TWO: THE INTERPRETATION

Chapter 7: Pre-Cathedral Church occupation 122

Chapter 8: Period 1: The Cathedral Church
Phase 1 – The 'Great or Old' Church *circa* AD 600 126
Phase 2 – The Cathedral Church *circa* AD 700 136
Phase 3 – Later alterations (Bishop Miel or Mielkuda and the Bishop Timotheus burial of AD 1371-72) 142

Chapter 9: Period 2: Post-Cathedral occupation and collapse *circa* AD 1480 145

Chapter 10: Period 3: Pre-Mosque building *circa* AD 1520 146

Chapter 11: Period 4: The Ottoman Mosque *circa* AD 1570-1811
Phase 1 - Original Mosque 147
Phase 2 - Later Mosque 147

Chapter 12: Period 5: Later occupation 149

Appendix 1 The tombs at the west front of the tower, *by Fred Aldsworth.* 150

Appendix 2 Human burials in and around the Cathedral, *by Fred Aldsworth and Hans Barnard.* 152

Bibliography 155

List of Figures

(Please note that Figures 16 and 23-32 are also included on the CD at the rear of this report)

		page
Figure 1:	Map of Christian Nubia	1
Figure 2:	The location of Qasr Ibrim	3
Figure 3:	The location and site plan of Qasr Ibrim	3
Figure 4:	Somers Clarke's sketch plan of the Cathedral	6
Figure 5:	The record plan prepared in 1963	9
Figure 6:	Reconstructed plan of the mosque and excavation trenches	11
Figure 7:	Plan and section of Trenches A1 and A2	16
Figure 8:	Record plan of collapsed columns and capitals prepared in 1964	24
Figure 9:	Plan of the pre-Mosque building	25
Figure 10:	Record plan of the upper level of the crypts	27
Figure 11:	Record plan of the lower level of the crypts and a cross section	27
Figure 12:	Plan of the upper level of the original arrangement of the north and south crypts	30
Figure 13:	One of the two sketches of the black basalt object	32
Figure 14:	Plan of the lower level and section of the original arrangement of the north and south crypts	33
Figure 15:	Tentative reconstruction plan of the features in front of the west entrance	38
Figure 16:	Przemyslaw Gartkiewicz's plan of the Cathedral (also on the CD)	42
Figure 17:	The locations of the excavations in 1972-1978	46
Figure 18:	Key diagram identifying the positions of the elevation and section drawings	56
Figure 19:	Simplified plan, identifying the principal elements of the Cathedral	57
Figure 20:	System of wooden bracing in the ring beams	59
Figure 21:	Types of carpentry joint employed in the wooden bracing frames	59
Figure 22:	Simplified plan showing the relationship between the original and the later apse	66
Figure 23:	Ground plan of the remains of the Cathedral Church in the 1970s (also on the CD)	82
Figure 24:	Elevation drawings AA, BB and CC (also on the CD)	83
Figure 25:	Elevation and section drawings DD, E and FF (also on the CD)	84
Figure 26:	Elevation and section drawings GG and HH (also on the CD)	85
Figure 27:	Elevation and section drawings JJ, KK, LL and MM (also on the CD)	86
Figure 28:	Elevation and section drawings NN, PP, QQ and RR (also on the CD)	87
Figure 29:	Elevation and section drawings SS, TT, UU and VV (also on the CD)	88
Figure 30:	Elevation and section drawings WW and XX (also on the CD)	89
Figure 31:	Elevation and section drawing YY (also on the CD)	90
Figure 32:	Section drawing ZZ (also on the CD)	90
Figure 33:	The classification of granite capitals in Nubian churches	91
Figure 34:	Motifs employed on granite capitals in Christian Nubia	92
Figure 35:	Granite capitals, shafts and bases, with eight types of motif employed on the shaft	93
Figure 36:	A revised version of the record plan produced in 1964, showing the locations of the collapsed shafts and capitals	95
Figure 37:	Large capitals in red sandstone	100
Figure 38:	Small capitals, a column, a column base, and an impost in sandstone	101
Figure 39:	Arches and *voussoir*s over the doors to the crypts and the baptistery tank	102
Figure 40:	*Voussoir*s of Group 2	104
Figure 41:	*Voussoir*s of Group 3	104
Figure 42:	*Voussoir*s of Group 4 (Nos 39-42)	105
Figure 43:	*Voussoir*s of Group 4 (Nos 43-56)	106
Figure 44:	*Voussoir*s of Group 5	108
Figure 45:	Arcade mouldings	110
Figure 46:	Fragment of window grille	110
Figure 47:	Stone capitals in the Nubian Museum, Aswan	113
Figure 48:	Inscription No 1	116
Figure 49:	The Christian symbols perhaps associated with inscription No 1	116
Figure 50:	Ground plan of the Cathedral, showing the locations of inscriptions Nos 1-8 and 10	116
Figure 51:	Inscription No 2	117

Figure 52:	Inscription No 3	117
Figure 53:	Inscription No 4	117
Figure 54:	Inscription No 5	118
Figure 55:	Inscription No 6	118
Figure 56:	Inscription No 7	118
Figure 57:	Inscription No 8	118
Figure 58:	Inscription No 9	119
Figure 59:	Inscription No 10	119
Figure 60:	Inscription No 11	119
Figure 61:	Inscription No 12	120
Figure 62:	Inscription No 13	120
Figure 63:	Topography of the bedrock prior to the commencement of quarrying and building	122
Figure 64:	The extent of bedrock and of features exposed beneath the Cathedral Church	123
Figure 65:	Then relationship between the house (X-1), the stone wall, the exposures of bedrock, and the original (Phase 1) arrangement of the Cathedral Church	123
Figure 66:	A generalised section through the south side of the Cathedral Church, looking north, showing the surface of the bedrock and the made ground between it and the paved floor of the building	124
Figure 67:	Simplified plan of the original (Phase 1) Cathedral Church	128
Figure 68:	Part reconstruction drawing of the original Cathedral Church, showing the walls to their surviving height	128
Figure 69:	Alternative cross-sections of the Phase 1 *naos*, looking east	131
Figure 70:	Adams' architectural evolution of the Nubian church	132
Figure 71:	Gartkiewicz's outline of Nubian church architecture	133
Figure 72:	The common elements in the internal plan of Nubian churches	134
Figure 73:	The functional uses of spaces in Nubian churches	134
Figure 74:	Adams' Type 1a, based on the Cathedral Church at Qasr Ibrim and the actual plan of the building	135
Figure 75:	Other Nubian churches with a passage behind the apse	135
Figure 76:	Simplified plan of the reconstructed (Phase 2) Cathedral	137
Figure 77:	Part reconstruction drawing of the rebuilt (Phase 2) Cathedral	137
Figure 78:	Hypothetical reconstruction of the interior of the Phase 2 building	139
Figure 79:	Reconstruction drawings of the north and south elevations of the Phase 2 building	140
Figure 80:	Reconstruction drawings of the east and west elevations of the Phase 2 building	140
Figure 81:	Simplified plan showing the later (Phase 3) alterations to the Cathedral	142
Figure 82:	The pre-Mosque building	146
Figure 83:	The first Mosque	147
Figure 84:	The later insertions to the first mosque	147
Figure 85:	Sketch plan showing the burial chambers, tombs, and graves associated with the Cathedral	153

List of Plates

Plate 1:	David Roberts' view of Qasr Ibrim	3
Plate 2:	Francis Frith's photograph of Qasr Ibrim	3
Plate 3:	Qasr Ibrim from the north in the early 1960s	4
Plates 4-5:	Qasr Ibrim from the south in the early 1960s	4
Plate 6:	Qasr Ibrim from the south-west in 1992	4
Plate 7:	Qasr Ibrim from the south-east in 1992	4
Plate 8:	The south wall of the Cathedral, from the south-east	10
Plate 9:	The north wall of the Cathedral, from the north-west	10
Plate 10:	The junction in the north wall between original fabric and reconstructed masonry	10
Plate 11:	Blocked window and heightened masonry at the east end of the north wall	10
Plate 12:	The west wall of the surviving structure, from the north	10
Plate 13:	The west wall of the standing structure and tower, from the south-west	10
Plate 14:	The partially collapsed tower, from the north	11
Plate 15:	The interior of the building from the west	11
Plate 16:	The interior of the building from the south-west	12
Plate 17:	The interior of the building, from the north-west	12
Plate 18:	The interior of the building, from the south-west	12
Plate 19:	The remains of the south arcade, with the *mihrab* and *minbar* beyond it	12
Plate 20:	The *mihrab* and *minbar*	12
Plate 21:	Side view of the *mihrab* and *minbar*, looking west	13
Plate 22:	The remains of the passage created down the west side of the building, looking north	13
Plate 23:	The wall linking piers 6 and 7, looking north	13
Plate 24:	The standing from the earlier building and part of the south arcade	13
Plate 25:	Trench A1, from above	15
Plate 26:	Part of trench A1 and trench A2, looking west	15
Plate 27:	The remains of the earlier apse	15
Plate 28:	The north end of trench B, looking east into the apse	17
Plate 29:	The north end of trench B, showing the bottom of the standing column and part of the base	17
Plate 30:	The south end of trench B, showing the bottom of the east pier of the arcade	17
Plate 31:	Trench C2, looking east to the opening into the south crypt	17
Plate 32:	Trench F looking north in 1964	19
Plate 33:	Excavations in the nave, showing the lower part of the fill and the paved floor of the Cathedral	21
Plate 34:	Excavations in the north aisle, against the north wall looking west	21
Plate 35:	Excavations in the north aisle, against the north wall looking east	22
Plate 36:	Excavations in the south aisle, near the *mihrab* in the south wall and the adjacent *minbar*	22
Plate 37:	Excavations in the north aisle showing the large pottery vessel	23
Plate 38:	Closer view of the large pottery vessel found in the north aisle	23
Plate 39:	Collapsed column amongst occupation debris in the north aisle	23
Plate 40:	Excavations of the pre-Mosque building, looking east	24
Plate 41:	Excavations of the pre-Mosque building, looking west	24
Plate 42:	The interior of the nave, looking east	26
Plate 43:	The interior of the nave, looking south-east	26
Plate 44:	The interior of the nave, looking south	26
Plate 45:	The opening indicating the existence of a north crypt	27
Plate 46:	The pavement over the north steps	27
Plate 47:	The broken stele with cursive Meroitic script	28
Plate 48:	The burial of Bishop Timotheos	28
Plate 49:	The burial of Bishop Timotheos	28
Plate 50:	The two scrolls found during excavations	30
Plate 51:	The north stairs and north antechamber	31
Plate 52:	The north crypt, looking south	32
Plate 53:	The granite pedestal or altar in the north crypt	32
Plate 54:	The south antechamber, looking west from the south crypt	34
Plate 55:	The south crypt with graves S1-S4, looking north	34
Plate 56:	Graves S2 and S3, during excavation	35
Plate 57:	The undisturbed female burial in Grave S2	36

Plate 58:	The inserted baptismal tank, with the earlier recess behind it	37
Plate 59:	The earlier baptismal tank, from the south-west	37
Plate 60:	The earlier baptismal tank, from the south-east	37
Plate 61:	The footings of the earlier apse, looking north-east	45
Plate 62:	The occupation layers against the west wall of the sacristy	46
Plate 63:	The south end of the earlier wall separating the sacristy from the nave	47
Plate 64:	The north end of the earlier wall separating the sacristy from the nave	47
Plate 65:	The foetus burials, from the south	47
Plate 66:	The foetus burials, from the north	47
Plate 67:	Structures and pottery under the *haikal*, from the north	48
Plate 68:	The north section of Area 4	48
Plate 69:	The junction of the tribune and the standing apse, looking east	48
Plate 70:	The junction of the tribune and the standing apse, from the north, with the stele exposed	48
Plate 71:	Area 6 and the paving alongside it, looking east	49
Plate 72:	Area 6 and the paving alongside it, looking south	49
Plate 73:	Area 7, looking east, and the masonry exposed beneath the later paving	49
Plate 74:	Area 8, looking east, with the wall foundation on the alignment of the column bases	50
Plate 75:	Area 8, looking west, with the wall foundation on the alignment of the column bases	50
Plate 76:	Area 8, looking south-east, showing the wall foundation	50
Plate 77:	The threshold of the south door, as found, from the south-east	50
Plate 78:	The threshold of the south door after excavation, from the south-east	51
Plate 79:	The threshold of the south door after excavation, from the north-east and showing the wooden door socket	51
Plate 80:	The threshold of the south door after excavation, from the east and showing the door socket wooden door socket	51
Plate 81:	Investigations in the southern part of the exonarthex, looking south	51
Plate 82:	Investigations in the southern part of the exonarthex, looking south-east	52
Plate 83:	Foundations of the west wall adjoining the tower, looking south-east	52
Plate 84:	Foundations of the west wall adjoining the tower, looking south	52
Plate 85:	Foundations of the west wall of the west ambulatory, looking north	52
Plate 86:	Foundations of the west wall of the west ambulatory, looking east	53
Plate 87:	Foundations of the west wall of the west ambulatory, looking from above	53
Plate 88:	Foundations of the west wall of the west ambulatory, looking east	53
Plate 89:	The stone walls exposed under the south arcade, from the west	53
Plate 90:	The stone walls exposed under the south arcade, from the south	53
Plate 91:	The stone walls exposed under the south arcade, from the east	54
Plate 92:	Area 12, as excavated	54
Plate 93:	The remains of the Cathedral, from the south-west, in the 1960s	55
Plate 94:	The remains of the Cathedral, from the south-west, in 1992	55
Plate 95:	The south wall from the south-west	57
Plate 96:	Part of the south wall where it survived to its highest level	58
Plate 97:	The interior face of the south wall, showing the ring beam and beam slots	58
Plate 98:	The west end of the south wall	58
Plate 99:	Pilgrim scrapes on the south wall	58
Plate 100:	Detail of the phase 2 stonework	59
Plate 101:	Samples of marginally-tooled stones from the phase 2 reconstruction	59
Plate 102:	One of the window openings in the south wall	60
Plate 103:	The east wall, looking from the north-east	60
Plate 104:	The north wall from the north-west	61
Plate 105:	The east end of the north wall	61
Plate 106:	Evidence for burning on the north wall	61
Plate 107:	The south end of the west wall	61
Plate 108:	Remnants of mud brick vaulting in the north crypt	63
Plate 109:	Remnants of mud brick vaulting in the north crypt	63
Plate 110:	The south antechamber, looking east to the arched opening to the south crypt	63
Plate 111:	The south steps, looking up from the south antechamber	63
Plate 112:	The east end of the slot in the south wall	64
Plate 113:	The west end of the slot in the south wall	64
Plate 114:	The slot and rebate on the south steps, looking west	64

Plate 115: The north steps, looking down towards the north antechamber with the niches on the right side 65
Plate 116: The south steps, looking down with the niches on the left side 65
Plate 117: The south steps, looking up with the niches to the right side 65
Plate 118: The lower courses of the two apses, showing the threshold on the south side of the original apse 66
Plate 119: The threshold on the north side of the original apse 66
Plate 120: Part of the threshold on the north side of the original apse and the return of the original apse under the one 66
Plate 121: The later apse, from the west 67
Plate 122: The later apse, from the south-west 67
Plate 123: The tribune, from the west side 68
Plate 124: The tribune from the south side 68
Plate 125: The pilaster and recess for a lamp on the south side of the baptistry 68
Plate 126: The small column base in the baptistery, from the east 69
Plate 127: The small column base in the baptistery, from the south 69
Plate 128: The north entrance into the crypts 69
Plate 129: The south entrance into the crypts 69
Plate 130: The north side of the north arch, seated in the earlier beam slot 70
Plate 131: Some of the column bases on the south side of the nave, looking west 70
Plate 132: One of the large column bases 70
Plate 133: The Greek letter *alpha* inscribed on one of the column bases 71
Plate 134: Some of the paving in the nave 71
Plate 135: The east end of the nave, showing the *haikal* to the left 71
Plate 136: The *haikal* from the west 72
Plate 137: The post sockets and rod holes for the altar 72
Plate 138: The setting of post sockets believed to have supported a pulpit 72
Plate 139: The south-east corner of the *naos*, showing parts of the south arcade and the south wall 73
Plate 140: The part of the south wall containing the inserted *mihrab* 73
Plate 141: The south ambulatory, looking east towards the steps to the crypt 74
Plate 142: Composite photograph of the south arcade, after the third pier had been dismantled 74
Plate 143: The base of one of the piers in the south arcade and its smaller footing 74
Plate 144: One of the piers in the south arcade 75
Plate 145: A timber lacing beam in the south arcade 75
Plate 146: A timber lacing beam joint in the south arcade 75
Plate 147: The south arcade in 1963 76
Plate 148: Part of the east end of the south arcade 76
Plate 149: Part of the south arcade 76
Plates 150-2: Details of the south arcade 77
Plate 153: The north wall, looking east from near the west end 78
Plate 154: The east end of the north wall, showing the two phases of construction, the ring beam, and the jambs of two windows 78
Plate 155: The most easterly of the intermediate pier bases of the north arcade, from the south 78
Plate 156: The west wall of the *naos*, looking north-west 79
Plate 157: The two forms of construction seen on the external face of the west wall of the *naos* 79
Plate 158: The rectangular pier base at the south-west corner of the nave, looking west 79
Plate 159: The north wall of the south-west tower, looking south 80
Plate 160: The first flight of stone steps in the south-west tower 80
Plate 161: Part of the stone-vaulted chamber under the stairs in the south-west tower 80
Plates 162-3: Granite capital No 1 92
Plates 164-5: Granite capital No 2 92
Plates 166-7: Granite capital No 3 94
Plate 168: The granite shaft (C1) still standing on its granite base (B1) at the east end of the south aisle in 1963 94
Plate 169: The complete Type A granite shaft, presumably C6, during excavation in 1964 95
Plates 170-1: Variations in the mouldings on the tops of the Type A granite shafts 96
Plate 172: Some of the designs of the carved crosses on Type A granite shafts 96
Plate 173: The Type C shaft re-used in the burial chamber under the south-west corner of the Cathedral 97
Plate 174: The Type B granite base from the baptistery 98
Plate 175: The Type C bases re-used in the burial chamber under the south-west corner of the Cathedral 98
Plates 176-7: The large sandstone capital No 13 99

Plates 178-9:	The sandstone capital No 14	99
Plate 180:	Fragment from red sandstone capital No 15	99
Plate 181:	Fragments from red sandstone capitals Nos 16, 17, 20 and 21	100
Plates 182-3:	Fragments of red sandstone capitals Nos 18 and 19	100
Plate 184:	Fragments of red sandstone capital No 22	101
Plates 185-6:	Group 1 *voussoir* stones over the south and north doors to the crypt	103
Plate 187:	Group 2 *voussoir*s Nos 28 and 29	103
Plate 188:	Group 2 *voussoir*s Nos 30 and 31	103
Plate 189:	Group 3 *voussoir*s Nos 33, 36 and 37	104
Plate 190:	Group 3 *voussoir* No 35	104
Plates 191-2:	Group 4 *voussoir*s Nos 38, 39 and 40	105
Plate 193:	Group 4 *voussoir*s Nos 42, 50 and 54	107
Plates 194-5:	Group 4 *voussoir*s Nos 49 and 51	107
Plate 196:	Group 4 *voussoir* No 56	107
Plate 197:	Group 5 *voussoir* No 57	107
Plate 198:	Group 5 *voussoir*s Nos 58 and 59	108
Plate 199:	Group 6 *voussoir*s	108
Plate 200:	Group 6 *voussoir*s Nos 61-63 and 68	109
Plate 201:	Group 6 *voussoir*s Nos 65-67 and 71	109
Plates 202-3:	Arcade mouldings Nos 73 and 75	109
Plate 204:	Fragment of hood mould No 76, with surviving chevron decoration	110
Plate 205:	Stone capitals Nos 1 and 2 in 1963	111
Plate 206:	Stone capitals Nos 1 and 2, repositioned in the nave in 1964	111
Plate 207:	Stone capitals Nos 3-6	111
Plate 208:	Stone capital No 4	111
Plates 209-10:	Granite capital NM1, from a 1930s photograph and as displayed at the Nubia Museum, Aswan in 1992	112
Plates 211-12:	Granite capital NM2, from a 1930s photograph and as displayed at the Nubia Museum, Aswan in 1992	112
Plates 213-14:	Sandstone capital NM3	113
Plates 215-16:	Sandstone capital NM4	113
Plates 217-18:	Sandstone capital NM5	114
Plate 219:	The Miel or Mielkuda inscription on the Church on the Point	115
Plate 220:	The Miel or Mielkuda insciption No 1	116
Plate 221:	The christian symbols associated with Miel or Mielkuda inscription No 1	116
Plate 222:	Inscription No 2	117
Plate 223:	Inscription No 3	117
Plate 224:	Inscription No 4	118
Plate 225:	Inscription No 8	118
Plate 226:	Inscription No 10	119
Plate 227:	Inscription No 11	119
Plate 228:	Inscription No 12	120
Plate 229:	Inscription No 13	120
Plate 230:	Typical pilgrim carving on a re-used stone block in the Cathedral Church	126
Plate 231:	The two tombs during excavation in 1964	151
Plate 232:	Tomb 11 during excavation	151
Plate 233:	The *gebel* sandstone cliff to the south of the Cathedral	153

PREFACE

The Cathedral Church at Qasr Ibrim, first erected in about AD 600 and probably dedicated to the Holy Apostles, was the largest church in Nubia and survived to serve a Christian community in the area at least until the fourteenth century. It was subsequently abandoned, used by squatters, and then adapted first as a dwelling and then as an Ottoman Mosque, which remained in use until the site was abandoned in the early nineteenth century.

The archaeological, architectural, and historical study of the Cathedral Church at Qasr Ibrim was commenced by the Egypt Exploration Society in response to the threat to the whole site of inundation by the construction of the Aswan Dam, on which work had been commenced in 1960, and the creation of the huge reservoir, to be known as Lake Nasser, which was to flood much of Nubia. The work was undertaken as part of the British contribution to the UNESCO International Campaign to Save the Monuments of Nubia.

A modest season of recording and small scale investigation in 1963 was followed by a major season of excavation in 1964, both under the direction of the Revd Professor J Martin Plumley, during which all the later deposits and structures overlying the remains of the Cathedral Church were investigated and removed. In the 1970s Professor Przemyslaw M Gartkiewicz, who had previously been involved in the works of the Polish Archaeological Mission at Old Dongola, in Sudan, was involved in three seasons of investigations at Qasr Ibrim, during which he drew and photographed the remains of the Cathedral Church and undertook some small-scale excavations.

In 1988 Paul Drury was invited to assist with the interpretation of the structure by the then director of the Qasr Ibrim excavations, Dr Mark Horton, and he was joined in 1992 by Fred Aldsworth to complete the work commenced by Professor Gartkiewicz in the 1970s. By 1992 the fortified promontory site of Qasr Ibrim was almost entirely surrounded by water, save only for a very narrow strip of ground linking it to the mainland, and by 1995 and 1998, when some additional recording was undertaken, it had become an island. It now seems, however, that the Cathedral Church will not be submerged, although the remains have been the subject of vandalism, and of collapse due to water penetration.

Although several interim notes have been published about the building, this is the first attempt to provide a full report on the investigations of the building, and it includes studies both of the Cathedral Church and its later use for domestic purposes and as a mosque. It has been prepared by Fred Aldsworth, with substantial contributions on the description of the standing structure (Chapter 4) and on the interpretation of the Cathedral Church (Chapter 8) by Paul Drury. It is based upon original site notes, drawings, photographs, and typescripts pertaining to the work undertaken in the 1960s and 1970s, held in 2007 by the Egypt Exploration Society at the McDonald Institute for Archaeological Research and in a basement store at the Faculty of Oriental Studies, University of Cambridge, and these include the Plumley Archives. In 2008 all this material was transferred to the British Museum and is henceforth referred to in the text as 'the archive'.

Additional research has been undertaken by the writer, who is grateful to the former director of investigations at Qasr Ibrim, Dr Pamela Rose, for providing access to the original documentation and for her help and support in the preparation of this report.

It is inevitable that this report is based heavily on reports written as long ago as 1963 and, during the 1970s, by Przemyslaw Gartkiewicz for whom English was not his first language. Some terminology has changed over the intervening years; some dating evidence may be capable of re-interpretation[1]; and a few of the original reports are difficult to understand. Generally speaking, the original terminology and datings have been employed and copious use has been made of quotations from original descriptions where their interpretation may be in doubt.

Professor W Y Adams *Qasr Ibrim: The Earlier Medieval Period* (EES Excavation Memoir 89. 2010) was published too recently for its results to be taken into account in the preparation of this study

[1] None of the finds recovered during the excavations have been re-assessed for this publication, but it is noted that some additional information may be available in original notes or on record cards.

INTRODUCTION

Medieval Nubia

Ancient Nubia extended along the Nile valley and covered that part of modern Upper Egypt and the Sudan roughly extending between Aswan, to the north, and to about 250 kilometres south of Khartoum, to the south (Figure 1).

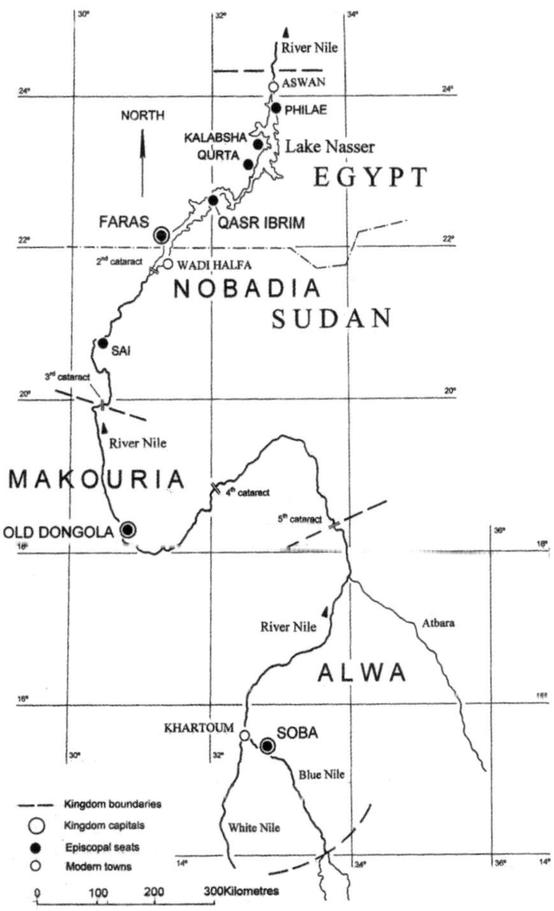

Figure 1: Map of Medieval Nubia.

It had formed part of the Kushite Empire, which existed for a thousand years, but this collapsed sometime before AD 350, bringing economic ruin and political chaos to what is now central Sudan. The effects were less severe in Lower Nubia, which was a frontier province, but the region became a battleground for local rulers and the fortified site of Qasr Ibrim changed hands several times (*Adams 1996*: 1-8).

In his publication on Qasr Ibrim in the late Christian period, William Adams has given an account of the historical and cultural setting of the site in the context of Medieval Nubia (*Adams 1996*: 22-26), and more recently Derek Welsby has published a detailed account of the conversion of Nubia and its eventual demise (*Welsby 2002*).[1]

By the latter part of the sixth century AD Medieval Nubia was divided into three kingdoms – Nobadia or Nobatia, named after the Nobadae tribe, extending from the First Cataract at present day Aswan to the Third Cataract at Hannek and with its capital at Faras and eventually with episcopal seats at Philae, Kalabsha, Qurta, Qasr Ibrim, Faras, and Sai; Makouria or Makuria, extending from the Third Cataract to the Fifth Cataract and with its capital and episcopal seat at Old Dongola; and Alwa or Alodia, extending from the Fifth Cataract to about 250 kilometres south of present day Khartoum with its capital and episcopal seat at Soba (Figure 1).

The usual date bracket attributed to the conversion of Nubia to Christianity is AD 540 to 580, and was the result of a series of missions led from Byzantium. The dates of conversion of the three Nubian kingdoms are generally accepted as Nobadia – AD 543; Makouria – AD 570; and Alwa – AD 580.

However, the people of Nubia had been exposed to Christianity some time before this, for in AD 524 the Byzantines pledged to supply the Ethiopian kingdom of Axum, which had declared itself Christian in the fourth century AD, with mercenary troops drawn from the Nubian tribes of the Blemmyes and Nobadae to assist in its invasions of Yemen. Thus, there was probably a Christian community in the Qasr Ibrim area of Nobadia by 550 AD and archaeological evidence from the site suggests that the Taharqo brick temple had been converted into a church 'nearer the beginning of the sixth century' (*Adams 1996*: 5 and see below Building No 287).

[1] Various sub periods and dates have been given in the past for the Medieval period in Nubia and not all these agree. For the purposes of this report the chronology adopted by William Adams and the Revd Professor J Martin Plumley in the 1960s is generally assumed, but has been adjusted to take account of Adams' divisions published in his volume on the later medieval period at Qasr Ibrim (*Adams 1996* Table 1). They are as follows :
Transitional AD 550-600; Early Christian I 600-750 (Adams subsequently has 700); Early Christian II 700 or 750 –850; Classic Christian I 850-950; Classic Christian II 950-1050 (Adams subsequently has 1172); Late Christian I and II 1050-1150 /1150-1250 (Adams subsequently has 1172-1400); and Transitional Christian latterly proposed by Adams as AD 1400-1500.

In AD 641-642 the Arab conquerors of Egypt tried to extend their domination into Nubia, but were repulsed by a strong Nubian army and, instead, agreed a peace treaty or *baqt* which was renewed in 652 following further aggressions. Christian Nubia then survived relatively intact as an entity, almost in isolation from the remainder of Christendom, for nearly a thousand years.

Over the centuries relations between the Nubian Church and the See of Alexandria were strong. In 1964 the discovery at Qasr Ibrim of the tomb of Bishop Timotheos of Faras, who died in 1371-2, revealed his instrument of episcopal consecration, at the hands of the Pope in the Church of the Virgin Mary Al-Moallaka ('the Hanging Church') in Old Cairo.

The Nubian churches soon began to develop their own architectural style and at Faras some magnificent wall paintings and stone carvings have been discovered, showing that they had a vibrant, but vernacular, iconography.

The late thirteenth century saw the gradual decline of the Nubian kingdoms. An Arab invasion in 1265 was the prelude to hostilities which led to the fall of Dongola and the capture of King David of Makouria. Over the next century the kings were effectively nominal, being clients of the sultans in Cairo who exploited the kingdom's internal divisions and a number of rival claimants. By 1315 the king had become a muslim and in 1365 the capital was transferred to Daw, presiding over a shrunken remnant known as the kingdom of Dotawo, although once more ruled by a Christian.

Less well documented is the decline of the southern kingdom of Alwa, although by the end of the thirteenth century there are references to its northern province as the kingdom of El-Abwab. Although distance spared it from attacks from the muslim armies of Egypt, Alwa seems to have fallen victim to attacks from nomadic tribesmen, the Funj from the south and the Abdallab Arabs. By the early sixteenth century its cities were in ruins and Christianity was no longer practised in Nubia.

Qasr Ibrim

As noted above, William Adams has suggested that an existing building at Qasr Ibrim had been converted into a church towards the beginning of the sixth century, though this can scarcely have been before the conversion of Nobadia in AD 543, and this may have been extended as a monastic complex shortly afterwards (*Adams 1996*: 5).

A major transformation subsequently took place when a new church, one of the largest in Nubia, was built at Qasr Ibrim in the most elevated position on the existing fortified, cliff-top site, and this was raised to the status of a cathedral when Qasr Ibrim was elevated to a Bishopric in the seventh century AD. [2]

The remains of Qasr Ibrim are located on the east bank of the, now flooded, Nile valley, about 160 kilometres south of Aswan, about 100 kilometres north of Wadi Halfa, about 50 kilometres north-east of Abu Simbel, and between a large bend in the river and, the now flooded, Wadi Tūshkah (Figure 2).[3] In the mid 1990s the Egyptian government commenced work on the creation of a new town alongside Lake Nasser and Wadi Tūshkah, almost immediately west of Qasr Ibrim, to be known as Tūshkah, Tushka, or Toshka. The development forms part of the New Valley Project which comprises the creation of a series of new lakes served by a canal cut from Lake Nasser, and the new town.

The fortified site was originally on the top of a tall outcrop of sandstone, rising to about 70 metres above the river, at the northern tip of a north-south promontory of high ground between two deep *wadis*. The highest exposure of natural sandstone on the site is under the south door of the Cathedral Church, and is at a height of about 183.6 metres above sea level (see also Chapter 7). The area enclosed by the defences, which were rebuilt on several occasions but always with the main entrance at the south-east corner, measured up to about 250 metres from north-south by 150 metres and contained about 2 hectares (Figure 3).

Both the main river valley of the Nile and the various *wadi*s which led into it have been inundated by the flood waters of the 485 or so kilometre-long Lake Nasser, an artificial reservoir created by the construction of the Aswan dam, on which work was commenced in 1960 and completed in 1971. By the mid 1990s much of the remains of Qasr Ibrim were covered by water and the higher ground at the south end, containing the remains of the Cathedral, formed a small island (Figure 3).

[2] Since there are doubts about precisely when the status was raised and when parts of the building were erected, the term 'Cathedral' is used only in places where the building is being referred to in a general manner and later in its life when it was known to have been in use as the seat of a Bishop. Otherwise the term Cathedral Church is employed to reflect those doubts.

[3] At latitude 22° 38' North and longitude 31° 59' East.

The site appears in several early views, prior to inundation but with the Nile in flood, and these include Thomas Legh's sketch, from the north, made in 1813 which is reproduced by Adams (*1996*: Plate 1b), and this can be compared with David Roberts' view from the north, produced in about 1844 (Plate 1); Francis Frith's photograph of 'The Traveller's Boat', being a view across the Nile, depicting the site from the north-west in about 1857 (Plate 2); and a photograph taken from the north in the early 1960s for the Egypt Exploration Society (Plate 3).

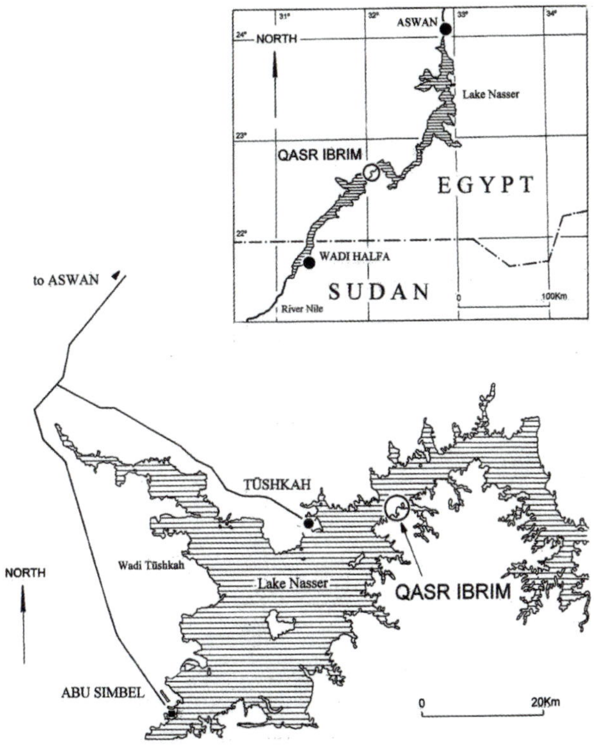

Figure 2: The location of Qasr Ibrim, showing the reservoir level in about 2005.

Plate 1: David Roberts' view of Qasr Ibrim, from the north, in about 1844.

Plate 2: Francis Frith's photograph of Qast Ibrim from the north-west in about 1857.

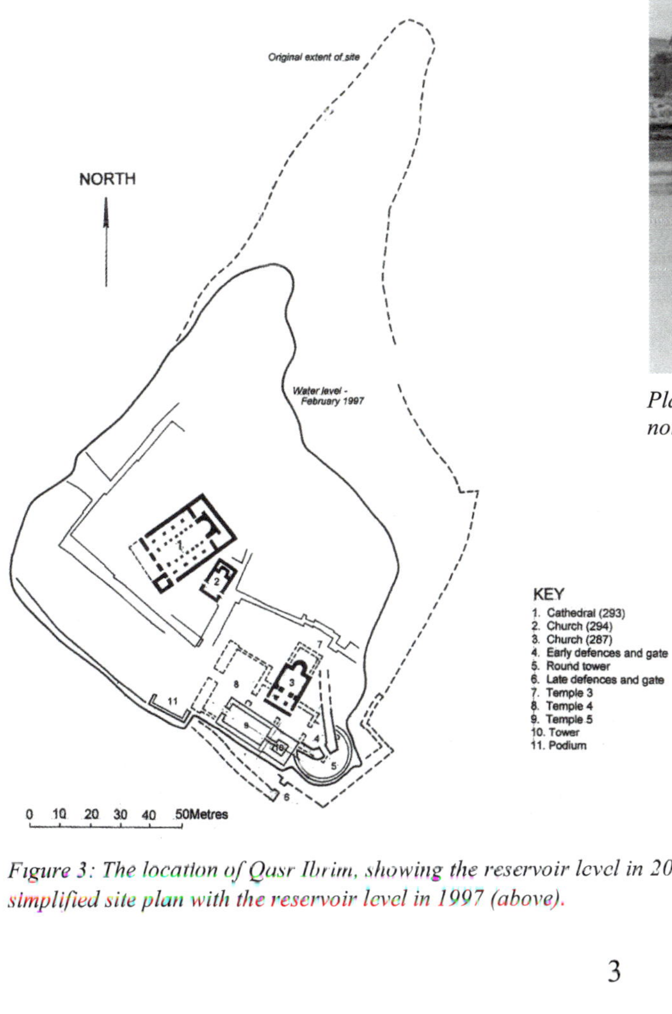

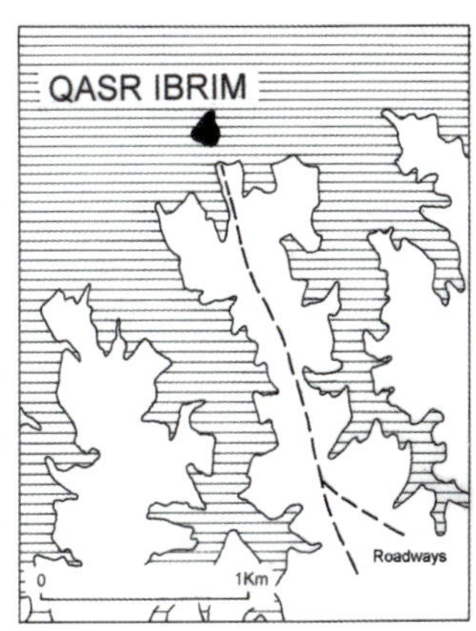

Figure 3: The location of Qasr Ibrim, showing the reservoir level in 2005 (right) and a simplified site plan with the reservoir level in 1997 (above).

Plate 3: Qasr Ibrim, from the north in the early 1960s (Unreferenced Egypt Exploration Society photograph).

A vertical aerial photograph taken prior to inundation recorded the site and the surrounding land to the south, the approach roadway, and the cemeteries to the west and south (see *Adams 1996*: Plate 1a and *Rose 1996*: Figure 1.1). Several photographs were taken of the site in the early 1960s and these include a general view from the south (Plate 4) and a closer view from a similar angle (Plate 5). These can be compared with views taken in 1992, from the south-west (Plate 6) and from the south-east (Plate 7).

Plate 4: Qasr Ibrim, from the south in the early 1960s (Unreferenced Egypt Exploration Society photograph).

Plate 5 : Qasr Ibrim, from the south in the early 1960s (Unreferenced Egypt Exploration Society photograph).

Although the level of the water in the reservoir has been allowed to rise several metres since 1992, it now appears that the remains of the Cathedral Church will not be submerged.

Plate 6: Qasr Ibrim, from the south-west in 1992 (Photograph by Fred Aldsworth).

Plate 7: Qasr Ibrim, from the south-east in 1992 (Photograph by Fred Aldsworth).

The fortified site was approached from the south by a roadway, and associated with this are a series of, what are believed to be, pilgrim foot outlines, some with Meroitic or Christian symbols and inscriptions, and on either side of it are a series of structures of varying dates (*Rose 1996*).

Historical resumés of occupation at Qasr Ibrim have been published by the British Museum (*James 1982*: 133-140); William Adams (*1996*: 1-8); and Pamela Rose (*1996*: 153-158 and *2007*: 1-4). Briefly, it appears to have been a place of some importance since at least the late New Kingdom, when during the Eighteenth Dynasty a temple was built on the summit which had been founded by the time of Tuthmosis III (1504-1450 BC) and was in use during the Twentieth Dynasty (after 1160 BC). Some time later, the penultimate king of the Twenty-Fifth Dynasty, Taharqo (690-664 BC), king of Napata, built a small temple on the site, which he dedicated to Horus of Miam – Miam being the fortified town on the opposite bank of the Nile, now modern Aniba.

Despite its modest size, the Taharqo temple remained in use for over 2000 years, first as a pagan shrine and later as one of Nubia's first Christian churches (see below and Figure 3 – Temple 3 and Building No. 287).

In the second or first century BC the site was fortified by the Ptolemaic rulers of Egypt, probably as a garrison town. The site is referred to as *Primis* in 23 BC, a name which survives as an inscription on a re-used block of sandstone in the east wall of the Cathedral, and for a short time it was a Roman garrison, taken from the Meroites and held from 25–21 BC by Augustus's general Caius Petronius. The name *Primis* was derived from the Meroitic name *Pedeme*, which was later mutated in Coptic texts to *Phrim* and then in the Middle Ages to *Ibrim.* The Arabic prefix *Qasr* 'castle' is a recent addition.

The Meroitic temple complex at Qasr Ibrim has been described and discussed by Pamela Rose (*2007*) and this includes detailed accounts of two of the Meroitic stelae found re-used in the Cathedral Church (*Edwards 2007*).

The site was re-occupied by Nubians in the Late Meroitic period, before the middle of the second century AD, and they repaired the Taharqo temple and extended it during the Ptolemaic period (Figure 3 - Temples 4 and 5). The balustraded platform in the south fortifications, known as 'the Podium' (Figure 3), has been dated to the Ptolemaic period and is believed to have been re-used as part of the Meroitic temple complex (*Rose* 2007: 9-11).

In the early X-Group period[4], *circa* AD 350, it was a major commercial and administrative centre, with a tight cluster of stone-built houses over most of the defended area.

As has already been noted, Christianity arrived in the area in the mid sixth century, and this was marked by the conversion of part of the old Taharqo temple to a church (Figure 3 – Building No 287) and then the construction of the 'Great Church' on the site of Meroitic structures and earlier X-Group houses, which had to be demolished to accommodate it, probably shortly after AD 550 (Figure 3 – Building No 293). It became a Cathedral Church when the site was elevated to a Bishopric in the seventh century AD.

Lower Nubia was invaded by the Ayyubid Shams ed-Dawla in 1172-73, which brought to an end more than five hundred years of uninterrupted peace between Christian Nubians and Muslim Egypt, made possible by the treaty negotiated after the Arab conquest of Egypt. The fortifications at Qasr Ibrim were rebuilt after the attack and the town was resettled and continued to thrive as a lively commercial centre at least until the middle of the fourteenth century, trading in a wide range of goods.

As will be seen, the Cathedral was rebuilt or repaired on several occasions, the latest possibly in about AD 960 or 1300, and it was certainly in use after 1323 at which time the ruler of the kingdom of Makouria was a muslim.

By the end of the fourteenth century Makouria ceased to exist and in its place were a series of warring principalities ruled by newly-arrived Arab nomads and a mysterious state called Dotawo. Textual finds indicate that Qasr Ibrim continued as the principal religious centre in Lower Nubia for a while, but the Dotawo period was a time of economic decline and by AD 1400 much of Qasr Ibrim had been abandoned. However, a leather scroll written in Old Nubian from Gebel Adda, the royal city of Dotawo, mentions that there was still a Bishop at Ibrim as late as AD 1484 (*Plumley Archive notes; Adams* 1977: 533).

Egypt was later conquered by the Ottomans and a garrison, believed to have been made up of Bosnian mercenaries, occupied Qasr Ibrim from about 1570. The Ottoman occupation continued into the beginning of the nineteenth century and during this time the remains of the old cathedral were refurbished as a mosque.

The Ottomans were finally evicted by Mamluk refugees in 1811, but a few months later the Mamluks were driven out and occupation of the site ceased. When the site was visited by Thomas Legh in 1813 it had been deserted.

Qasr Ibrim was visited by Somers Clarke in January and February 1894 and again in January 1899. His notebooks are preserved in the Somers Clarke papers, held at the Griffith Institute, Oxford.

[4] In order to avoid confusion, the term 'X-Group' is employed throughout this report, as this was used by the original excavators at Ibrim, although it is recognised that the term 'post-Meroitic' is now most commonly used for the period between the end of Meroitic and the beginning of the early Christian occupation of this area. The term 'Ballana' is also sometimes used.

The following notes and sketch (Figure 4) are taken from his Notebook O, compiled in 1899, and provide the earliest full description of the Cathedral on pages 68 to 78.[5] The comments in square brackets have been added for clarity.

> 'In the middle of the town stands a building rectangular in plan which has been a church and afterwards a mosque. There is a rectangular projection at the SE corner in which are the ruins of a stair.
>
> 'The lowest courses of the building are in stones of considerable size. Many are 1.40 metres long x 0.50 metres high. The lowest three courses are thus built. The courses of masonry above are in quite small stones. These are not however of a subsequent build and this is proved by the fact that at the NW & NE angles the large stones are carried up two or three more courses and the small ones are bonded in with them & so arranged that three courses of small stones range with one large or two with one as the case may be.
>
> 'At about 2.0 [metres] above the level of the floor of the building timber bond is [built] in the face shewing flush with the outside & inside of the wall. This bond timber are [sic] 10 x .18 laid flat (see sketch). At a height of 1.30 [metres] above the first range of bond timber lies a second set and between the two the window openings are arranged.

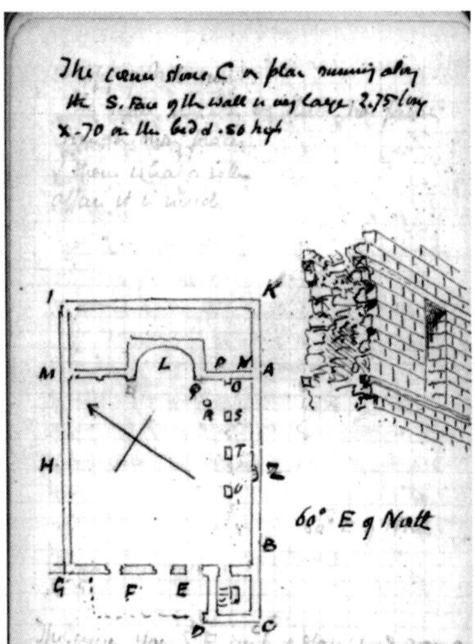

Figure 4: Somers Clarke's sketch plan of the Cathedral with his drawing of one of the windows.

> 'The ashlar on the outside face of the wall is neatly laid. The inner face is rough whilst in breaks in the wall it is too well seen that between these skins, the heart of the wall is of rough stones, chips & odds & ends set together with Nile mud, of which plenty is used. These walls have been easily overthrown being neither thick nor substantially built.
>
> 'The corner stone C in plan running along the S face of the wall is very large 2.75 [metres] long x 0.70 on the bed and 0.50 high.
>
> 'The wall with timber bond in it stands from A to B. Elsewhere it is too much ruined to show at this level.
>
> 'At D there seems to be a door jamb but the line of wall outward is quite gone. In build the base of wall is by stones they have in many places levelled up from below by putting in little ones. By grubbing out the small ones the spoilers have the more easily removed some of the large. Whether there was an atrium in front of the wall GE cannot now be seen. The pieces of wall E & F in which are door jambs are complete to a height of several metres & without timber bond. Against the face of this wall an earth platform has been set & the lowest courses are hidden, but at G big stones show once more standing on little ones.
>
> 'The outside face of the wall at G has been badly rebuilt, but the inner face is of the original ashlar.
>
> 'From G to H the wall has been completely overthrown to the bottom & built up again only using small masonry, most of it [illegible] old. From H to I the base course of big stones are perfect & a good deal of the wall above. Traces of timber bond are visible.
>
> 'From I to K the lowest & many of the upper courses remain. At the angle I the large stones are carried up seven courses [illegible] and at this point it is clearly to be seen that the smaller masonry is part of the original structure & bonded in with the larger. From K to A the wall remains the upper part much broken.'
>
> 'In a church which I think most undoubtedly [the] place was built for the building is not as well oriented as usual. It might be thought that its position was controlled by the foundation of an earlier building. This may be so, but [there] in so far as I see nothing to prove that any part of the existing structure is old foundations although of large stones.

---

[5] The author is grateful to Dr Pamela Rose for making this information available.

'The base of the wall is no thicker than the upper part. The base of an Egyptian wall [could] be three times as thick as are any part of these walls. I think the place has from the first been built as a church [illegible] if an older then a Roman building. Against this is the fact that we find timber bond in the rather thin walls that [for a] Roman work the masonry except the bottom courses, is small & the walls very ill built. That the timber bond is [halved] together exactly as we see it in early Arabic buildings.

'Then the spacing of the windows (which are not insertions) correspond exactly with the spacing of the arcades, & although rather worse built, the masonry of the walls & arcades corresponds in most respects.

'At the end opposite the door is the apse also in masonry, the walls of which stand up several metres high & are without timber bond. The space behind the apse in now subdivided by tumbledown walls of rough stone & mud. No traces of older walls are visible. No traces of a doorway into this part of the building can now be seen. The wall across the building at N [ie above the stairs to the south crypt] is of original masonry bonding in with the wall A [the south wall]. The lower part of the pilaster O is the same & I think the upper part above the abacus of the pilaster.

'The wall P has lost all its ashlar face. It may be a rebuild wall.

'At R stands a red granite column ill made with a cross on it in relief & a similar column has been used as a door sill in a neighbouring house. This column does not correspond with the spring of the apse, & on digging down I could not find that it stood on a base, but is merely planted in the ground, its base being below the floor level.

'STU are the piers of the [south] arcade. The arches just higher than round. The whole built of ashlar facing & the usual rubbish inside. The pier U has not the spring of another arch towards the west, but is carried up vertically. There is however a patch up. Judging by the window spacing there were two more arches.

'In the pier S & T timber bond has been built in at half the height & again under the abacus & under the abacus in the case of pilaster O.

'Stones with very [pretty] cross carved in relief are found on key stones to two of the arches & in the eastern arch two more are found half way up.

'In the other arches as in the piers are seen stones here & there with their faces carved with [strap] in knotwork evidently from some other & older building. The crosses are built in by intention where we see them.

'The Church. On the piece of timber bond inserted under the abacus of the north pier are traces of carving – a long leaf-like pattern. On another can be traced a pattern in circles with flowers in each circle.

'The rectangular piers carrying the arches are as ill built as the walls, ashlar facing but within mud & rubbish. The [illegible]-moulds of the [illegible] fit very ill to the abaci of the piers. I have no doubt that the building is not Roman. Its laid out from the beginning for a Church & it clearly was built when the Xtians were prosperous. The arcade is part of the original building. The detail is so simple that it may be very early, before the Arab conquest & is probably a very early example of an arch struggling towards pointed. There is to each arch a key stone & this conceals the degree of [pointedness] there is in the arches.

'The place was turned into a mosque. A *kibleh* [*mihrab*] was cut into the E wall at Z & clumsily formed with a decidedly pointed arch. On its right as we face it are the steps of a *minbar*.'

In 1910, or shortly afterwards, some repairs are believed to have been undertaken on the remains of the Cathedral, following a visit from the Director General of Antiquities in Egypt (*Adams 1996*: 12), but the extent of these works has not been ascertained.

The commencement of construction work on the Aswan High Dam in 1960 brought a threat of destruction to Qasr Ibrim and in 1961 a licence to excavate on the site was granted to the Egypt Exploration Society as a contribution to the International Campaign to Save the Monuments of Nubia.

The excavations were directed by the Revd Professor J Martin Plumley until 1976, who was assisted by Dr William H C Frend and later by Dr William Y Adams of the University of Kentucky and he continued to work on the site until 1984.

More recently the investigations have been directed by Dr Mark Horton from 1988 until 1995 and subsequently by Dr Pamela Rose until 2008.

The programme of work, which has been summarised by Adams (*1996*: 12-14), was commenced with the riverside cemeteries and in 1963 and 1964 moved to within the walls and began with an investigation of the Cathedral Church (see below Chapters 1 and 2).

In the period 1972-1978 the structure was further excavated and recorded by Przemyslaw M Gartkiewicz (see below Chapter 3) and in the period 1990-1998 further recording was undertaken on the standing structure and architectural fragments associated with it by Paul Drury and Fred Aldsworth.

The late medieval occupation of Qasr Ibrim has been described in some detail by William Adams (*1996*) and he has included summary descriptions of the Taharqa temple-church (Figure 3 Building No. 293 – *Adams 1996*: 69-73); the Cathedral (Figure 3 Building No 293 – *Adams 1996*: 73-78); and a further church immediately to the south of the Cathedral which has been completely demolished (Figure 3 Building No 294 – *Adams 1996*: 78-79).

The early documents found during excavations at Qasr Ibrim have been discussed by a number of writers including *Plumley 1975; Hinds & Sakkout 1986; Plumley & Browne 1988; Browne 1989 & 1991; Hinds & Ménage 1991;* and *Ray 2005.*

The two parts of this volume comprise a more detailed account of the evidence for the Cathedral Church - Part One, as derived from original excavation records and surviving material on the site, and then an interpretation of that evidence - Part Two, in terms of pre-Cathedral occupation; the construction and alteration of the Cathedral Church during the Christian period; and its subsequent abandonment and re-use as a domestic dwelling and as a mosque.

Appendices 1 and 2 then deal with tombs and burials associated with the cathedral.

PART ONE: THE EVIDENCE

Chapter 1: 1963 SEASON

The first season of excavations took place between the 20th January and the 26th February 1963.[1]

The works undertaken on the Cathedral Church appear to have comprised the production of a plan and a photographic record of the building, as found; the dismantling of some of the internal walls and stone piers; and the excavation of six trenches (see below Trenches A1, A2, B, C1, C2, and F). The work on the Cathedral was supervised and recorded by Dr George F Dales, assisted by Ali el-Kholy.

The archive documents relating to the work include a folder of drawings containing a record plan of the building, and details of the *mihrab*, the *minbar*, and the south arcade by Dales; descriptions of the *mihrab* and *minbar*; a diary; architectural notes by Plumley and Dales; photographs; albums of contact prints and negatives, including Dales' photographs (prefixed '63 GD') and Plumley's photographs (prefixed 'QI 63'); and an interim report.

In 1978, William Adams prepared a short typescript entitled 'Synoptic Notes on Churches – Supplementary Comments on the 1963 Excavations' and this includes a summary of the excavations in the Cathedral, based on the excavation notes by Dales, together with photographs, registered objects, and potsherds.

Using all this material, an attempt is made here to reconstruct the layout of the structures in the interior of the Cathedral as they existed at the commencement of the first season of work in 1963, and then to discuss the excavations undertaken at that time.

THE STANDING STRUCTURE

In 1963, all four external walls of the latest structure on the site survived intact or had been rebuilt to something like their original height (Figure 5).

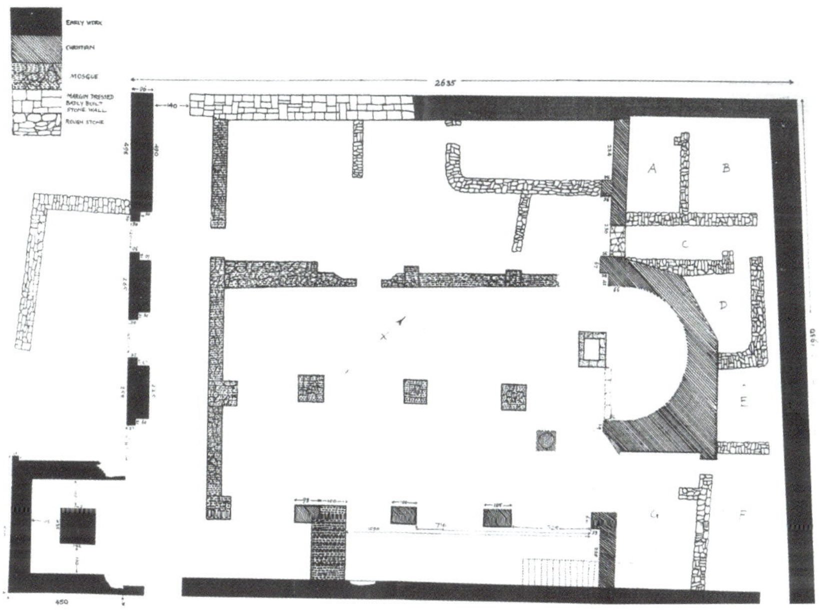

Figure 5 : The record plan prepared at the commencement of the 1963 season.

These included almost the entire length of the south wall, which had been rebuilt in part at its east end (Plate 8); the east wall; the north wall, which had been rebuilt at its west end for about one third of its length (Plates 9, 10 and 11); and the west wall, which was pierced by original openings into the former *narthex* (see below and Plates 12 and 13).

The tower at the south-west corner had partially collapsed by this time (Plates 13 and 14).

The record plan of the structures surviving in 1963 distinguished five phases of construction - 'early work' being the external walls of the Cathedral and the tower at the south-west corner; the 'christian' phase, including the later apse, the adjoining walls to the north and south, and the south arcade; the 'mosque' phase, being the inserted piers and linking walls; a later section of the north wall of the Cathedral which had been rebuilt; and, finally, 'rough walls' which appear to have been substantially later insertions.

[1] The works which were commenced in December 1963 are described under the 1964 season – see Chapter 2.

Plate 8: The south wall, from the south-east (EES Photo QI 63/1/1).

Plate 11: Blocked window and heightened masonry at the east end of the north wall (EES Photo QI 63/1/29).

Plate 9: The north wall, from the north-west. Note the change in construction of the wall part way along its length and the crude steps to the entrance in the foreground (EES Photo QI 63/1/27).

Plate 12: The west wall of the surviving structure, from the north. Note the inserted wall running inside and parallel to it (EES Photo Reference QI 63 1 24).

Plate 10: The junction in the north wall between the original fabric to the left and the reconstructed masonry to the right (EES Photo QI 63/1/28).

Plate 13: The west wall of the standing structure and the tower, from the south-west (EES Photo QI 63/1/30).

Plate 14: The partially collapsed tower, from the north (EES Photo 63 GD/I/9).

Within this outer shell, the apse, the walls separating the nave from the rooms to the north and south of the apse, part of the south arcade, and one standing column of the Cathedral Church survived.

THE MOSQUE

The archive contains a typewritten description of the late mosque as it existed in 1963, presumably compiled by Plumley and Dales, and some comments on its history. Below, the structure is described first from the evidence of the plan and photographs, and this is followed by extracts from the description prepared in 1963. The comments on the history of the building are included in Chapter 11.

There are some inconsistencies between the photographs and the plan produced at the time of excavations. Setting aside the 'rough walls', which appear to represent use of the building after the mosque had been reduced in size or abandoned, the remaining features comprise a series of inserted stone piers and stone walls dividing the interior of the building into a series of smaller spaces.

A pier at the west end of the south arcade and a line of four piers extending east-west across the body of the building were each a little over one metre square at the base, reducing in size as they rose above the floor level and were about four metres in height (Figure 6 Piers 1-5 and Plates 15-18).

Mirroring three of them to the north were three further piers (Piers 6, 7 and 8), each of about the same dimensions, but two of them (Piers 6 and 7) are shown much smaller on the plan, whilst the third (Pier 8) is not shown on the plan at all. It is clear from contemporary photographs, however, that all three existed and that they were all of similar size to those to the south. Given the layout of the other piers, there is a strong likelihood that a further pier had existed to complete a line of four (Pier 9), mirroring those to the south, though it does not appear on the plan and has not been identified in photographs. It is conceivable that it was removed when the later walls were added.

In his notes on excavations undertaken in 1964, Plumley refers to the fact that the mosque was built 'directly over its [the pre-mosque building's] foundations' (see Chapter 2) and, as far as can be determined, two of the pier bases (Pier 3 and Pier 4) appear to be very close to, if not directly on top of, two pier bases of the pre-mosque building (see below Piers B and C) and other masonry associated with that earlier building appears to have been incorporated into at least two of the later piers (Piers 6 and 7).

Some of the piers were linked by walls up to about three metres in height, and these appear to be later insertions, possibly at two different dates.

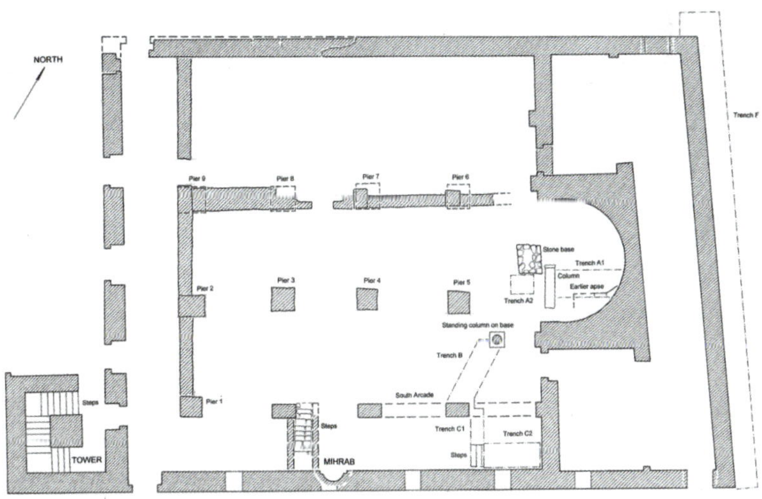

Figure 6: Reconstructed plan, showing the features associated with the conversion of the building to a mosque and the excavation trenches. Based on the 1963 record plan and photographs taken at that time.

Plate 15: The interior of the building from the west, showing the one standing column and some of the inserted piers and walls (EES Photo QI 63/1/25).

Plate 16: The interior of the building from the south-west, showing the one standing column, the south arcade, and some of the inserted piers and walls (EES Photo 63 GD/I/7).

Plate 17: The interior of the building from the north-west, showing part of the south arcade and some of the inserted piers and walls (EES Photo 63 GD/I /2).

Plate 18: The interior of the building from the south-west, showing the one standing column and some of the inserted piers and walls (EES Photo 63 GD/I/0).

The impression gained from the plan and photographs is that the area contained within the surviving walls, which was approximately 18 metres square internally, was converted for use as one large space, presumably intended as a mosque. It had entrances at the west end of the north and south walls and a roof supported on the external walls, the remains of the south arcade, one surviving standing column, and the nine inserted piers (Figure 6). The earlier apse of the Cathedral was evidently incorporated into the east wall of this structure, and had an earthen floor with traces of some paving on it.

The Cathedral's south-west tower may have been used as a *minaret,* and a niche or *mihrab* was inserted in a central position in the south wall. Immediately to the west of the *mihrab* was a flight of stone steps presumed to have been a pulpit or *minbar* built mostly from re-used margin-dressed blocks re-used from the walls of the Cathedral.

Plate 19: The remains of the south arcade, with the mihrab *and* minbar *beyond it to the right. (EES Photo 63 GD/I/3).*

Plate 20: The mihrab *and* minbar *(EES Photo QI 63/I/3).*

Plate 21: Side view of the mihrab *and* minbar, *looking west (EES Photo QI 63/I/4).*

At a later date the enclosed space was reduced in size, possibly on more than one occasion, by the insertion of dividing walls. A wall linking Piers 1, 2 and 9 and the north wall, and running parallel to and inside the west wall, appears to have been intended to create an external passage down the west side of a smaller building (Plates 12 and 22) and have reduced the enclosed space to about 15 metres east-west, entered by doorways towards the north and south ends of the west wall.

The opening at the north-east corner of the nave, which had previously given access to a room to the north of the apse, may have been blocked at about this time, whereas that to the south of the apse appears to have remained open but a dividing wall was at some time inserted into the room beyond it (Figure 5 and Plate 8).

Plate 22: The remains of the passage created down the west side of the building, looking north. The inserted wall is on the right (EES Photo QI 63/I/22).

Perhaps later still, Piers 6, 7, 8 and 9 appear to have been linked together by another inserted wall, reducing the enclosed space to about 15 metres east-west by about 11 metres north-south. This may have contained an opening directly opposite the *mihrab* (Plate 17 and 23).

Plate 23: The wall linking Piers 6 and 7, looking north (EES Photo QI 63/I/14).

The standing column from the earlier building appears to have survived *in situ* at this time (Plate 24). A small square stone base was set near the opening of the apse, which was originally tentatively described as an 'altar' (see Trench B below).

Plate 24: The standing column from the earlier building and part of the south arcade beyond it (EES Photo 63 GD/II/8).

The 1963 description of the surviving building includes the following remarks, in which the comments in square brackets have been added in light of the evidence referred to above.

'When the builders of the Mosque adapted the standing building remains of the Cathedral, the level of deposit in the building had risen to a level of just over 100 cms above the original floor. Since the south wall and its arcading were still standing, the task of constructing a simple flat roof of beams thatched over with reed matting was comparatively easy for the builders, who needed only to construct six [this should perhaps read nine] stone piers to carry the ends of the roofing beams and two walls, one on the west and the other on the north [probably added later], to enclose the area of the Mosque. The piers each about 105 cms square and the walls an average thickness of 60 cms were constructed of sandstone from the ruined Cathedral. Mud was used in lieu of proper mortar to bind the courses together.

'A pointed prayer niche or *mihrab*, 230 cms high and 85 cms wide was cut into the inner face of the south wall beneath the third window which had been partially blocked [Note: There are detailed drawings of the *mihrab* and *minbar*, prepared by G F Dales in February 1963, in the archives]. Since the Cathedral had not been orientated to the east, the axis of the apse being towards the north east, the south wall had been chosen as being nearer to the direction of Mecca. The niche forming the *mihrab* is semi-circular in section and 55 cms deep. It is lined with burnt red bricks (24 x 12 x 4.5 cms) and was originally coated with white plaster.

'The bottom of the *mihrab* had been formed by cutting into the top of one of the large blocks of sandstone upon which the courses of the smaller blocks of the south wall rested. Over the top of the *mihrab* a mason worked block projected from the blocking of the window above. A hole drilled in the end of this block may have been intended to act as a socket to hold a support for a hanging lamp.

'To the right of the *mihrab* a nine stepped pulpit or *minbar* had been erected. The two lowest steps abutted on to the third pier of the south arcading. Constructed very crudely from margin dressed sandstone blocks which certainly came from the Cathedral, the *minbar* rose to a height of 155 cms. The base was 285 cms long and 130 cms wide. A portion of a small red sandstone pillar bearing a couple of incised signs had been erected to the left of the lowest stair [possibly that surviving on the site in 1992 as two pieces – see Chapter 5, Figure 38, Nos 23 and 24]. It is, however, not possible to be certain if this portion of the pillar was an original feature of the *minbar* or had been erected quite fortuitously later. Its purpose is obscure. Possibly it might have been intended as a lamp stand.

'The floor of the Mosque was hard compacted earth which formed an effective seal over the levels beneath.

'The space between the enclosing north wall of the Mosque and the north wall of the Cathedral had been divided by roughly built stone walls to form four rooms. Likewise the area behind the apse and its flanking walls had been divided to form seven small rooms. It is, however, possible that these rooms may antedate the building of the Mosque and belong to the immediately preceding period. The space between the west enclosing wall of the Mosque and the triple entranced west wall of the cathedral had been left uncluttered to serve as a kind of vestibule.

'No attempt at any internal decoration of the Mosque seems to have been undertaken. The remains of some incised inscriptions in Arabic were noted but they do not afford any certain evidence for dating the building of the Mosque.

'When the work was undertaken, the tower at the west end of the Cathedral with little major adaption would have served as an elevated place from which to call the faithful to prayer. This would account for Çelebi's description of a minaret in the old style.'

At a later date, and possibly even after the mosque had been abandoned, walls were inserted in the north and east sides of the building, perhaps to provide domestic accommodation, and a suggestion has been made that these parts of the building may have formed a dwelling for the Imam.

THE EXCAVATIONS

The Cathedral was referred to as *Church 1* and also as *Building No 293* during the 1963 season.

The excavations appear to have commenced before the internal walls and piers had all been demolished and were undertaken both inside (Trenches A1, A2, B, C1 and C2) and outside the building (Trench F). The following comments are based on Adams' 'synoptic notes' which were prepared in 1978 from Dales' original notes and drawings prepared on site in 1963.

Trench A1

This was located within the southern half of the apse and was a little over 1 metre wide and up to about 3.5 metres long. Its east end was formed by the curve of the apse and its west end was formed by part of a granite shaft (Figure 6 and Plates 25 and 26). It was excavated down to and beyond the original floor level of the building.

Plate 25: Trench A1, from above. North is to the top of the photograph (EES Photo 63 GD/II/13).

Plate 26: Part of Trench A1 and Trench A2, looking west. The stone base can be seen to the right of the photograph, just behind the collapsed column (EES Photo 63 GD/I/10).

Dales prepared a plan of the trench with adjacent features; a 'west' section, which is in fact of the north side of the trench; and a drawing of details of the earlier apse. The archive contains copies of these drawings as photographs (*EES Photos QI 6/ 6/35, 36 and 38*). The drawings, together with that of Trench A2, have been merged and redrawn below (Figure 7).

Immediately north-west of the west end of the trench was a stone base, about 1.2 metres square, with a 'dirt fill', which Dales had tentatively identified as an 'altar' (Plate 26). Apart from identifying the substantial depth of soil over a plaster floor, the principal discovery in the trench was the remains of the footings of what has subsequently been confirmed to be an earlier apse beneath the one still standing (Plate 27).

Plate 27: The remains of the earlier apse (EES Photo QI 63/2/8).

Dales identified four 'levels' in Trench A1 and in light of Adams' comments and subsequent discoveries these can now be commented on further.

Level I was about 20 cms thick and comprised a fine, wind-blown deposit, over compacted occupation debris, which included stone fragments and reed matting, but no pottery was recovered. It presumably represents the latest occupation in the building.

Level II was about 50 cms thick and appeared to be occupation fill with a compacted upper surface, probably the floor of the mosque, which sealed the stone base or 'altar' beneath it. Since the fill included part of a large granite column and three fragments of smaller red sandstone columns, it must post-date the abandonment and collapse of the Cathedral. The date given by Adams to the latest pottery in this deposit is after 1350 and he gave a date bracket of *circa* 1350 to 1500 for its deposition.

Immediately under Level II were the remains of a hard, white plaster floor which now appears, on comparative grounds, to represent part of a Late Christian or post-Christian refurbishment of the building. It was not separately numbered in 1963 but is referred to here as floor level IIA (for further discussion see below).

Level III was a deliberate fill of stone and brick, up to about 170 cms wide and 130 cms deep, at the east end of the trench and is thought to be part of an extensive artificial platform constructed as a foundation for parts of the east end of the Cathedral using debris from Meroitic and X-Group houses which had formerly occupied this part of the site. It included some X-Group pottery and early Christian wares and was tentatively dated by Adams to perhaps *circa* AD 600.

Level IV was attributed to the foundations of the earlier apse, but no dateable material was found here.

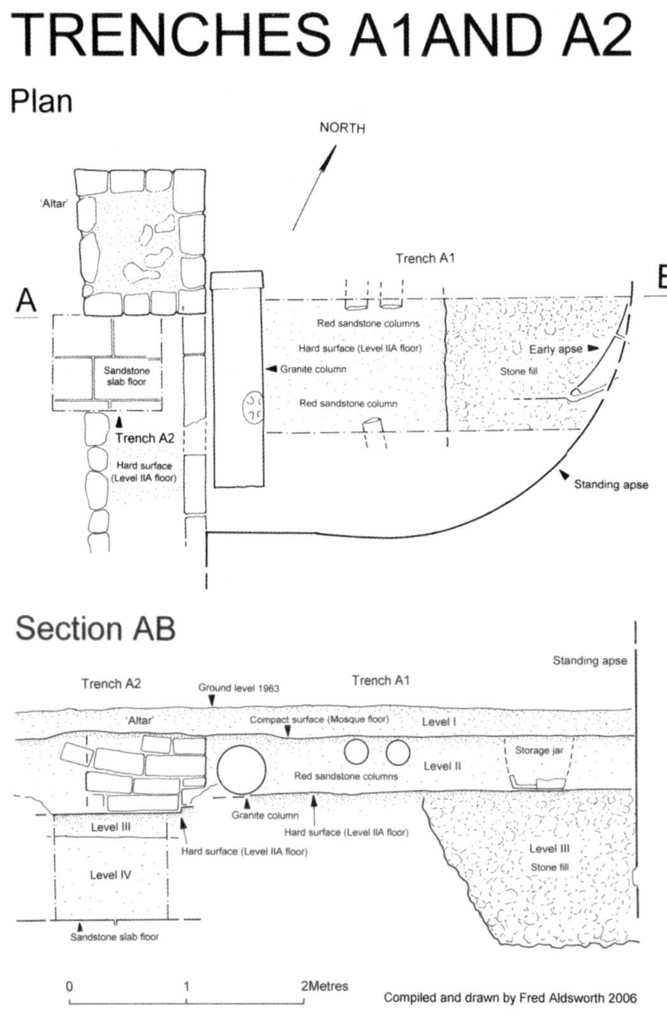

Figure 7: Plan and section of Trenches A1 and A2 Based on Dales' 1963 drawings.

Trench A2

This was a western extension of Trench A1 into the east end of the nave of the Cathedral. It was immediately south of the stone base noted above. It measured about 90 cms east-west by 80 cms, and was excavated down to the sandstone slab floor of the Cathedral (Figures 6 and 7, and Plate 26).

Dales prepared a plan of the trench and a drawing of the north section, though the latter does not include all the levels noted, and the archive holds a photograph of this drawing (*EES Photo QI 63/6/37*).

Level I was about 5 cms thick and is believed to have been post-occupation debris, presumed to correspond with Level 1 in Trenches A1 and B.

Level II was about 50 cms thick and appeared to be occupation debris mixed with ash and straw.

Immediately under Level II were the remains of a white plastered floor, on which the stone base and some stone paving were set. As in Trench A1, it was not separately numbered in 1963 but is referred to here as floor level IIA (for further discussion see below).

Level III was about 20 cms thick and consisted mostly of stone chips. It is seen as a bedding layer for the floor and it was suggested by Adams that it may have been a intended to bring the floor level in the nave up to the same level as that in the apse. It can probably best be seen as part of a late or post-Christian refurbishment of the building.

Level IV was about 70 cms thick and comprised refuse which included straw, ash, animal droppings and small stones but, evidently, no pottery sherds. It appeared to Adams to be the same as Level II in Trench B, which is dated to the late Christian period or later.

Level V equates with Level IV in Trenches B and C1 and was identified as the sandstone paved floor of the Cathedral.

Trench B

This was a narrow trench, about 1.5 metres wide and up to 3 metres long, which extended diagonally across the inner south aisle of the Cathedral, from the base of the only standing column to the east pier of the south arcade. It was excavated down to the sandstone slab floor of the Cathedral (Figure 6 and Plates 28, 29 and 30).

Dales drew a dimensioned sketch plan and a section along the south-east side of the trench and a photograph of his drawing is held by the archives (*EES Photo QI 63/6/39*).

Plate 28: The north end of Trench B, looking east into the apse (EES Photo Reference 63 GD/I/5).

Plate 29: The north end of Trench B, showing the bottom of the standing column and part of the base. (EES Photo 63 GD/II/10).

Plate 30: The south end of Trench B, showing the bottom of the east pier of the arcade (EES Photo 63 GD/II/11).

Four levels were distinguished in the trench.

Level 1 was about 10 cms thick and of fine wind-blown material, as in Trenches A1 and A2.

Level II was also about 10 cms thick but of compacted material thought possibly to be the floor level of the mosque. Pottery sherds included early, late and post-Christian pieces.

Level III was about 94 cms thick and was made up of occupation debris similar to that in Level IV in Trench A2. It included a few late and post-Christian pottery sherds, none dateable to before AD 1200, to which Adams assigned a date range of AD 1200 or later.

Level IV was the paved floor of square-cut sandstone slabs of the Cathedral.

At its north end the trench exposed the bottom of the standing column and part of the base on which it was standing (Plate 29) and at the south end it exposed the bottom of the east pier of the arcade (Plate 30).

Trench C1

This was cut across the outer south aisle of the Cathedral, from the most easterly pier of the south arcade to the face of the south wall. It was about 60 cms wide and about 2.7 metres long (Figure 6).

Dales prepared a plan of the trench and the archive contains a copy of this in the form of a photograph (*EES Photo QI 63/6/40*).

The levels encountered in Trench C1 were described as essentially the same as in Trench B. Level III contained a few late Christian sherds and the deposit was dated by Adams to 1350 AD and later.

At the bottom of the trench the excavations encountered a pavement of irregular flagstones at the same level as the square-cut slabs in Trench B.

Trench C2

This was an extension of Trench C1 to the east, along the south wall of the Cathedral, in order to expose the stone steps leading down to the south crypt (Figure 6 and Plate 31). It was about 1 metre wide and about 2.5 metres long.

Plate 31: Trench C2, looking east to the opening into the south crypt (EES Photo 63 GD/II/1).

Only three levels appear to have been recorded in this trench. The first (Level I) was about 115 cms thick and appears to correspond to Levels I-IV in Trenches B and C1. The next deposit (Level II) was up to 250 cms thick, without any bedding or occupation surface, and appears to have been a loose fill deliberately intended to cover the stairs and fill the space above them, thus obscuring the opening into the south crypt. The few pottery sherds retrieved were Late Christian, and Adams assigned a probable date for the deposit of AD 1200-1350. A further deposit was described by Dales and Adams suggested that it was probably at the bottom of the stairs and ascribed a Late Christian date of AD 1150-1200 to the pottery contained in it.

A number of objects were recovered from the deposits in Trench C2 and these were described by Dales as:

Level I	63/34	Five reed pens
	63/42	Paper with Arabic writing
Level II	63/11	Wooden key
	63/12	Late Christian cooking bowl
	63/13	Bronze bowl
	63/28	Late Christian saucer lamp
	63/29	Late Christian saucer lamp
	63/30	Late Christian saucer lamp fragment
	63/31	Late Christian cup lamp fragment
	63/32	Classic Christian saucer fragment
Level II	63/38	Paper with Greek inscription
	63/40	Paper with Coptic inscription
	63/41	Christian ostrakon
	63/138	Gourd fragment with incised decoration
	63/146	Wooden key handle
Others	63/33	Wooden spindle
	63/148	Perforated wooden block
	63/152	Wooden spoon handle

Discussion

Given that the remains of Bishop Timotheos were buried in the fill above the north crypt steps shortly after he died in AD 1371 or 1372 (see Chapter 2), it can be reasonably assumed that both the north and south crypts had been abandoned and, at least partly, filled by this date. This would seem to correlate with the dating ascribed by Adams to the fill over the south steps of about AD 1150-1200 (Level III) and AD 1200-1350 (Level II).

There is a problem, however, with the dating of both the Level IIA white plaster floor or floors that were encountered, at slightly different but probably contemporary levels in Trenches A1 and A2, which might be Late Christian or post-Christian in date, and the possible floor encountered as Level II in Trench B and C1, which was thought to belong to the mosque.

The white plaster floor or floors found in Trenches A1 and A2 were not observed in Trenches B, C1, and C2 and may be unique to part of the east end of the nave and the apse, and none of the floor surfaces observed and, indeed, none of the stratigraphy, was related to the internal piers and walls before they were removed. The plaster floor in Trench A1 did, however, appear to pre-date the collapse of the stone columns of the Cathedral but this is by no means certain. All the other large granite shafts were found in the 1964 season lying on the stone paved floor of the Cathedral and the one in Trench A1 could have been re-located here at a later date, some time after the Cathedral had collapsed and after the floor had been laid. The plaster floor appears to have been intended to support the stone base, which was centrally placed in the opening of the apse and may conceivably have been the base for a small altar serving the Late Christian Cathedral.

The thick deposits beneath the identified floors, which are presumably to be interpreted as deliberate build-up, are variously dated to the Late Christian period or later (Level IV in Trench A2), AD 1200 or later (Level III in Trench B), and AD 1350 or later (Level III in Trench C1).

On balance it is probably safest to assume that the plaster floors observed in Trenches A1 and A2 were contemporary; that they were perhaps unique to a small area or areas of the building; that they date to the late Christian period; and that they were a late modification to the east end of the nave and the apse, which included the provision of a small stone altar. The reason for raising the floor surface in the nave by some 90 cms at this time is not clear.

The possible floor encountered in trenches B and C1 is much more likely to belong to the mosque.

Trench F

This was excavated alongside the external face of the east wall of the Cathedral Church for its entire length and extended around the north-east corner to the adjoining portion of the north wall. It was about 1 metre wide, about 20 metres long, and was carried to a depth of 150 to 200 cms in order to expose the foundations of the building (Figure 6 and Plate 32).

Plate 32: Trench F looking north in 1964 (Unreferenced EES photograph).

It revealed that the foundations of the Cathedral Church had been laid in a trench which was cut through an older, Meroitic or X-Group, building subsequently designated as House M-2 and X-2.

The following comments are essentially Adams' 'synoptic notes' based upon Dales' field notes.

Dales had evidently indicated that four stratigraphic levels could be recognized in the trench, but no relative depths were indicated in his notes and no drawing appears to have been prepared. The levels were designated as I - Bosnian; II and III - Islamic, and IV - Christian Nubian, but this reading was not confirmed by the sherd collections seen by Adams, which contained material only for levels I and II. The registered objects, listed below, included X-Group, Christian, and post-Christian items, but the sherd material seen by Adams was overwhelmingly X-Group, with a small admixture of Early Christian pottery and nothing later.

Adams thought that it was noteworthy that Early Christian sherds were somewhat more numerous at Level II than at Level I; i.e. the expected stratigraphy was reversed. He thought that this was probably due to the fact that the collections from these two levels were taken from different parts of the trench, there being no effort to separate the collections on the basis of horizontal controls.

The collections from both levels, but especially Level II, therefore, probably included fill material which was thrown into the Christian foundation trench when the Cathedral Church was built, mixed with occupation deposit from the underlying X-Group house.

Adams' reading of the evidence was that there was an X-Group house (House X-2) on the site, which was already deeply filled with X-Group refuse before it was cut through by the foundation trench for the Cathedral Church. Earth which was used to refill the trench after the building of the Cathedral Church included some early Christian sherds. Objects of later than early Christian date, which are recorded from Trench F, must have either been from the surface or present due to subsequent disturbance of the deposit. Adams was adamant that there was definitely no evidence of occupation in the Classic or Late Christian periods in this area.

The registered objects from Trench F were as follows:

Level 1	63/144	Mouth of X-Group amphora with mud stopper attached
Level II	63/18	Pottery beaker of unfamiliar ware, probably pre-Christian
	63/20	Base of pottery lamp, X-Group or Early Christian
	63/22	Wooden spindle whorl
	63/23	Leather strap with tooled decoration, possibly Christian
	63/24	X-Group pottery lid
	63/25	Spindle whorl made from pottery sherd, perhaps X-Group
	63/27	Classic Christian embossed sherd
	63/39	Part of a Christian letter on paper
	63/147	Notched wooden peg
	63/150	Lathe-turned wooden furniture piece
	63/151	Wooden archer's loose fragment, possible X-Group
Unstratified		
	63/26	Islamic glass bracelet fragments
	63/145	Piece of shaped wood, probably part of a door bolt mechanism
	63/154	Point of a wooden peg
	63/159	Perforated disc of bronze, possibly Islamic
Surface find		
	63/19	X-Group pottery goblet

SUMMARY OF 1963 EXCAVATIONS

The following comments are based on Adams' 'synoptic notes'.

The very limited trial excavations carried out within and alongside the building in 1963 did not reveal a great deal about the Cathedral Church, but the following observations can be made :

1. The foundation at the east end of the Cathedral Church was laid in a trench cut down through earlier buildings (Houses M-2 and X-2), as revealed in Trench F. The absence of very early Christian deposits here suggested that the building of the Cathedral Church took place early in the Christian period, but not actually at the beginning of it.

2. The surviving apse was built upon the dismantled foundations of an earlier apse, which were revealed in Trench A1.

3. The south crypt and steps of the Cathedral Church were kept open and clear of refuse until the end of the Classic Christian period. They were then filled in the Late Christian period, as revealed in Trench C2.

4. If the Level IIA floor identified in Trench A1 represented the original floor of the apse, then it was nearly one metre above the original paved floor of the nave revealed as Level IV in Trenches B and C1. It seems more likely, however, that the Level IIA floor was contemporary with that added in the nave which was identified in Trench A2.

5. In the Terminal Christian period a new, hard white plastered floor, revealed in Trench A2, was laid in the east end of the nave at almost the same level as that in the apse, with which it is probably contemporary, but on top of a substantial accumulation of refuse. A small stone base was laid on top of this floor, possibly as the base for an altar.

For a fuller discussion of the interpretation of the features revealed in 1963 see Chapters 7-11.

Chapter 2: 1964 SEASON

The second season of excavations took place between the 21st December 1963 and the 26th February 1964, and the results were summarised in an interim report published in 1964 (*Plumley 1964*: 3-5).

The work on the Cathedral was under the general direction of Professor Plumley and supervised by William H C Frend, who was assisted by Kenneth Frazer and Ali el-Kholy. Archive documents relating to the work include a folder of drawings; various diaries and notebooks; a report on survey and architecture by Frazer, which includes a detailed description of the building; photographs (those of Frend prefixed WF); and albums of contact prints and negatives.

The excavations undertaken inside the Cathedral during this season were very extensive and included the removal of any surviving remnants of the internal walls and piers of the Mosque; the excavation of all the deposits inside the nave and aisles of the building down to the level of the stone-paved floor, which were up to 1.6 metres thick and contained the collapsed granite columns; the excavation of the fill of the north crypt, including the removal of the burial of Bishop Timotheus and the investigation of the graves cut in the crypt floor; the excavation of the south crypt, including the investigation of the graves cut in the crypt floor; and the investigation of the room to the south of the apse, which was then referred to as the south sacristy.

A space about 1.5 metres wide was cleared around the outside of the building and this showed that the Cathedral Church had been built partly on the solid sandstone bedrock and partly on an earth platform over the foundation walls of earlier structures. At the east and west ends of the building these included parts of Meroitic and X-group buildings, that at the west end had been modified in the Early Christian period and then filled with soil and rubble to form part of the foundation platform (*Plumley 1964*: 4).

Two brick tombs located immediately west of the west tower were also excavated in the 1964 season (see Appendix 1).

THE NAVE AND AISLES

The removal of the deposits from within the main body of the building was a large undertaking, since they comprised an estimated 480 cubic metres of soil, masonry, and domestic refuse.

It would appear from photographs that, following the removal of the last vestiges of the internal partitions and piers of the Mosque, the interior of the building was laid out as a series of large trenches and that the intention was to excavate these in turn (Plates 33, 34, 35 and 36).

Plate 33: Excavations in the nave, showing the lower part of the fill and the paved floor of the Cathedral (EES Photo QI 64/I/8).

Plate 34: Excavations in the north aisle, against the north wall looking west, showing the lower part of the fill and the paved floor of the Cathedral. Note the single course of stones on the edge of the trench, which formed part of the pre Mosque building (EES Photo QI 64/I/11).

However, it was soon realised that the internal piers and walls of the Mosque (Period 4) were built directly on top of an earlier building (Period 3), and that in turn this had been built on a substantial layer representing 'squatter' occupation and the collapse of the roof and columns, which in turn overlay a layer of wind-blown silt, representing the abandonment of the building (Period 2). This lay on the paved floor of the Cathedral (Period 1).

Plate 35: Excavations in the north aisle, against the north wall looking east, showing the lower part of the fill and the paved floor of the Cathedral. Note the single course of stones on the edge of the trench, which formed part of the pre Mosque building (EES Photo QI 64/I/22).

Plate 36: Excavations in the south aisle, near the mihrab *in the south wall and the adjacent* minbar, *showing the depth of deposit (EES Photo QI 64/I/29).*

In addition to the published interim report (*Plumley 1964*), a general note on the excavations was produced by Frend and Plumley after completion of the excavations, and this forms the basis of the following description of the findings. Inevitably, this starts with some general comments and then follows the deposition sequence from the earliest to the latest levels.

The contents of the levels which covered the floor of the Cathedral to a depth of 1.15 metres on the north side and 1.60 metres on the south side, clearly demonstrate the increasing poverty of the successive occupations during the period which followed the abandonments of the Cathedral and which ended with the final abandonment of the site in AD 1811.

Post-Cathedral Squatter Occupation

The general impression given by the accumulated layers of deposit above the floor of the Cathedral is one of occasional squatter occupation (Period 2).

After the final abandonment of the Cathedral as a place of Christian worship sufficient time elapsed for a layer of wind-blown silt mixed with animal droppings and pieces of palm fronds to accumulate to a depth of 5-8 cms over the floor of the nave and the side aisles. It was in this deposit that fragments of Greek and Nubian texts were found, which had presumably been held in the Cathedral library (*Plumley 1964*: 3).

Above this layer was the first of several deposits of wind-borne debris. In these layers intermittent squatter occupation was evidenced by small areas of beaten-earth flooring and hearths. The hearths were particularly numerous near the flanking walls of the apse, leaving considerable traces of burning on the lower parts of the walls adjacent to the north and south crypts. There was also extensive burning in the stairway of the south crypt. Near the wall of the north aisle was a small handmade cooking pot, about 9.1 cms high and 9.4 cms in diameter with a straight rim and a rounded base, resting on an earth floor.

Of the small amount of pottery discovered, the greatest part was coarse, crudely made cooking pots and storage jars of poor fabric. Decorated or glazed sherds were few in number. Personal possessions were represented by coloured beads, fragments of bone and glass bracelets, wooden spindles and whorls. There were many fragments of rush or palm floor matting. A small pot lid of fine red ware, broken in antiquity and carefully mended with string, served to indicate the poverty of the former occupants of the ruined structure. The general squalor of the later occupation of the Cathedral is emphasised by an accumulated layer one metre thick of animal droppings over the south aisle.

The earliest of the occasional squatter levels varied in depth from 12 to 25 cms, and contained, apart from fragments of cooking pots, a small amount of green- and blue-glazed 'Islamic' pottery fragments, spinning whorls of wood and pottery, beads, a bronze ring, a small round lamp of Arabic design, and a small fragment of paper inscribed with six lines of Arabic, which was found in the debris to the east of the *minbar*.

In the debris over the south aisle, about 30 cms above the floor of the Cathedral, was found what appears to have been the cover of a book, probably Arabic, which had been made from paper fragments of a Bohairic Coptic manuscript, pasted together to form a kind of cardboard consistency.

The earliest phase of squatter occupation was also represented by three large cooking pots which were found *in situ* where they had been left. Two of these were handmade of a thick coarse friable fabric without decoration. Both were found resting on an earth flooring, 30 cms above the Cathedral floor, one near the south-west corner of the north aisle and the other near the west wall of the nave. Both had been used long enough for their rims to have been broken.

The third vessel, a large globular pot, was found complete and resting on animal droppings and a layer of hard compacted brown earth some 20 cms above the Cathedral floor, towards the western end of the north aisle. This pottery vessel, some 129 cms in circumference and 41 cms high with a mouth 13 cms in diameter, had been made by hand and decorated by two sets of three parallel lines incised in the neck. When found it had, before its final use, become silted up to within a centimetre of the neck. Thus with its mouth protruding through the floor of a room (probably Room 5) in the late building which proceeded the Mosque (Period 3), it provided a means for storage. In fact, three 'wicker dishes' were found concealed in this pot. The vessel and its partial context appear to be depicted on two photographs (Plates 37 and 38).

Plate 37: Excavations in the north aisle showing the large pottery vessel (EES Photo QI 64/I/17).

Plate 38: Closer view of the large pottery vessel found in the north aisle (EES Photo QI 64/I/6).

This early level contained the fallen granite columns and at least four of the capitals which once stood in two rows in the nave (see below and Chapter 5).

A plan of the layout of the collapsed columns and capitals was prepared in 1964 (Figure 8), but it is not absolutely clear, from the contemporary account of the findings, whether the granite columns had fallen before the squatter occupation had commenced or afterwards. However, several photographs appear to show granite shafts resting on occupation debris (Plates 34 and 39).

Plate 39: Collapsed columns amongst occupation debris in the north aisle (EES Photo QI 64/I/12).

A serious fire seems to have terminated this early phase of occupation, as a layer of ashes, between 3 and 5 cms thick, covered most of the area of the nave. In places the burning had been intense and it is possible that it resulted from the destruction of the roof, presumed to have been of wood. However, it is significant that nothing which could be assigned with confidence to the remains of roofing material was found during the excavations within the Cathedral. Some large beams were found during the 1964 season about 50 metres to the south-east of the Cathedral, but there is no direct evidence to indicate that they originated from the Cathedral.

It may well be, therefore, bearing in mind the evidence for a large fire occurring during the squatter occupation, that the shell of the Cathedral was occupied for a while when the roof was still, at least partially, intact and the columns were still standing, and then continued after the fire, at which time both the roof and all but one of the columns collapsed (for further discussion see Chapter 9).

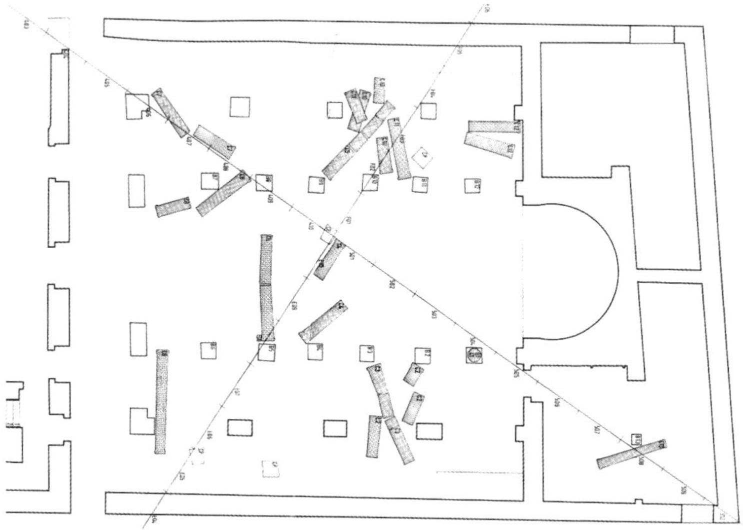

Figure 8: The record plan prepared in 1964 showing the collapsed columns and capitals.

The foundations of this building rested on the underlying deposit, between 0.8 and 1.0 metres above the floor of the Cathedral. A general plan of the building was provided by a single surviving course of walling, which consisted of small rectangular sandstone, marginally-tooled blocks taken from the Cathedral and laid directly on top of the debris below.

Whilst no attempt had been made to lay down proper foundation trenches, the remains of the surviving piers of the Cathedral were used to strengthen the wall at the west end of the new structure.

At least two substantial but crudely-built piers, each about 1.05 metres square (Piers B and C), had been constructed to carry beams from the top of the surviving south arcade. On the north side, the fallen columns of the nave and the remains of the third arcade pier on the north side of the Cathedral formed the foundations for the room partitions.

Above the deposits terminated by the burning was a layer of sterile dark brown, sandy earth, between 20 and 25 cms thick. Here and there this was broken by the remains of small isolated hearths. On top of this layer lay evidence of further squatter occupation was found. Its character was similar to that of the earlier phases in yielding beads and crude pottery. However, in this layer there were no less than 23 fragments of Arabic texts, some evidently magical, scattered about the area within the Cathedral walls, and these may provide a *terminus post quem* for the more elaborate building which was constructed on top of the successive squatter levels.

It now seems most probable that the occupation within the Cathedral immediately after the fire occurred after the roof and the columns had collapsed.

The Pre-Mosque Building

The altar-like stone base discovered at the entrance to the apse in the 1963 season was subsequently identified by Frend and Plumley in 1964 as the base of a pier (Pier A), forming part of a large, roughly-built structure which covered almost the whole of the area of the nave (Figure 9 and Plates 34, 35, 40 and 41). However, there are lingering doubts in the mind of the present writer as to whether the stone base, which is known to sit directly on a hard mortar floor, may have been adapted for the purpose at this stage (for further discussion see Chapters 8 and 9).

The pre-Mosque building, referred to in 1964 as 'the late habitation', is recorded on a plan prepared in 1963-64 and described in a typed report prepared in 1964.

Plate 40: Excavations of the pre-Mosque building, looking east (EES Photo QI 64/1/1).

Plate 41: Excavations of the pre-Mosque building, looking west (EES Photo QI 64/1/3).

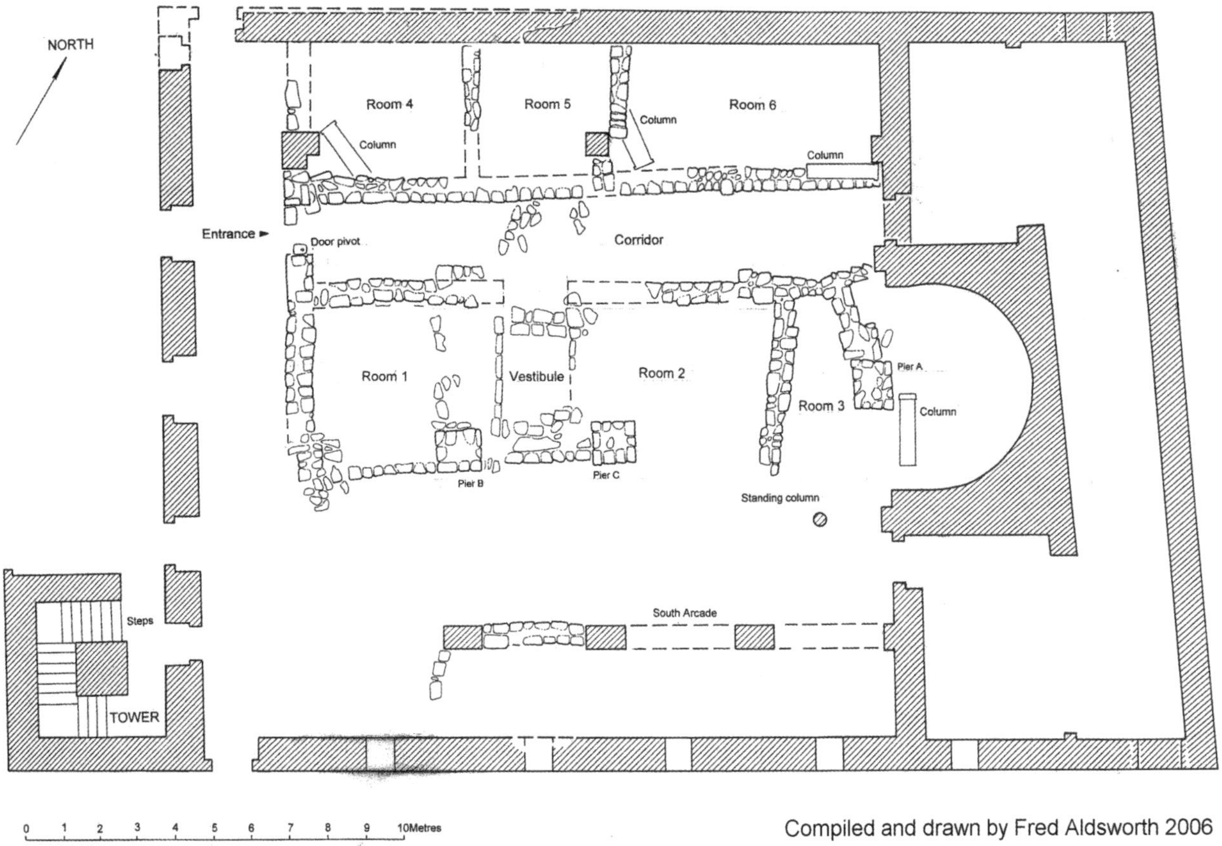

Figure 9: Plan of the pre-Mosque building, based on the 1963-1964 survey drawing.

The entrance to the building was on its west side, at the beginning of a long irregular corridor, approximately 2 metres wide and 15 metres long, which ran the whole length of the north side of the Cathedral, roughly on the line of the column bases. The actual entrance was further indicated by the existence of a sandstone block in which a hole, 12 cms in diameter, was made to contain the door pivot.

About half way along the entrance corridor, on the right hand side, was an opening leading into a rectangular lobby or vestibule, measuring internally about 1.7 metres wide and 3 or 4 metres in length. At the far end of the vestibule were the two stone piers (Piers B and C). On each side of the vestibule were rooms, that to the west (Room 1) about 4.8 metres long and 4 metres wide, whilst that to the east (Room 2) was about 5 metres long by 4 metres wide. Beyond the east room was a small apse-like compartment (Room 3), which was only 1.5 metres wide at its widest point where it abutted Pier A, and separated from the adjoining room (Room 2) by a rough stone wall which may have been a later addition. Beyond this small compartment was the apse of the Cathedral which was still standing to its full height when this building was in use.

On the north side of the corridor were three rooms (Rooms 4, 5 and 6). Room 4 measured about 4 metres by 3.5 metres internally; Room 5 was a little over 3 metres square; and Room 6 was 6.5 metres by 3 metres. At some time, possibly when the building was erected, some attempt was made to reinforce the west part of the north wall of the Cathedral with re-used material, while at the east end of the corridor a fallen column from the Cathedral was used for this purpose.

Beyond the end of the corridor was the space forming a room to the north of the apse of the Cathedral, but it is not known whether this was in use at this time as the door opening into it was blocked. This, however, may have happened at a later date.

The area between the south side of Rooms 1 and 2, the vestibule, and the two piers (B and C), which may have formed the south side of the building, and the south wall of the Cathedral seems to have been used for domestic purposes, as can be demonstrated by the discovery of a large open clay platter sunk into the beaten earth surface, possibly intended for kneading dough. In this area, too, the remains of oxen and goats would imply that this part of the house was concerned with the preparation of food.

At least part of the south arcade of the Cathedral was still standing at this time, with a wall built between at least two of the piers, and the implication appears to be that this area was covered by a roof supported on the arcade and the two piers to the north of it, perhaps as an open-sided, but covered, yard.

To the east of the yard was the space forming a room to the south of the apse of the Cathedral, and this may have been in use at this time, as no evidence was noted to demonstrate that it was ever blocked.

The inhabitants of the building left little behind. Possibly their stay was short-lived, since the building was removed to provide for the construction of the Mosque, at which time a cleaning-up of the area followed the actual dismantling. Among the debris in the west room (Room 1) was a piece of carved wood, which may have come from the handle of a pistol. Some glazed Islamic potsherds and some fragments of multi-coloured glass bracelets and a number of beads suggest that this building might be associated with the initial phase of the Ottoman occupation of Ibrim (i.e. *circa* AD 1570).

For a further discussion of the building see Chapter 10.

Discussion

At the completion of the excavations in the nave and aisles during the 1964 season, all the soil and refuse deposits had been removed. The Cathedral had been excavated down to the sandstone paved floor, and the granite bases for six pairs of columns had been revealed flanking the nave (Figure 8 B1 – B12 and Plates 42, 43 and 44). With the exception of one granite shaft which was still standing on its base at the east end of the south side of the nave (B1 and C1), the remainder were lying either complete or broken on the paved surface, mostly where they had fallen (C2 – C12). Either four or five capitals were also found (Caps 1, 2 and 3 and Caps A and B - for further discussion of all the bases, columns and capitals from the Cathedral see Chapter 5).

On the south side, part of the south arcade was still standing to something close to its original height, separating the inner from the outer aisles, whilst the bases for their counterparts on the north side, also separating the inner and outer north aisles were also found. There were more substantial bases for piers inside the west end of the building.

Plate 42: The interior of the nave, looking east, on the completion of the removal of all the deposits in the nave and aisles. Note the dark stain on the end walls marking the level of the deposits that had been removed (Unreferenced Egypt Exploration Society photograph).

Plate 43: The interior of the nave, looking south-east, on the completion of the removal of all the deposits in the nave and aisles. Note the dark stain on the piers and walls marking the level of the deposits that had been removed (Unreferenced Egypt Exploration Society photograph).

Plate 44: The interior of the nave, looking south, on the completion of the removal of all the deposits in the nave and aisles. Note the dark stain on the piers and wall marking the level of the deposits that had been removed (Unreferenced Egypt Exploration Society photograph).

THE NORTH CRYPT

The north and south crypts, along with their stairwells and antechambers, were fully explored during the 1964 season and record drawings were made (Figures 10 and 11). At that time they were referred to as the west and east crypts, with the burials within them being referred to as west tombs (W1 and W2) and east tombs (E1 to E4).

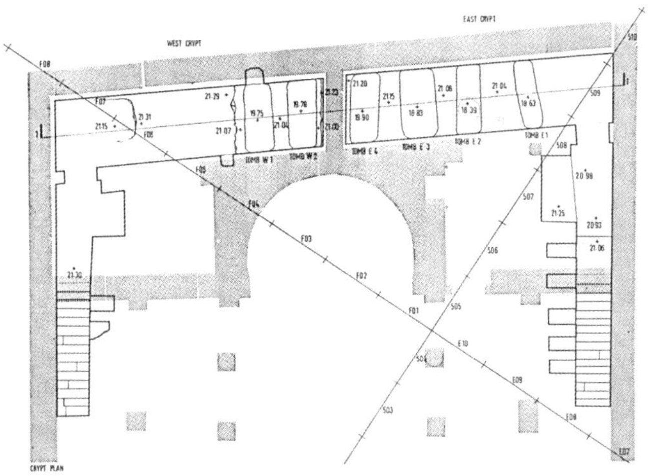

Figure 10: Record plan of the upper level of the crypts.

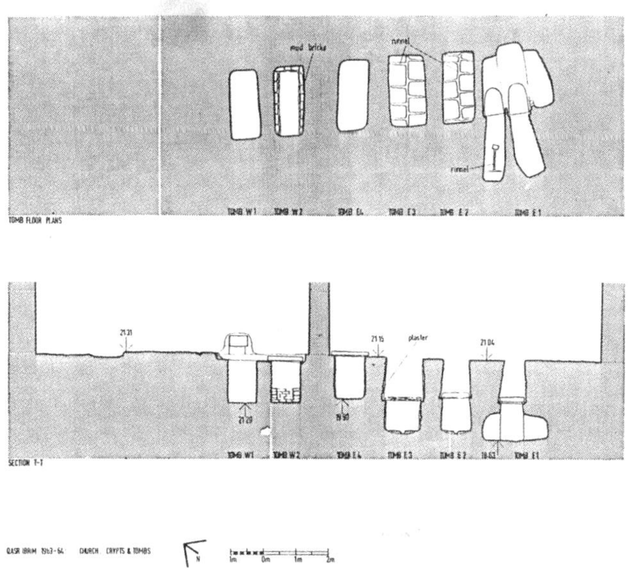

Figure 11: Record plan of the lower level of the crypts and a cross section.

They were subsequently referred to as the north and south crypts and as the north and south tombs, and these orientations are adopted here (Figures 12 and 13).

North Steps

The top of an opening indicating the existence of a north crypt was revealed during the removal of the deposits in the north aisle (Plate 45).

Plate 45: The opening indicating the existence of a north crypt (EES Photo QI 64/1/10).

The stair-well leading to the north crypt was sealed by a rough stone pavement, laid at the same level as that of the paved floor of the Cathedral, but of a very different character (Plate 46).

Plate 46: The pavement over the north steps. Note the broken slab in the foreground, which appears to be the broken stele with a Meroitic inscription. (EES Photo QI 64/2/1).

The paving extended for a distance of 5.2 metres, from the east face of the second pier of the north arcading to the north wall of the apse, and was 2.11 metres wide, from the north face of the same pier to the interior face of the north wall.

It was constructed out of blocks of building material, parts of flagstones, and some pieces of burnt brick, and at its west end it contained two parts of a large, nearly complete Meroitic *stele* (Plates 46 and 47; *Plumley 1964*: 4; and *Edwards & Rilly 2007*: 82-90). The paving gave every appearance of having been laid 'hurriedly'.

Plate 47: The broken stele with cursive Meroitic script (EES Photo QI 64/2/37).

Beneath the pavement, a short distance to the east of the commencement of the steps, a length of rough stone walling had been laid alongside the interior face of the north wall, and in front of this, on top of the stairway itself, was a burnt clay door socket. Presumably at some time a structure of some kind had been built around the well of the stairs, but no evidence remained to show for what purpose it was intended.

It was evident that the stairway was still open until immediately prior to the laying of the pavement, because the material beneath it was not a series of occupation levels but a deliberate fill of soft, grey earth containing plant remains, pieces of broken masonry, broken bricks, and a few fragments of coarse pottery. At the bottom of this fill, in a layer of silt near the north wall, were a number of fragments of manuscripts in Greek, Old Nubian, and possibly Coptic. It is probable that these considerably antedated the time of the fill.

The Burial of Bishop Timotheos

The reason for the fill was explained by the finding of a burial almost immediately inside the entrance to the crypt. It was located about 1 metre beneath the roofing behind the arched entrance of the north antechamber, and was covered by the same kind of grey soft fill as that in the well of the stairway (Plate 48).

The garments in which the burial was dressed and associated objects indicate that the body was that of a bishop, whilst accompanying scrolls identify him as Timotheos, Bishop of Faras and Ibrim, who died and was buried in AD 1371-72 (*Plumley 1975*: 3-4).

Plate 48: The burial of Bishop Timotheos (EES Photo QI 64/2/10).

It was clear that some attempt had been made to orientate the body towards the apse of the Cathedral, but because of the restricted space available it had not been possible to effect a fully extended position. Instead, while the upper part of the body lay on its back, the lower part of the trunk had been twisted towards the right and the legs bent sharply.

Two pieces of sandstone had been inserted beneath the head to form a support. The rest of the body lay on a deep layer of soft fill. Near the feet lay the two halves of a plain, unornamented palm wood staff, 147 cms long and 4 cms in circumference at the top, tapering down to a blunt point (Plate 49).

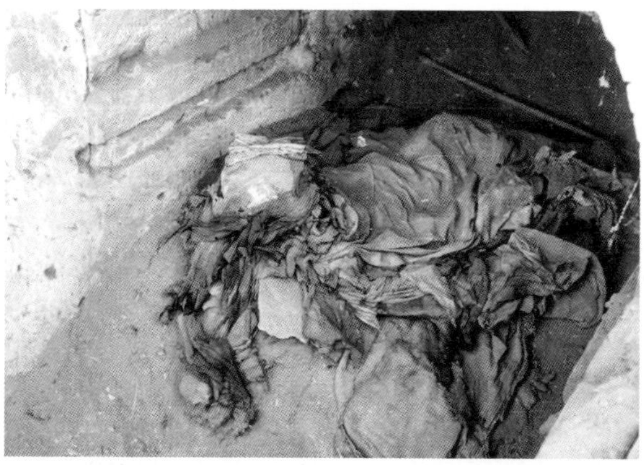

Plate 49: The burial of Bishop Timotheos (EES Photo QI 64/2/11).

On examination, it was seen that the body had been covered above and below by a shroud of coarse white linen.[1] Although the end of this shroud near the feet had greatly decayed, it is almost certain that the covering had originally consisted of one single length of linen, without a seam, which had been doubled back over the body. Since the length of the surviving portion over the body measured 1.06 metres, it is possible that the covering may have been as much as 3 metres in length. The width of the shroud was 55 cms. Along one end of the shroud, where it had been gathered at the neck, a single line of blue thread had been woven in.

When the preparations for the burial had been carried out, the ends of the shroud were gathered round the neck and the four corners knotted together. On each edge of the upper half of the shroud, about 70 cms from the neck, a plain round button was sewn. Similar buttons were also sewn on the lower portion of the shroud. Short pieces of string were wound round the buttons to bring together the covering on each side of the body.

Around the head, and completely veiling the face, was a scarf of fine linen, originally turquoise blue in colour, but faded mostly to 'veridian' green. The ends of the scarf were tucked in at the neck.

A handkerchief of very fine woven linen, measuring 84 cms by 70 cms and decorated at the two ends with five parallel lines of dark blue silk weave, was arranged loosely at the join of the neck with the chest. The handkerchief had been suspended from the neck by means of a plaited leather cord, attached to one corner by a knot.

Beneath the shroud and covering the upper part of the body was all that remained of the outer garment, a sleeveless cape-like garment of coarse, dark brownish red material, lined at the edges with a turquoise blue cloth, similar in colour to that of the head scarf. To the back of this garment was sewn a hood of the same material and similarly lines with turquoise blue. Where the hood joined the cape-like garment, a band of white material, about 21 cms wide and decorated with a design in blue and black silk, ran across the back from one shoulder to the other.

Detailed examination of this garment indicated that most of what survived of the outer garment was in fact the inner stiffening, the main part of the garment, which had been of black wool, having been almost completely destroyed, probably by insects.

The original garment, long and sleeveless with an attached hood, is undoubtedly the medieval Egyptian version of the *paenula,* which in the early centuries of the Christian church had become the normal official attire of a bishop. In the Coptic Church this garment was also the accepted outdoor attire of a bishop and other articles found with the burial confirm that the wearer held this position.

Under the outer garment, the dead man wore a long white garment made from a number of wide strips of linen and lined throughout. The sleeves widened from the shoulders to a width at the wrists of no less than 28 cms. The only decoration on the garment was a narrow strip of material in black and orange which formed the binding of the neck. This garment, which is the equivalent of the present-day *alb* - one of the earliest of liturgical vestments - was gathered in by a leather belt, about 65 cms in length and 2.5 cms wide. Three small cylindrical objects of leather, which probably formed part of the fastening of the belt, were found lying among the folds of the *alb.*

Suspended from the neck by a plaited cord of blue material, probably flax, and lying on the left breast was a finely wrought iron benedictional cross, an essential item of bishop's ensignia. The cross, 32.5 cms in length and 3.6 cms in width across the arms, lay pointing downwards. The lower end of the shaft was thrust under the belt. The first part of the blue cord, which was attached to the small ring at the end of the shaft, ended in a knot from which six cords ran to join two leather crosses plaited from the same material, and from each of these crosses two further loops of the same material ran to encircle the neck of the dead man.

Beneath the *alb* there was a pair of knee-length pantaloons, 84 cms in length and 28 cms wide, of rather coarser woven white linen than was the case of the *alb.* Draw strings had been inserted in the waistband and at the bottom of each leg. Two linen body belts completed the dead man's wardrobe. No shoes were found with the burial.

Concealed under the left side of the body, between his clothing and the lower part of the shroud, lay two paper scrolls, each 34 cms wide and 482cms long but rolled to a diameter of 4.5 cms (Plate 50). These proved to be the consecration deeds of the dead man, one written in the Bohairic dialect of Coptic and the other in Arabic, bearing the bishop's name and See (*Plumley 1964*: 3).

[1] The following description of the textiles and their significance in the Coptic Church is based entirely on the original account by Plumley. Elizabeth Crowfoot's full study of the textiles will be published in 2010 by the Egypt Exploration Society (EES Excavation Memoir 96, forthcoming)

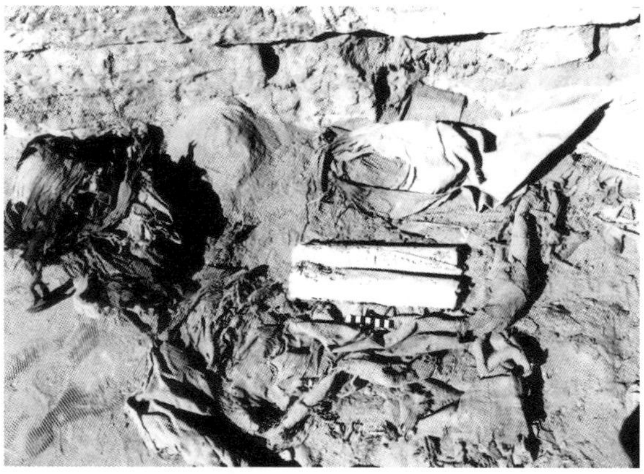

Plate 50: The two scrolls found during excavations (EES Photo QI 64/2/16).

The two scrolls confirm that the dead man was a bishop and that he was Nubian by birth, and almost certainly Timotheos, Bishop of Faras and Ibrim (*Plumley 1975*: 3-4). From the evidence afforded by measurements taken of one of his femurs, he was about 1.73 metres (5 feet 7 inches) in height. The teeth were complete, though the tops of the molars, in particular, were worn flat. This fact could not be taken to indicate an advanced age, since such dental wear is more likely to be the result of the coarse diet. At the time of the excavation, it seemed not unreasonable to assume that he was in the prime of his life when he died. Apart from the evidence contained in the scrolls buried with him, no other memorial has been found of this Bishop of Ibrim, Timotheos the Nubian.

There are indications that Timotheos' burial was unusual, and that his death may have been violent. The fact that he had to wait for some time in Egypt after his consecration in Cairo and that the rite of his enthronement took place in Upper Egypt and not at Ibrim, would suggest that times were troubled, and that it was difficult, if not perilous, for other bishops to accompany him into Nubia.

Writing in the 1960s, Frend and Plumley thought it not unlikely that Timotheos met with a violent end When his remains were examined, noticeable features of the skeleton were that the arms were fully extended on each side of the body and that there was a marked curved contraction of the bones of both hands. No attempt seems to have been made at burial to straighten them and to place the hands in a crossed position over the pubic region, as was customary with all other Christian burials found at Ibrim. In addition it was noted that the bones of the right foot were missing.

Possibly the burial was both hasty and carried out in secret. The body was not placed, as might have been expected in a proper grave, but in a makeshift burial under the entrance to the north crypt which no longer in regular use. What was surprising to the original excavators was to find that some attempt had been made to lay down a pavement over the fill of the stairwell, to the same level as the original pavement of the Cathedral. This seemed to suggest that when Timotheos died in AD 1372, the Cathedral, or a significant part of it, was still in use.

The garments and the objects associated with the Bishop Timotheos burial, including the benedictional cross, are in the British Museum (*Crowfoot* forthcoming), and the scrolls are believed to be held in Cairo.

North Antechamber

The entrance to the north antechamber and crypt was originally under the portcullis-like block set behind the later round-headed opening, a feature of both crypts. It was blocked by a rough stone wall, which rested on a layer of greyish silt, 11 cms thick (Figure 12 and Plates 48 and 51). The wall, 39 cms in thickness, and extending upwards on the left (north) side to a height of 127 cms and on the right (south) to 87 cms, was constructed with stone blocks, rough stones, and a few large bricks.

The outer face of the wall still retained the remains of a plaster of mud and straw. Although it was not easy to decide whether the wall was built at the time of the bishop's burial, or whether it antedated that event, the balance of evidence, especially the fact that the body lay on debris which was higher than the lower edge of the portcullis-like entrance, would seem to favour a date prior to the insertion of the burial for sealing up the entrance to the crypt.

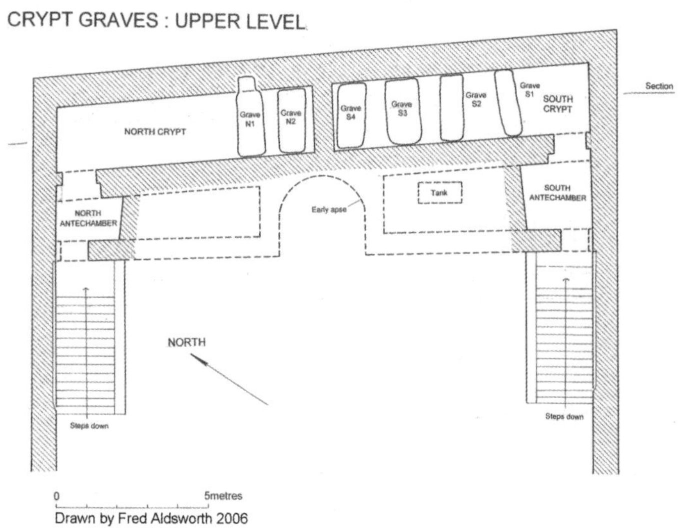

Figure 12: Plan of the upper level of the original arrangement of the north and south crypts. Based on the 1963-64 record drawing and a new survey in 1992.

Plate 51: The north stairs and north antechamber in 1992. Note the 'portcullis-like' block immediately behind the arch, which was above the burial and, at a lower level, the lower part of the wall blocking the access into the antechamber (Photograph by Fred Aldsworth).

The burial of Timotheos may have been placed over the remains of the blocking wall and in the small vaulted chamber, measuring 2.2 metres by 1.6 metres internally, and here referred to as the north antechamber (Figure 12). This had already been filled to a depth of 1.3 metres with soft brownish, sandy debris containing some vegetable matter. Included in the debris near the entrance to the chamber was a footed pot of greenish, white ware, and lying a little way into the chamber against the north wall was a small complete pot of polished orange-red ware, decorated in black geometric linear design. Also there were fragments of an 'Islamic' bowl of glazed yellow ware, bearing traces of Arabic script on the outside, and a stamped impression on the inside. From the debris in the chamber also came the remains of a red ware, well-fired pot with the symbol 'N' incised on the outside; a shallow bowl; a handled flask of greenish white ware; part of a camel saddle and a number of mud amphorae seals, although not in such quantity as in the south crypt.

Most of the pottery was found near the floor, covered with about 1.2 metres of light, wind-borne dust particles. The greater part of the deposit had penetrated into the chamber from a hole in the roof of the adjoining room of the north crypt, although a smaller amount had probably penetrated into the chamber via the archway of the stairway entrance.

Deep in the debris a number of fragments of manuscripts in Greek and Old Nubian were found. Of these, one, a fragment of parchment measuring about 10 cms by 8 cms, proved to be part of a service book in Greek, containing part of the *Anaphora of St Athanasius*. More importantly for the purposes of dating was the finding of part of a letter on paper written in Arabic and bearing the date AD 1348-49. This would suggest that the crypt may have been open up to that date, and that it was not finally closed until the burial of Bishop Timotheos some thirty years later.

To the right of the entrance of the chamber and on the west face of the wall, there is a block of stone bearing the remains of an inscription, now upside down, which may form part of an inscription found on the west face of the west wall of the lower part of the apse, exposed during excavations in the south crypt (see below).

North Crypt

On the east side of the antechamber is a doorway, bearing a lintel 1.05 metres wide, giving access to the innermost portion of the crypt, which extends north-south to finish at a cross wall that not only separates the north crypt from the corresponding return of the south crypt, but also serves as a buttress wall to the rear of the apse.

In the north crypt, two distinct levels of fill could be distinguished quite clearly. The uppermost of these was a deposit of light, dark brown loam and dust, which had been blown down from a hole in the roof of the crypt. The top of this deposit was about 1.05 metres below the top of the vaulted ceiling. The lower fill consisted of a succession of occupation levels, of which there were at least fifteen, characterised by matting floors and coarse pottery. These levels were 1.10 metres deep, and rested on a layer of grey barren silt, 10 cms thick.

A considerable quantity of pottery sherds was found in the occupation levels. The finds in these deposits, so different from the majority of post-Christian and pre-Christian levels discovered elsewhere in the Cathedral, can perhaps be explained by some later, but still pre-Ottoman, occupation of the building. Given that the crypt appears to have been sealed before AD 1372, the most likely scenario seems to be that this material found its way into the crypt, from above, through the hole in the floor of the room above it.

The floor of the north crypt, which is cut into the natural bedrock and has been polished in places by wear, slopes downward by about 25-27 cms from its north end towards the dividing wall at its south end.

In the corner of the return passage, opposite the entrance, lay two fragments from an object carved out of black basalt, in the form of a square or rectangular basin approximately 66 cms wide, 28 cms tall, and more than 45 cms long, which may have once formed the top of a small shrine (Figure 13). There seemed little doubt when this was first discovered that it was probably late in date.

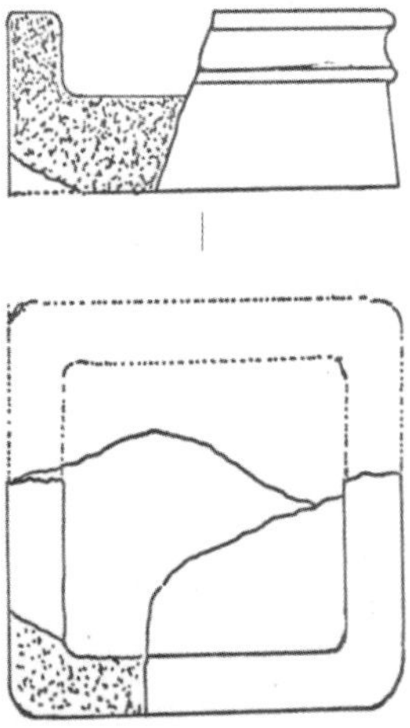

Figure 13: One of two sketches of the pieces of the black basalt object, drawn in 1964. The other sketch gives the scale indicating that it measured about 60 cms across.

Just under 3 metres from the north wall is a shallow depression, about 15 cms deep, cut into the floor of the crypt (see Figure 10), which appears to be the first cutting for a tomb shaft that was never completed.

The roof of the crypt had collapsed at two places in the return passage. The probable cause of one of these falls was a large granite pedestal or altar, measuring 95 cms high, by 78 cms in both directions at the base, without ornament apart from a simple roll moulding under the cornice top (Plates 52 and 53).

Plate 53: The granite pedestal or altar in the north crypt, as photographed in the 1970s (EES Photo Gartkiewicz 171).

This was thought to have fallen through the floor of the room to the north of the apse, and lay on its side with its base near to the west wall. However, the excavators found it difficult to account for its use in the room above, now identified as the sacristy, and it is unlikely that it was dragged there after the final abandonment of the Cathedral as a place of Christian worship, since it was found lying directly on the floor of the crypt and not on debris which had built up on it.

The basalt basin and the granite altar are both tentatively attributed to the Meroitic period by Pamela Rose, who suggests that they may have come from the Meroitic temple complex on the site (*Rose 2007*: 102, Figures 17.3 and 17.4).

The south end of the north crypt contained two graves, both cut down into the bedrock from the floor level to a depth of about 1.3 metres (Figures 12 – 14 Graves N1 and N2, previously referred to in the 1964 drawings as Tombs W1 and W2).

Plate 52: The north crypt, looking south in 1992. Note the large granite pedestal or altar and the two graves at the far end (Photograph by Fred Aldsworth),

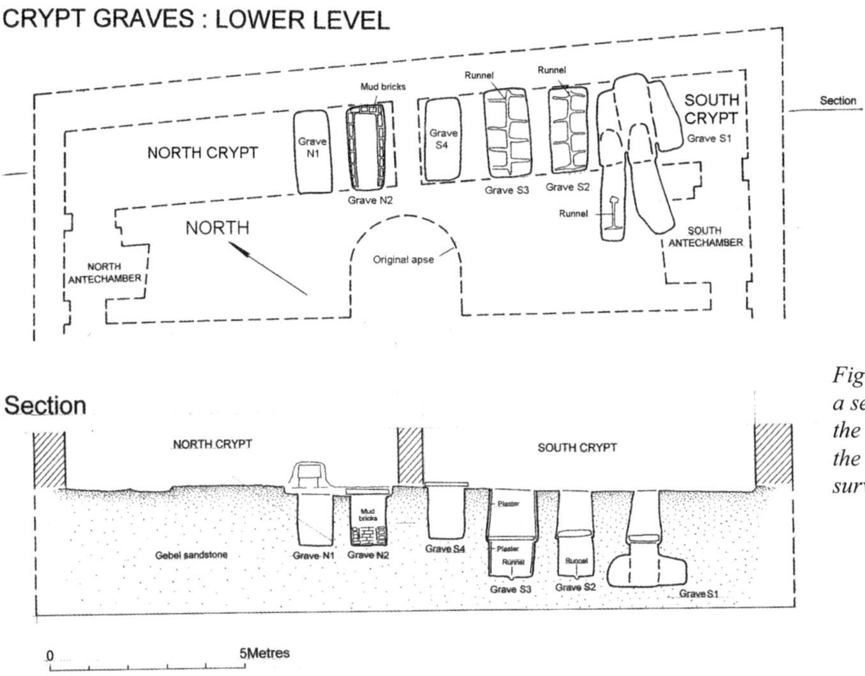

Figure 14: Plan of the lower level and a section of the original arrangement of the north and south crypts. Based on the 1963-64 record drawing and a new survey in 1992.

Grave N1

The more northerly of the two graves (N1) had been disturbed in ancient times. However, part of the original sealing was in position. The seal, which consisted of two slabs of stone, had been improvised out of the remains of an early New Kingdom *stele*, of which the top portion was missing. This was subsequently identified as showing Amenophis I and his wife worshipping Horus of Mi'am, and dated to the eighth year of his reign (*Plumley 1964*: 4 and Plate I,3).

The fill of the grave contained a mixture of both painted Christian pottery, and some green and yellow glazed 'Islamic' ware.

The bones of the burial had been thoroughly disturbed, but whether this was due to the activities of grave robbers or to the collapse of debris into the grave after the removal of part of the covering, is not easy to determine. It was noted, however, that the skull showed signs of burning.

Grave N2

The second grave (N2) appears to have been undisturbed. The four sides of the lower part of the grave cut were lined with five courses of mudbrick, which rose to a height of 40 cms. The average size of a brick was 38 cms long, 16 cms wide, and 8 cms high. The brick lining formed a support for four sandstone slabs of irregular shapes and differing sizes.

Above the slabs was a fill, about 70 cms deep, containing much broken pottery. Above this fill a second series of stone slabs were placed, but only one of these was still in its original position. The removal of the upper slabs raised the problem as to how far the fill below them remained uncontaminated.

There was no doubt, however, that the burial was undisturbed. The remains were interpreted as that of a man, lying on his back with head to the west. There was no trace of clothing. However, alongside the lower part of the left leg was placed a mud-sealed amphora, with the seal end pointing to the west. It was 64 cms long, including the seal, and about 65 cms in circumference. A small hole was pierced under one of the handles. The vessel was empty. In shape and style the amphora appeared to be similar to that found in Grave S1 in the south crypt (see below).

South Antechamber

The entrance steps to the south crypt had been cleared during the 1963 season of excavations (see Chapter 1 Trench C2 and Plates 31 and 54). The notes from the 1964 season commence on the 27th January with descriptions of the types of stonework employed in the construction of the south crypt and the nature of its fill. The implication would appear to be that either the south antechamber had been cleared during the previous season or it was cleared at the beginning of the 1964 season. In either case no records have been found of the work.

Plate 54: The south antechamber, looking west from the south crypt in 1992 (Photograph by Fred Aldsworth).

South Crypt

A sketch section accompanying the original notes suggests that the south crypt was found to be completely full of layers of silt and occupation debris when investigated.

The roofing of the crypt consisted of mud brick vaulting, above which was laid a thick layer of reeds, which in turn supported a layer of fine sand upon which the flagstones of the room to the south of the apse were placed. A large part of the north end of the floor of this room had collapsed into the crypt below. In view of the dangerous conditions, work was commenced by clearing the crypt from above.

Immediately below the level of the flagstones the deposit consisted of brown dust and sand, which contained much broken pottery. Among this debris was found part of a platter of red ware decorated with painted floral and geometric designs. Below the brown dust and sand, the sketch section records layers of occupation debris, over brown silt, then more occupation debris over shallow deposits of brown silt and then greenish silt on the floor.

Once the crypt was cleared, its walls and ceiling were shown originally to have been covered with plaster and then whitewashed. In places the plaster had fallen away exposing the large re-used stone blocks of the outer walls. Some of these blocks were incised with representations of hands and occasional graffiti. In particular on the inner surface of the external south wall, just within the second arched doorway of the crypt, had been incised an inscription in Greek letters and possible Meroitic cursive script, as well as the representations of two hands, and this has recently been discussed and illustrated by Penny Wilson (*2007*: 114 CTH 14, Figure 18.27).

On the west wall of the apse, on a stone block adjoining the dividing wall of the crypts measuring 66 cms by 43 cms, were the remains of an inscription carved in monumental-like letters, 9 cms high, with a *graffito* above it. A possible reading of the *graffito* appeared to be 'Castor and Pollux', suggesting that the inscription derived from an earlier Roman building on the site associated with one of the Roman Cohorts stationed in Egypt. It was further suggested in 1964 that another part of this inscription might be preserved in a stone block built into the north antechamber (see above).

The floor of the south crypt was formed by levelling off the bedrock on which the Cathedral Church is built. Excavated in it were four grave cuts (Figures 12 and 14 Graves S1-S4, referred to in 1964 as Graves E1-E4, and Plate 55). No flagstones were laid, so that the top of the fill of each grave was level with the floor of the crypt. Although numbered, and perhaps investigated, in 1964 from south to north, the graves were presumably cut in the reverse order from north to south.

Plate 55: The south crypt with Graves S1-S4, looking north in 1992 (Photograph by Fred Aldsworth).

Grave S1

This grave was located towards the south end of the crypt (Figures 12 and 14). It was undisturbed and measured 2.20 metres in length and 0.65 metres in width at the top. As the excavation descended the width increased until it reached nearly 1.0 metre.

At a depth of about 1.30 metres, a ledge of an average width of 12 cms projected from all four sides of the grave cut.

Two large sandstone slabs were placed on the ledge, the smaller of the two being about 1.0 metres square, whilst the larger one was about 50 cms longer. Each slab averaged about 10 cms thick, and each had a circular hole cut through it to facilitate lifting in the event of further use of the burial space below.

The fill which covered the slabs up to the level of the crypt floor was very similar to that in Grave N2, that is sandstone chippings mixed with earth. Very little pottery was found in this fill, and only then in a very fragmentary condition.

About 1.2 metres below the slabs, the grave cut opened out into an irregularly-shaped space, just over 1.0 metre at its greatest height and about 2.0 metres square, to create burial chambers to the north and south (Graves S1a and S1b).

In the west end of this space were two more narrow vaulted burial chambers cut into the bedrock, each averaging 2.0 metres in length, 60-70 cms in width, and about 55 cms in height (Graves S1c and S1d). The entrance to these burial chambers were intended to be sealed by means of sandstone slabs, averaging 6 cms in thickness. The top of each slab was semi-circular, in order to fit into the vaulted entrance.

When the grave was opened the burial chamber nearest the south wall (S1c) was sealed by one of these slabs, with mud plaster having been spread thickly around its edges. Within the burial place lay a skeleton, its feet pointing to the east. The burial, which appeared to be that of a male, was covered with a few fragments of what had been a garment of some kind, but the remains had so decayed to a powdery consistency that it was impossible to hazard even a guess as to what was their original composition. Nothing else was found with the burial.

The adjoining burial chamber (S1d) was empty. It seems certain that it had never been used, for the slab door was found lying immediately in front of the entrance. The floor of this burial chamber contained a groove or runnel, about 60 cms in length, which was connected with a cross runnel at the west end of the chamber, and led eastwards to join with a small square depression, that would have been positioned under the pelvis of the body. This simple system of channels, which also occurs in a different form in Graves S2 and S3, was probably intended to drain off liquids from the decomposing body.

It is probable that this large rock-cut grave was intended for at least five burials. As already noted, the provision of two holes in the large slabs which sealed the grave support this intention. However, it is quite clear that only one interment (S1c) was ever made.

The reason for this is unknown, but one possibility is that, as floor of the south crypt was almost fully occupied by graves, and no more space was available here, this particular, and last, cut was made to accommodate more than one burial, but only one occurred.

As to the dating of the cutting of this grave and its one and only burial, some indication may be afforded by the discovery in the grave of a sealed amphora, placed against the east wall of the large chamber before the whole complex had been sealed in antiquity. The amphora was 64 cms in height and about 65 cms in circumference. A large conical mud stopper, impressed in three places with seals, had closed the mouth, but when opened there was no evidence of the original contents.

Grave S2

This was 2.20 metres long and 0.88 metres wide and was undisturbed. A pair of ledges, each about 7-10 cms wide, ran the whole length of each side of the grave, about 1.2 metres below the floor of the crypt. The ledges supported six sandstone slabs, each about 10 cms thick and between 30 and 40 cms wide, which formed the roof over the burial (Plate 56).

Plate 56: Graves S2 (right) and S3 (left), during excavation in 1964 (EES Photo WF4/109).

The body, of which only the skeleton survived, was laid upon the rock floor into which was cut a pattern of runnels, with one aligned down the centre of the grave and branches on either side feeding into it, four to the north and five to the south. The remains appeared to be of an adult female, about 1.62 metres tall, but there were no surviving vestiges of the garments in which the body had been buried and there were no associated objects (Plate 57).

The fill above the sandstone slabs was largely composed of sandstone chippings mixed with a certain amount of earth. There were some fragments of coarse pottery in the fill.

However, two finds of special significance were part of a moulded lamp and a 'typical Early Christian goblet'. The remains of the lamp were found about 1 metre below the top of the grave. In addition to the usual elaborate pattern, the lamp bore a Greek inscription. The goblet was found deep in the fill in the north-east corner of the grave. Part of the rim was broken, but its overall dimensions were 10.5 cms in height, 9.5 cms in diameter at its widest point, and 4.5 cms in diameter at the foot. The presence of these two objects in an undisturbed fill suggested to the excavators a possible 6th-7th century date.

Plate 57: The undisturbed female burial in Grave S2 (Unreferenced EES Photograph).

Grave S3

This was 2.20 metres long and 1.43 cms wide and was disturbed.

At a depth of 1.33 metres was a pair of ledges, each 8 cms wide. Originally a number of thick wooden planks rested on them to protect the body of the deceased from the fill above (Plate 56). Two of the planks were still in position (Figure 9) and three others had been displaced and leaned into the bottom of the grave. Each plank was 7 cms thick and of those still in position the widths were 44.5 cms and 33 cms. Originally there were probably seven planks in all.

The grave cut continued down for a further 0.92 metres and the floor was divided lengthways by a runnel, 11 cms wide, which had four branches on either side running into it. All the sides of the grave were covered with white plaster, 5 mms thick. No remains of a body were found.

The fill of the grave was composed of the same kind of light, dark brown loam which was found in Grave S4. This fill contained a considerable quantity of coarse pottery, possibly Late Christian in date, some green glazed ware, the stem of a cup, a shallow bowl with decoration, and a piece of coloured glass, possibly the bottom of a *kohl* bottle.

Grave S4

This was 2.11 metres long by 0.94 metres wide and had been excavated down into the bedrock to a depth of 1.29 metres. It was found to be undisturbed. This was the least deeply-excavated grave in the floor of the south crypt, although the two graves in the north crypt had been excavated to a similar level. The walls of the tomb were covered in white plaster.

Of the original interment there remained only a few bones. Some fragments of wood found with them may be either the remains of planking or intrusive. The 1964 drawing appears to show either planking or slabs at the level of the crypt floor (Figure 9), but these are not described in the notes made at the time.

The dark brown, light loam which filled the grave contained some fragments of rough, hand-made pottery.

It was contaminated by fallen material from the area above, behind the apse. Amongst it were several bases of large hand-made cooking pots, much burned internally, possibly used as lamps; fragments of three or more amphorae, all wheel-turned, well-fired, and of a grey-brown fabric; a handled pot with corrugation; several bowls, with internal painted decoration; a large bowl of whitish fabric, with black and white linear decoration on the interior; and a platter of light brown fabric, with painted decoration (pink on rim and brown or black on the interior) in a linear pattern.

THE BAPTISTRY

This room is located to the south of the apse, and was referred to in 1964 as the South Sacristy. It was accessed from a door in the east end of the innermost south arcade of the Cathedral, and no evidence was found to indicate that it was blocked prior to the commencement of investigations on the site in 1963. There is, however, photographic evidence to indicate that a dividing wall was inserted from north to south across the enclosed space, perhaps at the time that the building was adapted for use as a mosque (see Chapter 3, Figure 5 and Plate 8).

Excavations were started in this room to facilitate safe access to the south crypt, but the only record of the investigations are some handwritten field notes prepared by Frend. The following comments are based on those notes.

Baptismal Tanks

A tank, hollowed out of a single block of sandstone and plastered on the inside, was set next to an earlier recess cut into the external south wall of the apse (Plate 58).

Its external dimensions were 1.0 metres long, 0.60 metres wide, and 0.45 metres high, and its internal dimensions were 0.88 metres long, 0.46 metres wide, and 0.39 metres high.

Plate 58: The inserted baptismal tank, with the earlier recess behind it (EES Photo QI 64/4/30).

The recess in the south wall of the apse was surmounted by a round archway, similar in construction to the arches which are above the entrances to the north and south crypts. This arch, which is slightly smaller at 1.08 metres in diameter, differs from those of the crypts in that only *voussoirs* are employed, and there is no cross carved over the centre of the arch (Plates 59 and 60).

When the inserted tank was removed in several pieces, it was seen that its base rested on a fill of rubble composed of stone chippings and earth.

Beneath this fill, at a distance of about 1.2 metres from the level of the pavement of the baptistry, lay a large *stele* containing thirty-seven lines of cursive Meroitic writing. It was evident that the recess exposed by the removal of the inserted tank had once formed an earlier baptismal tank, of which the *stele* had formed the bottom, for both the *stele* and the sides of the cavity carried the remains of hard plaster. Parts of the inscribed surface of the *stele* had been deliberately defaced by chisel marks before the plaster had been applied (*Edwards 2007*: 90-92).

Frend evidently considered the possibility that the arched recess may at one time have formed the head of a doorway into the apse and noted that the lower part of the apse might be older than the upper part.

Since the edges of the *stele* forming the base of the tank lay under the masonry which formed its sides, it was not possible to determine if a threshold block to the doorway remained, and an attempt to remove it would have called for major dismantling of part of the baptistry. This was not attempted. There is no sign that a similar door was present in the exterior of the north wall of the apse into the sacristy.

Plates 59 and 60: The earlier baptismal tank, from the south-west and south-east (EES Photos GP421 and 422).

Column Base and Shaft

No further written records have been found relating to the 1964 investigations in the baptistry, but on the plan produced at the time (Figure 6) a small granite base was marked as found *in situ* with a small granite shaft lying beside it (see Chapter 5).

THE SACRISTY

This room is located to the north of the apse, and was referred to in 1964 as the North Sacristy. It was accessed from a door in the east end of the innermost north arcade of the Cathedral and there is photographic evidence to indicate that it was blocked prior to the commencement of investigations in 1964. This was perhaps as part of the works associated with the adaptation of the building as a mosque (Plates 35 and 37 and Figure 4).

No records have been found of the excavations undertaken here.

AREA IN FRONT OF THE WEST ENTRANCE

Amongst the records of works carried out here are several very sketchy plans of the area, and these provide the basis for a tentative reconstruction plan of the features encountered (Figure 15).

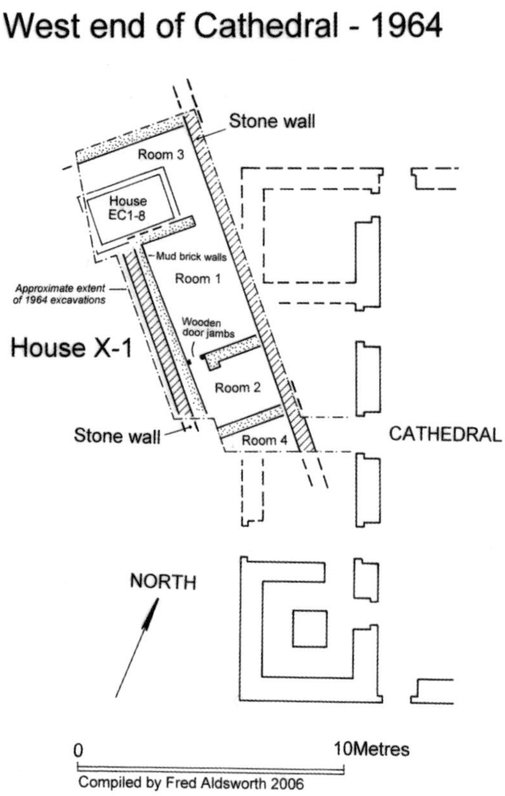

Figure 15: Tentative reconstruction plan of the features encountered in front of the west entrance to the Cathedral in 1964.

The following account is based on the original notes and the reconstructed plan.

A roughly paved area, measuring about 9.25 metres by 4.5 metres, lay in front of the three western entrances into the surviving portion of the Cathedral. This area was bounded on the south by the surviving south-west tower, and on the north by another tower or building of similar dimensions as to length and width. No certain traces of the foundations of this northern structure were found during the excavation, but the rough state of the exterior of the west wall at this point, together with the remains of a door jamb, are strong indications of the former existence of some kind of structure here to counter balance the surviving tower to the south.

'Retaining Wall'

A narrow exploratory trench was laid down at the entrance to the central door and extended westwards for a distance of 2.0 metres. At a depth of 0.8 metres below the level of the west front paving stones, which had been floated on a bed of light dusty earth, the top of a massive roughly-built, stone wall was uncovered. This wall, 0.6 metres in width, was seen to run at an angle from the north door of the tower and was traced for a distance of 11.0 metres (Figure 15). Although referred to by Plumley in his interim report as a retaining wall for the platform of earth and rubble on which the western and most of the northern part of the Cathedral was built (*Plumley 1964*), it is clear from the excavation notes and photographs that the stone wall not only pre-dated the Cathedral Church but also pre-dated the mud-brick X-Group house (X-1) which was built up against it on its west side.[2] In fact it now appears that the stone wall was built on the natural bedrock surface at the base of the rock-cut cliff face, exposed to the south of the Cathedral, which is believed to have been formed by quarrying in or before the the Meroitic period (see Chapter 7 and Appendix 2). The stone wall presumably formed part of an extensive early structure identified and discussed by Gartkiewicz (see Chapter 3).

X-Group House (X-1)

Built immediately against the west face of the stone wall were the remains of mud brick walls with plastered interior surfaces forming part of a house complex (House X-1). Owing to lack of time it was not possible to excavate the whole of this building, and there was some danger that the removal of too much earth at this point might cause the west walls of the Cathedral, which stood on poor foundations, to collapse.

[2] The author is grateful to Dr Pamela Rose for this information.

The house complex had been deliberately filled in by the builders of the Cathedral to provide extra support to the retaining wall of the platform.

Two main levels could be clearly distinguished in the fill of the house. The lower of these, which could be subdivided into four, rested upon the bedrock, 3.05 metres below the level of the paving.

The upper main level, 2.0 metres in depth, was made up of greyish fine earth, containing broken pottery, stones, vegetable remains, animal droppings, and much roof debris. One of the rooms excavated contained in addition a considerable amount of ash.

It is not impossible that the rooms excavated may have formed cellars, but whatever their original purpose there is no doubt that they were filled in prior to the construction of the west end of the Cathedral Church, and to provide an open space in front of it which at this point seems to have been approached by some kind of processional way, entrance to which was by way of the north stairway leading up from the Podium site.

The area cleared measured 11.0 metres by 3.0 metres and consisted of an L-shaped passage at the north end (Room 3), of an average width of 1.5 metres, which led into two rooms by means of a doorway, 0.5 metres in width. Each of the two rooms (Rooms 1 and 2) was further connected by a doorway at the south end of the separating cross wall. The doorway still retained in position the two wooden jambs and the section of palm trunk which served as the threshold. Originally there would have been a wooden lintel, for the top of each jamb had been cut to form substantial tenons for the mortice at each end of the lintel. This doorway was a later addition, since it stood 27 cms above the *gebel* and is to be associated with the floor beneath the hard mud floor which formed the final level of occupation.

The east face of the west wall of the first room which, in common with all the internal walls, had been plastered with mud, contained two square niches at a height of 1.10 metres from the hard mud floor. The niches, each about 35 cms square and about 25 cms deep, would appear to have been used as cupboards. There was no blackening of the top of the niches to suggest that they may have held lamps.

At a height of some 10 cms above the top line of the niches were five smaller niches cut into the wall. The purpose of these was to carry large cross beams of palm trunks, one of which was found in position, and it was not considered impossible that they were intended to support a substantial storey above. As some of the plaster had fallen away from the lower part of the interior face of the west wall, it was possible to observe the method of construction employed in laying the courses of mud bricks and it was noted that this method of brick laying was also employed elsewhere at Ibrim. A sketch accompanying the typescript shows four stretcher courses and then one header course on edge.

A terminal date for the disuse of this house was afforded by the discovery of several caches of pottery which had been concealed at the time when the interior of the structure was filled in. All the pottery was assigned to the X-Group period, probably the last phase of the same.

It seemed probable to the excavators in 1964 that, if the house was filled in to buttress the platform upon which the Cathedral Church was built and to provide an open space in front of the west entrance, the possibility of assigning a fairly early date for the building of the Cathedral Church must be considered.

Early Christian House (EC 1-8)

A structure over the south-west corner of Room 3 was interpreted as a later building which intruded into the fill of the room at a high level.

SUMMARY OF THE 1964 EXCAVATIONS

The investigations undertaken during the two-month period which comprised the second season of excavations in and around the Cathedral were extensive. All the deposits and structures overlying the paved floor of the Cathedral Church were removed, and these included squatter occupation prior to and after the collapse of the roofs and columns; a pre-Mosque building, which may have existed for only a short period of time; the late Mosque, which may have been remodelled on several occasions prior to abandonment at the beginning of the nineteenth century; and some walls inserted into the Mosque at a very late date to provide some domestic accommodation (for further discussion see Chapters 9, 10, 11 and 12).

The contents of the north and south crypts were also removed, including the burial of Timotheos dating to AD 1371-1372 and the rock-cut graves contained within them were excavated.

The baptistry was investigated and it was found that the original (Phase 1) baptismal tank had been accommodated in the later (Phase 2) reconstruction and then replaced by a new one at a later date.

Investigations at the west end of the Cathedral Church showed that it overlay an earlier masonry structure with a probable X-Group mud-brick house built against it.

Chapter 3: EXCAVATIONS AND INVESTIGATIONS BY P M GARTKIEWICZ 1972-78

Przemyslaw M Gartkiewicz was involved in three seasons of investigations at Qasr Ibrim, in 1972, 1976 and 1978, having previously participated in the Polish Archaeological Mission in Old Dongola since 1968. As a result of his work at Old Dongola, he published a report on the Cathedral there in which he drew parallels with that at Qasr Ibrim (*Gartkiewicz 1990*).

The 1972 season took place between 9th October and 4th December; the 1976 season between 21st January and 11th March; and the 1978 season between 17th January and 29th March. Gartkiewicz was not present during the 1974 season and there are no indications that any work took place on the Cathedral at that time. The excavations were again supervised by Professor Plumley, assisted for part of the time by R D Anderson, with Gartkiewicz, then chief architect of the Polish Centre of Mediterranean Archaeology in Cairo, supervising work on the Cathedral.

The archives for these seasons include interim reports; a brief report by Gartkiewicz on his investigations in 1972 in the north and south aisles; various notebooks and diaries; an extensive photographic record produced by Gartkiewicz; and photographs for the 1972 and 1976 seasons. Faulty cameras in 1978 resulted in the survival of only a few photographs taken at that time.

At Qasr Ibrim, Gartkiewicz undertook a detailed architectural study of the cleared Cathedral. He prepared a photographic archive of the building and the decorated stone from it, and undertook a series of modest excavations to clarify issues about the extent of the building and its predecessors. His work remained unfinished at the end of the 1978 season. At the time of writing, no detailed written record is available of Gartkiewicz's work at Qasr Ibrim, apart from the summary of his investigations in 1972, already mentioned, and entries in a site diary for 1978 (see below). This review of his work is based on that material as well as his drawings, which have for the most part been integrated into those prepared in 1992 (Chapter 4), and his photographs, which are used throughout this volume.

PLAN

Gartkiewicz produced a very detailed plan of the Cathedral in 1972 at a scale of 1:50, with an accompanying key and legend which records a great deal of information about the building (Figure 16). The detailed legend for his plan is given below using his identifications and descriptions. The plan and the contents of the legend are incorporated into the description of the standing building (Chapter 4).

KEY

O - walls of the Old Church adapted to the Cathedral's structures
/? - parts not recognized to the full;
1 - walls in section;
2 - elements above the pavement level;
3 - pavement slabs and other elements in view;
4 - negative of not-preserved piers appointed by paving slabs;
5 - lack of the original stone pavement;
6 - stone pavement measured by Kenneth Frazer, and dismantled before 1972;
7 - position of the corners of later piers;
8 - profiles of arches or barrel vaults;
9 - holes cut originally in stone pavement;
10 - door-sockets and traces made by moving door-leaf;
11 - mason's letter marks on the bases;
12 - levelling;
13 - stairs;
14 - main points of geodetical measurement.
15 - numbering of the interiors:
A – apse, with tribune;
B – *haikal*;
C – baptistry;
D – eastern isolated part of the baptistry named south-eastern chamber;
E – *prothesis*;
F – isolated part of the *prothesis* named north-eastern chamber;
G – nave;
H – aisles;
I – *essonarthex*/western part of the ambulatory;
J – ambulatories;
K – staircases leading to the roof;
N – chamber under the stairs;
O – place of not-preserved north-western corner room/tower.
16 – detailed description:
a – position of the wooden legs of the altar and accompanied it elements;
b – position of the wooden vertical elements of the *ciborium*;
c – position of the wooden vertical elements of an unknown structure, possible a screen surrounding the *ciborium*;
d – position of the wooden main vertical elements of the *haikal*'s rail/screen;
e – entrances to the *haikal*'s dais;
f – baptistry basin of the Old Church adapted and used in the Cathedral;
g – standing stone slabs framing the hollow/step surrounding the basin;
h – base of the column both sides cut in for fixing the vertical elements of a rail/screen, laid originally or later on the paving slabs;
i– hole in the vault covering the underground chamber serving as a window;
j – holes in the pavement and walls, probably to fixing the elements of a screens;

k – position of the wooden vertical elements of the *ambo* and stairs leading to its landing;
l – round stone slab with sloping edge;
m – door-sockets;
n – deep recess of an unknown function situated in the wall between *essonarthex* and staircase. In the north-western corner of this recess there is a slit, perhaps originally closed by a mud, connected it with the interior of the staircase;
o – outer landing/dais in front of the southern entrance to the church, originally framed by standing stone plates/to right preserved two, to left only the negative cut in the rock/;
p – outer pavement of the s.c. Bishop's Necropole;
q – mud floor surrounded by thrown up stone foundations and threshold;
r – stone plate under the foundations of cathedral's walls covering three red bricks laid there as a foundation deposit;
s – southern jamb of the southernmost entrance to the *exonarthex*;
t1 – remains of the foundation of the outer wall of the *exonarthex*;
t2 – the lowest, only preserved layer of the foundation of the partition wall between *exonarthex* and north-western corner room/tower;
u – holes for setting up wooden guide rails;
v – wooden guide rail for bar closing the door;
w- entrance to the north-western corner room with landing high above the pavement level : preserved door socket and traces of moving the door-leaf;
x – substruction [*thus Gartkiewicz, 'Foundation' would be better term*] for an outer landing/dais in front of the northern entrance to the church;
y – supposed position of door-socket – a hole for fixing an element with it;
z – inner corner of door recess preserved in negative;
aa – edge of pavement showing the original position of the inner face of the outer wall of the church;
bb – two lowest course of stones of the wall collapsed outerwards;
cc – position of wooden lintels situated behind the arches upon the staircases leading to the underground.

PHOTOGRAPHS

Gartkiewicz produced a collection of photographs of Qasr Ibrim and the majority of these are of the Cathedral Church or objects associated with it. The remainder are of the mud-brick church, which was located close to the south-east wall of the Cathedral and has since been demolished (Figure 3 Building No. 294), and of the Taharqa temple church (Figure 3 Building No.287). Copies of the photographs and of a typewritten inventory, prepared in both English and Polish in 1986, are held in the archives. The photographs are mostly numbered between 1 and 578, but a few have a letter added after the number, hence the total number of photographs is a little over 580. The photographs taken of the Cathedral Church in the 1972 and 1976 seasons are numbered 299-553, whilst those taken in the 1978 season are numbered 1-257. The Gartkiewicz photographs are identified in this report by the prefix *EES Photo GP* ... and the original captions given to the photographs by Gartkiewicz can be identified by the unique number in his inventory. The photographs taken by Gartkiewicz are used here to illustrate a brief review of his excavations, and elsewhere in this report to illustrate the description of the standing building (Chapter 4); the architectural components (Chapter 5); and the Bishop Miel or Mielkuda inscriptions (Chapter 6).

EXCAVATIONS

It is difficult to determine from the photographs precisely when the excavations they depict were undertaken, since some work may have been carried out before 1972. However, Gartkiewicz produced an interim report on his observations and investigations in the Cathedral in 1972. Unfortunately, the English employed is, in places, difficult to follow and it is likely that it was never intended to be published in its original form. However, it is the only written record of investigations undertaken at this time and for this reason it is repeated here in full, with references added to specific areas of the building identified from his photographs (see below Figure 17 Areas 1-12), so that the original descriptions comments are available for re-interpretation. The comments in square brackets have been added by the author to clarify the original text.

> 'In connection with Professor Plumley's suggestion that an earlier building had previously existed in this place, I made a preliminary analytical study of the present building and dug six trial pits in the aisles [*perhaps Areas 4, 6, 7, 8, 11 and 12 referred to below*] in order to clarify the above mentioned suggestion.
>
> 'The Earlier Building [*Gartkiewicz is evidently referring here to the first phase of the Cathedral Church, and makes a clear distinction between this building, which he refers to as the Great Church, and referred to henceforth in this report as Phase 1, and its later reconstruction, perhaps as a Cathedral, henceforth referred to as Phase 2*].
>
> 'Research proved that the cathedral walls differ and that the dissimilarity runs horizontally one metre above the church floor. The whole eastern section of the cathedral was built on previously existing walls which were almost wholly filled up by masonry blocks, nearly all of which had been re-used. Few remains of pharaonic [*in fact Meroitic*] decoration may be found on their surfaces. The thick and heavy stone pieces were very carefully interlocked and a few undercuts had been made in them for better further stone adaption.'

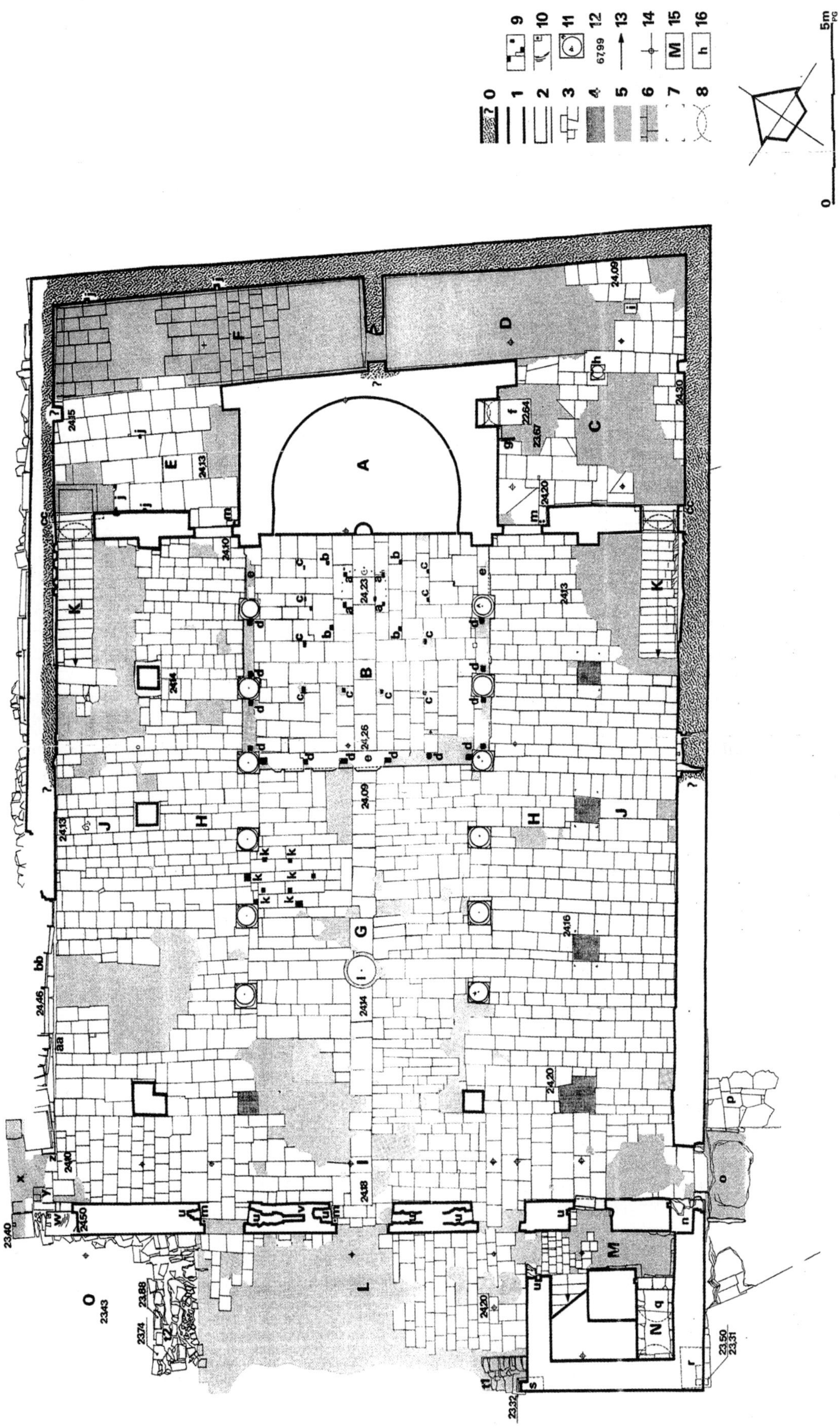

Figure 16: Przemyslaw Gartkiewicz's plan of the remains of the Cathedral (also on the CD).

'The run of individual block courses is free, only the height of the horizontally arranged course being mutable. Examination *in situ* proved that the lower storey walls were bound and set up as a whole. They constituted two similar chamber rows accessible from two staircases located symmetrically along the southern and western walls [*This is evidently referring to the north and south crypt, the antechambers, and the stairs leading down to them*].

'In three trial pits [*probably including Areas 6 and 11*] I discovered and identified the original walls, parallel to the outer ones, which bounded the staircases from the interior. The original stairs were wider and led to a slightly lower level than the present church floor. I found that the gebel on which the building was founded slopes quite abruptly towards the North East for almost a half the length of the present cathedral. That the place was previously built over is proved by the walls the remains of which were discovered outside the building [*presumably south of Area 11*]. Inside the cathedral two trial pits [*presumably Areas 7 and 11*] revealed further remains. These were stone structures [*now identified as probably Meroitic and post-Meroitic in date*] constructed from poorly dressed blocks and laid directly up on bedrock. The run [*alignment*] of these walls differs from the later layout of the building for they were built parallel to the rock escarpment bounding line [*presumably referring to the rock-cut cliff face containing the burial chambers*].

'The original [*Phase 1*] walls, i.e. those existing before the construction of the cathedral, were founded on bedrock. They contained the previous construction walls and its mud floor.

'The lower storey of the [*Phase* 1] edifice was founded on the gebel slope. The inner south staircase wall should be examined together with the previous construction that bounds the rock plateau from the west. I did not detect any inner face of the wall [*presumably that flanking the south steps in Area 11*]. It seems that at this height it constituted one side of a staircase boundary and on the other the floor basis of the central portion of the building. The floor in the central portion must have been previously laid higher than the present one and that is why it was levelled and reconstructed during the church building [*i.e. the construction of Phase 2 of the Cathedral Church*].

'In all of the preserved walls I verified the existence of outer offsets – the one that run [*ran*] along the wall – and also some grooves in the wall faces.

'I identified these as foundations of barrel vaults which previously existed in all the chambers examined. These offsets and grooves constituted a clear system of brick vault buttresses.

'Some of these vaults, which were made of a mud brick, ca [*circa*] 37 x 17 x 7.6 cms in size, have been preserved till now. The rest, and especially the vaults under the staircases, were reconstructed most probably during the cathedral erection. I came across primary wall dressing fragments which were whitewashed several times. In the higher storey of the existing cathedral I found the remains of the above mentioned building walls and constructions. The small pilasters in the south and north of the present vestry [*baptistry and sacristy*] walls are fragments of the previous [*Phase 1*] constructions. The corresponding somewhat bigger ones, attached to the [*Phase 2*] apse walls and the apse itself, seem to be in the present state of research a Christian construction. It was [*they were*] most probably contemporary with the cathedral [*Phase 2*] erection.

Conclusion [*Phase 1*]

'In reconsidering the results achieved in my research it can be asserted that before the building of the [*Phase 2*] cathedral there had been a monumental two storey stone edifice [*Phase 1*] which was constructed over the remains of a [*pre-existing Meroitic and post-Meroitic*] building that might have served residential purposes. Its [*the Phase 1 Cathedral Church's*] western boundary was not clearly pronounced, nevertheless its eastern part was very carefully researched with the exception of the middle portion.

'In its lower storey it constitutes two chamber rows adjacent to two staircases which bound the middle part. The interiors were vaulted, plastered and painted. The style of the masonry dates them [*no*] earlier that [*than*] the beginnings of Christianity in Nubia. That this building was constructed later than the pharaonic [*Meroitic*] period is supported by the fact that the stone blocks were twice used (for its construction), /once during pharaonic [*Meroitic*] times and then during the pre cathedral construction/.

'The Cathedral [*these comments clearly refer to the Phase 2 reconstruction of the Cathedral Church*]

'It is constructed on the remains of the previous [*Phase 1*] edifice.'

'The northern wall was partly surrounded by the western section built on the new foundations which did not reach the rock level, which falls here vertically [*this seems to suggest that the courses of large stone blocks at the west end are a Phase 2 rebuild – an aspect discussed further in Chapter 8, and also identifies the vertical face of the quarried gebel surface in this area*]. The widened lower part of the foundation was placed on secondary layers which had accumulated during the occupation of this area by the previous inhabitants. The lack of hard and firm foundations contributed to the deflexion of the building in its western part and probably caused its eventual collapse.

'The Cathedral was mainly based on the remains which bounded the building on the west and these partly conditioned the space arrangement in this part of the building, mainly traceable through the structures of both western vestries [*the north-west and south-west towers*]. During the process of adapting the preserved fragments the transverse walls were erected and the western access to the aisles was closed.

'The new entrance to the underground sections [*the north and south crypts*] was arched. The width of both previous staircases [*north and south steps*] was narrowed by a ⅓, thus extinguishing the previously existing vaults and building over the corresponding offset and grooves [*Gartkiewicz appears to have mistakenly identified the slots and rebates designed to take timbers forming false floors over the north and south steps as having been designed to take vaults*].

'I also found out [*in Area* 11] that during the construction of the piers that divided both of [*the*] south aisles, the foundation fragment of the previous inner face southern stair wall was used. In the northern part of the cathedral the piers were built at a certain distance from the analogical northern stair wall. The piers construction was quite different, they were put on special, wider bases which were supported by rough stone construction. Very untypical of church building rules was the differentiation in shape of the northern and southern piers, the former being square and the latter rectangular. This might be explained by the different foundation circumstances [*now seen as a later rebuild in Phase 3 of those in the south arcade – see Chapter 4*].

'I detected the technical homogeneity of the masonry in the new walls constructed on the remains. It can be asserted that the cathedral masonry was done by highly qualified masons who followed other than the native tradition.

'The walls were constructed in "opus emplectum" technique in which the rule of keeping the same level of the courses is most crucial. The masonry blocks were relatively small and constituted the ashlar-stone courses. Their faces were usually very carefully worked out. In the western lower part huge masonry blocks were used. Here the levelling method was followed. They [*the walls*] were generally one side faced with the exception of the walls between the Exonarthex and Esonarthex due to their spacial position in the building layout. According to the opus emplectum technique the masonry blocks used in the inner faces were poorly worked out since they were intended to be faced with mortar and plaster, inner parts of the wall being filled up by stones with mud mortar poured on.

'In addition to the usual kind of mortar the presence of one containing gypsum, used mainly for the crucial constructions, was detected.

'I made some research on the wood used in the cathedral structure. The main walls and piers contained horizontal bindings. These occur in both faces in each of the walls. In the preserved parts of the walls, the binds [*bindings*] run above and below the window apertures. In the piers on the other hand, they run in mid height and at the top. Such constructions constituted the general stiffening frame for the whole building and for some of its most important parts. They also served a decorative purpose especially in the cathedral elevation. Dom palm timber was used in the wall stiffening and tamarisk in the piers. Many different types of timber bar joints were observed, thereby verifying that the cathedral masons were highly skilled in the use of wood working.

'[*The*] Other building material used during the cathedral construction was burnt brick. This appears in the northern crypt vault, in the staircase vault of the cathedral, and in the apse tribune fill. Occasionally it occurred in the south western tower foundation.

Conclusion [*Phase 2*]

'The church layout, as well as its examination from the technical point of view, proved that it was the product of highly skilled masons. The traces of the former existence of another [*north-west*] tower in the western façade and the exonarthex between them leads to the conclusion that the builders of the cathedral were strongly influenced by the north-Syrian architecture.'

'I am of the opinion that the plan and the arrangement of the western elevation can be treated as an example of the classical "double tower rule" dating from the Vth and the VIth century. Similarly, when examining the technique and the masonry of the western walls, I am of the opinion that it was built by north-Syrian masons who came to Qasr Ibrim not later than the end of the VIIth or in the first half of the VIIIth century. The Christian edifice re-placed the old, pre-Christian monumental edifice which might have been a pagan temple [*Gartkiewicz appears to erroneously refer to the Phase 1 building as pre-Christian*].'

The relevant diary entries read as follows, with comments added in square brackets to clarify the text.

'6th February - Dr Gartkiewicz removed upper courses of the north wall of the Cathedral as it was unsafe.'

'4th March – Dr Gartkiewicz closed down operations on Church 2 [*to the south of the Cathedral*] and returned to study the Cathedral within the guidelines laid down by Dr William Adams.'

7th March – Dr Gartkiewicz completed his work on the apse of the Cathedral [*see below Areas 1, 4 and 5*] and his gang started to rebuild the inner wall of the tribune. At the west front [*see below Area 10*] he noticed a wall running parallel to the west wall of the Cathedral and noted that there was a possibility that this might be connected with the first [*ie Phase 1*] Cathedral [*this appears to have been the 'retaining wall' found in 1964 which has since been shown to pre-date the Cathedral Church – see above Chapter 2*].'

'8th March – Gartkiewicz filled in the southernmost of his trenches at the west front of the Cathedral and asked the Administrative Director for permission to clear a little to the north.'

'9th March – He [*Gartkiewicz*] completed his excavation to the west of the Cathedral and was planning the area before filling in the trench.'

'19th March – Dr Gartkiewicz found a wall in the sacristy which confirmed theories about the layout of the earlier Cathedral [*see below Area 2*].'

Apart from Gartkiewicz's plan and some elevations of the building, no other drawings have been found which locate the areas investigated by him.

DISCUSSION

The following description, based on photographs and the comments noted above, attempts to identify the areas investigated in the 1970s and the features exposed within them. The area numbers have been allocated by the present author.

Area 1: The Apse

A trench had been excavated across the apse in the 1963 season, and at that time it was recognised that the standing apse was a replacement for an earlier one of which the footings survived (Chapter 1 Trench A1).

At some subsequent date, the area contained within the later apse was fully excavated to reveal the full extent of the earlier structure, as well as part of the paving of the floor and thresholds in the side walls that served former openings on the north and south sides and gave access to adjoining rooms (Figure 17 and Plate 61).

Plate 61: The footings of the earlier apse, looking north-east, with the floor paving and thresholds on either side (EES Photo GP 489).

It is not known precisely when these investigations took place, but there are photographs of the fully excavated apse in the Gartkiewicz collection from the 1972 and 1976 seasons (for example GPs 489, 491, 494, 495, and 501). There is a strong likelihood that this part of the site was excavated in the late 1960s, prior to Gartkiewicz's first visit to the site in 1972.

The remains of the earlier apse are further discussed and illustrated below in Chapter 4.

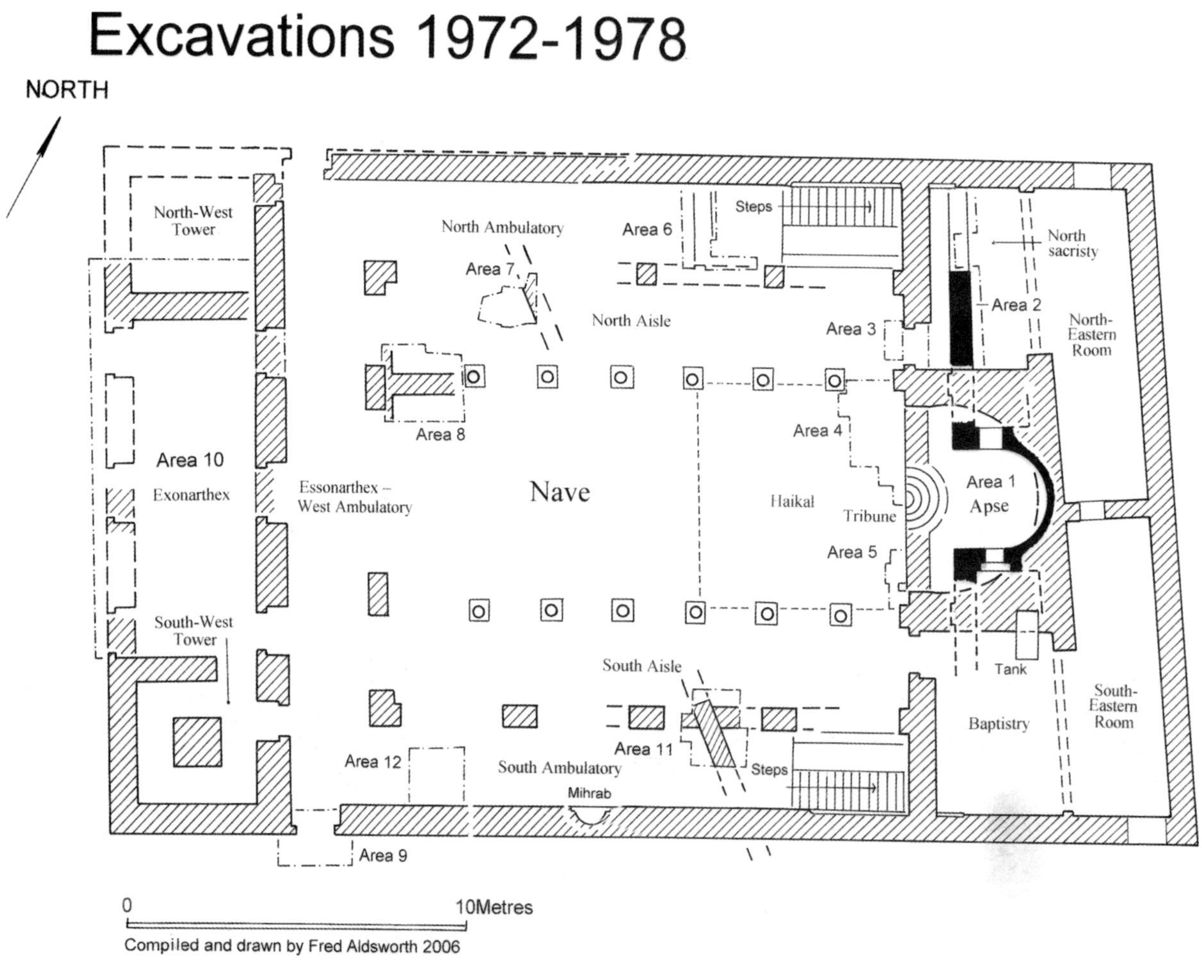

Figure 17: The locations of the excavations believed to have been conducted by Gartkiewicz in the period 1972-1978, with his identifications of elements of the plan.

Area 2: The Sacristy

This room, located immediately north of the apse, was referred to by Gartkiewicz as the North Sacristy (Figure 17).

It is not clear whether the room still contained occupation debris over the whole of the floor area in the 1970s, but a photograph, looking west, shows that the west door was still blocked until the 1978 season and that against it was a section of what Gartkiewicz referred to as 'preserved layers of Post Christian occupation', up to 1.5 metres in height (Plate 62).

The condition of the floor and the section suggested that they had only recently been exposed and cleaned and the likelihood is that the deposits in this room were not excavated until the 1978 season. The diary entry for the 19th March of that year may refer to them.

Plate 62: The occupation layers against the west wall of the sacristy (EES Photo GP 7).

The paving slabs against the west wall of the sacristy were evidently taken up after the removal of the remainder of the occupation debris, and revealed the entire length of the foundation of an earlier wall which had separated the sacristy from the main body of the earlier (Phase 1) Cathedral Church (Plates 63 and 64). This may have extended at full height to within 2.3 metres of the north wall of the building, at which point it appears to have terminated at an opening marked by paving slabs.

Plate 63: The south end of the earlier wall separating the sacristy from the nave (EES Photo GP 85).

Plate 64: The north end of the earlier wall separating the sacristy from the nave (EES Photo GP 84).

Area 3: The North Aisle (East End)

This appears to have been a very small excavation undertaken in 1978, immediately adjacent to the door into the sacristy. It was achieved either by removing one or two floor slabs, or by cleaning an area from which they had previously been removed (Figure 17).

It revealed two pottery vessels containing the remains of human foetuses, which were either buried before the paving of the Cathedral Church was laid down or inserted under a deliberately lifted area of paving that was then replaced (Plates 65 and 66).

Plate 65: The foetus burials, from the south (EES Photo GP 78).

Plate 66: The foetus burials, from the north (EES Photo GP 79).

Area 4: The *Haikal* (North Side)

This was a larger excavation undertaken in 1972 or 1976 at the east end of the nave, under the pavement on the north side of the *haikal*. It was bounded by the tribune on its east side and the first column base of the nave on its west side (Figure 17).

Masonry structures and pottery are depicted in photographs (GPs 515, 516 and 518) and these are simply referred to in his descriptions as 'Pre-Christian structures' (Plates 67 and 68). Nothing more is known of them.

Plate 67: Structures and pottery under the haikal, *from the north (EES Photo GP 518).*

Area 5: The *Haikal* (South Side)

This appears to have been a small investigation made in 1972 or 1976 against the west face of the tribune, at its junction with the standing apse (Figure 17).

A small number of paving slabs appear to have been lifted to reveal a part of a stele with Meroitic inscription, partially under the tribune, which had evidently been re-used as paving or sub-structure in the earlier building (Plates 69 and 70). It is referred to but not described by David Edwards in his recent account of Meroitic stelae from the site (*Edwards 2007*: 92).

Plate 69: The junction of the tribune and the standing apse, looking east (EES Photo GP 508).

Plate 68: The north section of Area 4 (EES Photo GPs 515A and 516).

Plate 70: The junction of the tribune and the standing apse, from the north, with the stele exposed at the bottom (EES Photo GP 502).

Area 6: North Ambulatory

This was a small area lying a short distance to the west of the north steps (Figure 17). It was probably one of the trenches in which Gartkiewicz investigated the wall flanking the south side of the north steps, referred to in his interim report for 1972.

The two photographs taken by Gartkiewicz (GPs 144 and 146) depict an L-shaped slot where paving had been removed and, what appears to be, some earlier paving alongside it (Plates 71 and 72). In his descriptions, Gartkiewicz refers to the photographs as showing the 'original pavement of the Old Church and the foundation of its partition wall', but it is not clear which features were thought to be a wall.

Plate 71: Area 6 and the paving alongside it, looking east (EES Photo GP 144).

Plate 72: Area 6 and the paving alongside it, looking south (EES Photo GP 146).

Area 7: North Aisle (West End)

This was a small area towards the west end of the north aisle, which was investigated in 1972 (Figure 14).

The photograph taken by Gartkiewicz (GP 303) shows a small area investigated after the removal of paving (Plate 73). A piece of masonry has been exposed which was described by Gartkiewicz simply as 'Pre-Christian structures'.

This is likely to have been the piece of masonry shown on a general survey plan for the 1972 season, which seems to have been a continuation of the walls found to the south-east, both within and outside the Cathedral (Figure 17 and see below area 11).

Plate 73: Area 7, looking east, and the masonry exposed beneath the later paving (EES Photo GP 303).

Area 8 : Nave (West End)

This was an area investigated in 1978 towards the west end of the north side of the nave, following the removal of paving slabs (Figure 17).

It appears to have exposed an L- or T-shaped foundation for a wall extending east-west, close to the line of the column bases, and another at right angles at its west end, on the line of the pier bases forming the west arcade (Plates 74, 75 and 76). They may have formed part of the earliest phase of the Cathedral Church or have been introduced as footings for the extended building (for further discussion see Chapter 8).

Plate 74: Area 8, looking east, with the wall foundation on the alignment of the column bases (EES Photo GP 58).

Plate 75: Area 8, looking west, with the wall foundation on the alignment of the column bases, in the foreground, and that at right angles to it under the pier base at the far end (EES Photo GP 61).

Plate 76: Area 8, looking south-east, showing the wall foundation (EES Photo GP 64).

Area 9: South Door

The threshold of the main door into the building towards the west end of the south wall was investigated in 1972 or 1976 (Figure 17).

Here a later threshold, formed of large blocks of stone, was removed to expose an earlier threshold at the west side of which was a wooden door socket containing three circular holes (Plates 77, 78, 79 and 80).

Plate 77: The threshold of the south door, as found, view from the south-east (EES Photo GP 339A).

Plate 78: The threshold of the south door after excavation, from the south-east (EES Photo GP 337).

Plate 79: The threshold of the south door, after excavation, from the north-east and showing the wooden door socket (EES Photo GP 341).

Area 10 : West End

The area outside the west end of the standing remains of the building, and referred to by Gartkiewicz as the *exonarthex*, was investigated in 1972 or 1976 and in 1978 (Figure 17). The work is referred to in the diary entries made in March 1978 (see above). The wall 'running parallel to the east wall of the Cathedral' in the 7th March 1978 was probably the stone wall found in 1964 which pre-dates the Cathedral Church (see Chapter 2).

Plate 80: The threshold of the south door after excavation, from the east and showing the wooden door socket (EES Photo GP 451).

Features exposed here included the foundations for parts of the west wall of the building (Plates 81 and 82); its junction with the north-west corner of the surviving tower (Plates 83 and 84); the foundations under the surviving west wall of the west ambulatory or, as Gartkiewicz referred to it, the *essonarthex* (Plates 85-87); and foundations for the south wall and south-west corner of the north-west tower (Plates 81 and 88).

Plate 81: Investigations in the southern part of the exonarthex *in 1978, looking south. Note the remains of the foundations for the west wall of the* narthex *in the foreground (EES Photo GP 6).*

Plate 82: Investigations in the southern part of the exonarthex *in 1978, looking south-east. Note the remains of the foundations for the west wall of the* narthex *in the foreground (EES Photo GP 9).*

Plate 84: Foundations of the west wall adjoining the tower, looking south (EES Photo GP 350).

Plate 83: Foundations of the west wall adjoining the tower, looking south-east (EES Photo GP 345).

Plate 85: Foundations of the west wall of the west ambulatory, looking north (EES Photo GP 1).

Plate 86: Foundations of the west wall of the west ambulatory, looking east (EES Photo GP 2).

Plate 88: Foundations of the west wall of the west ambulatory, looking east (EES Photo GP 446).

Plate 87: Foundations of the west wall of the west ambulatory, looking from above (EES Photo GP 31).

Area 11: South Ambulatory

This was a trench excavated alongside the second pier from the east of the south arcade and is probably one of the six referred to by Gartkiewicz in his 1972 report.

A folder of site notes and photographs relating to the 1966 to 1972 seasons, compiled by Professor Plumley, includes two photographs taken on the 9th November 1972 in the south aisle of the Cathedral (Photographs 528 and 530). The first is captioned 'wall of earlier building under south aisle of Cathedral Trial Pit 4'. They both record an earlier stone wall running diagonally across that part of the building, possibly aligned on the wall recorded in Area 7, with a stone footing butting up to it on either side. This appears to be on the line of the south arcade and a continuation of the wall forming the north side of the south steps.

Three further photographs show similar, but not identical, views of the same features in the contact print and negative albums for the 1972 season (Plates 89-91).

Plates 89 and 90: The stone walls exposed under the south arcade, from the west and from the south (EES Photos QI 72/4/ 6 & 7).

Plate 91: The stone walls exposed under the south arcade, from the east (EES Photo QI/72/4/8).

The 1972 survey plan mainly records the work undertaken to the south of the Cathedral, but it shows the diagonal wall continuing south to form part of a building which extended under Church 2 (see Figure 3 Building 294) and formed part of a structure referred to as House X-3.

Area 12: South Ambulatory

This trench lay against the inner face of the south wall, a short distance to the east of the south door, and is probably one of the six referred to by Gartkiewicz in his 1972 report.

It is recorded on a photograph taken on the 9th November 1972 and is captioned 'Pit 5' (Plate 92).

Plate 92: Area 12, as excavated in 1972 (EES Photo QI 72/4/9).

The purpose of the investigation in this position is unclear, but it was next to the change in fabric in the lowest courses of masonry in the south wall, which can be seen in the photograph, and it may have been intended to investigate this feature. The photograph indicates that there was a flat surface of bedrock immediately under the paved surface, and this may have been levelled to take the paving slabs, or possibly to create a threshold for an opening through the original (Phase 1) wall at this point (for further discussion see Chapter 8).

SUMMARY

During his three seasons of excavation and recording at Qasr Ibrim, Gartkiewicz demonstrated that the Cathedral Church had been built on the site of earlier structures, perhaps designed for residential use, of which extensive remains survived under and around the building. He was also able to demonstrate that there were two principal phases of construction of the existing building – the first (Phase 1) of which he considered to have been a Church, and the second (Phase 2) to have been a Cathedral. He suggested that the form of the existing plan of the west end of the building (perhaps Phase 1) might date to the fifth or sixth century AD and that the technique of their construction (perhaps Phase 2) could not be later than the end of the seventh century or the first half of the eighth century AD. He prepared a detailed record of the surviving building in the form of a plan, accompanied by a detailed key and legend; a series elevation drawings; and a photographic record, accompanied by a written inventory, all of which contribute to an understanding of the building.

Chapter 4: THE STANDING BUILDING

The Cathedral Church was built on the highest point of the bedrock at Qasr Ibrim and constituted the most imposing structure left standing when the site was finally abandoned in 1811 (Plates 93 and 94).

Plate 93: The remains of the Cathedral, from the south-west, in the 1960s (Unreferenced EES Photo).

Plate 94: The remains of the Cathedral, from the south-west, in 1992 (Photograph by Fred Aldsworth).

The structure had been excavated and partially recorded between 1963 and 1978 (Chapters 1-3), but because the investigations conducted by Gartkiewicz in the 1970s were incomplete, Paul Drury was invited by Dr Mark Horton, then Field Director of the Qasr Ibrim expedition, to assist in the interpretation of the major architectural monuments. After an initial reconnaissance in 1988-1989, work concentrated on the interpretation of the second phase of the Cathedral Church (substantially the existing structure) in 1990, and of the earlier (Phase 1) building in 1992. The results of Gartkiewicz's detailed survey became available at the end of the 1990 season, and the opportunity was taken by Fred Aldsworth in the 1992 season. to complete the detailed drawings of the walls and to record architectural fragments lying on the site.

This part of the report, which includes substantial contributions from Paul Drury, provides a general description of the standing building, mostly as it existed in the 1990s. The following part deals with the architectural components that were lying on the site at that time, or are believed to have derived from the Cathedral Church (Chapter 5). In both cases heavy reliance is placed on the photographs taken by Gartkiewicz and the captions that he prepared for them.

A general description of the Cathedral and its history has already been published (*Adams 1996*: 73-78) and a full discussion and interpretation of all the evidence presently available is included below (Chapter 8).

THE SITE

The site chosen for the Cathedral Church had previously been occupied by earlier buildings (see Chapter 7). Similar structures were excavated immediately to the south, where they directly overlie, and indeed are partially cut into, the natural bedrock; and short lengths of wall and occupation levels directly underlie the latest paving of the body of the Cathedral. However, towards the east end of the church the bedrock falls away by about 3 metres, and advantage was taken of this to provide crypts around the east end of the sanctuary .

A burial chamber had also been cut into the bedrock under the south-west corner of the Cathedral and there were others further south (Plate 93 and Appendix 2). Their date is uncertain, although they were certainly used in the Christian period.

THE GROUND PLAN

The building falls short of accurate orientation and in January 1963 its axis was measured as lying on a magnetic bearing of 57° 30', i.e. about 12½° east of north-east.

In the early work on the Cathedral, however, it was accepted that the apse was at the north end of the building. This was subsequently changed and it was assumed to be conventionally orientated, so that the apse was assumed to face west.

The ground plan of the external north, south, and west walls is in the form of a rectangle, but the east wall is at an angle of about 85 degrees to the south wall

The overall dimensions of the building, complete with its two west towers and *narthex* is approximately 32.0 metres by 19.6 metres.

It was recognised as early as the first season of excavation in 1963 that there were at least two major phases of construction of the standing building. These were first identified in the apse (see Chapter 1 Trench A1) and then explored further during later investigations both in the apse and in the sacristy to the north (see Chapter 3 Areas 1 and 2).

The standing masonry also falls into two distinct elements: the lower parts of the walls, of massive, often re-used, ashlar blocks, and the upper parts, faced externally and, in important areas, internally, using smaller rectangular ashlar blocks very tightly jointed.

Discontinuities of plan between the later and the earlier structure at the east end, and the fact that the present east nave wall abuts the lower element of the north and south walls but bonds with the upper part, make quite clear that the break in masonry implies two distinct periods of construction, rather than a change in the supply of building materials or a short hiatus in the building work.

The two stages of work are referred to here as Period 1, Phases 1 and 2 and are discussed in greater detail below (Chapter 8). Accepting that these two phases of construction exist, it is proposed to describe and illustrate the principal elements of the structure.

For ease of handling, the record drawings of the standing structure completed in the 1990s are placed at the end of this chapter. There is firstly a ground plan (Figure 23 on p. 82) and then a series of elevation and section drawings which are lettered AA-ZZ (Figures 24-32, see pp. 83-90).

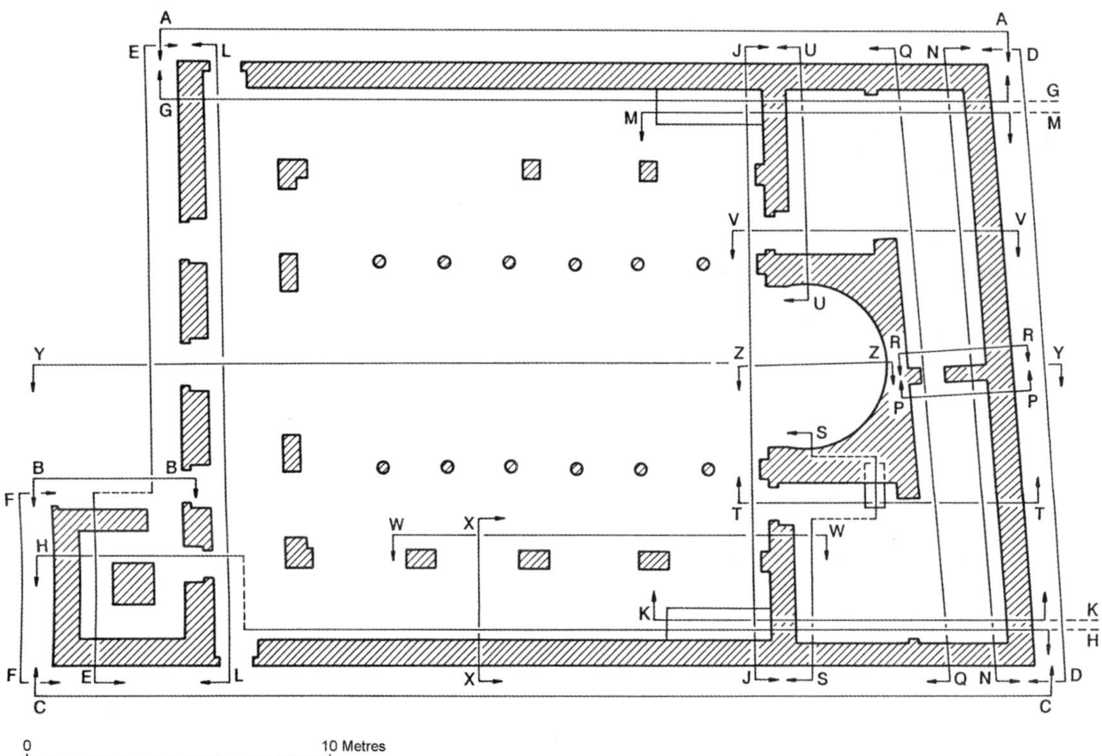

Figure 18: Key diagram identifying the positions of the elevation and section drawings.

The relevant figure numbers are as follows:
Figure 24 (p.83) AA, BB and CC;
Figure 25 (p.84) DD, EE and FF;
Figure 26 (p.85) GG and HH;
Figure 27 (p.86) JJ, KK, LL and MM;
Figure 28 (p.87) NN, PP, QQ and RR;
Figure 29 (p.88) SS, TT, UU and VV;
Figure 30 (p.89) WW and XX;
Figure 31 (p.90) YY;
Figure 32 (p.90) ZZ.

The ground plan (Figure 19) identifies the principal elements of the standing structure and these are described, mostly in the condition that they survived in the 1990s, in the following order – the external walls; the crypts; the early apse; the later apse, the tribune, and the adjoining rooms; the nave, including paving, column bases, pulpit and *haikal*; the south aisle and ambulatory; the north aisle and ambulatory; the west ambulatory; the west towers; and the *narthex*.

Plate 95: The south wall from the south-west, in 1992 (Photograph by Fred Aldsworth).

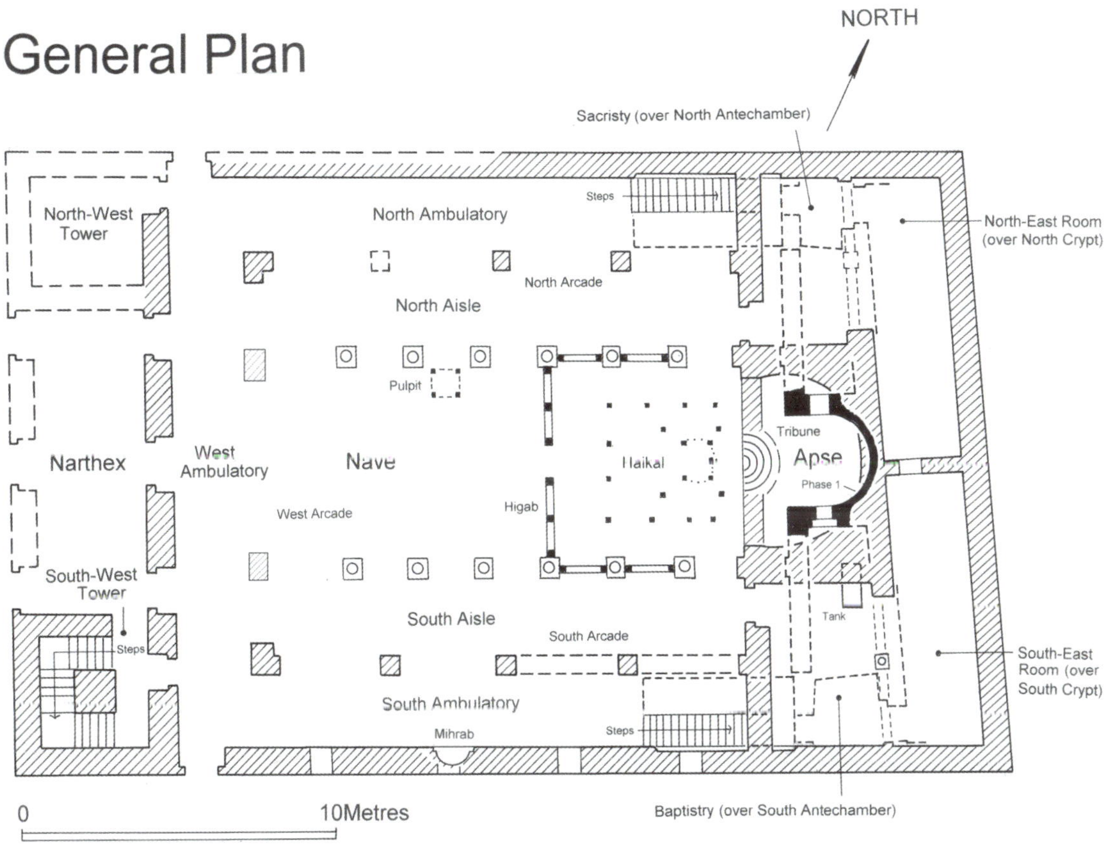

Figure 19: Simplified plan, identifying the principal elements of the Cathedral Church, and showing the two phases of construction of the apse and of the adjoining spaces to the north and south.

THE EXTERNAL WALLS

The south wall survives to its full height, with parapet, of 6.18 metres above the paved floor level for a distance of 5.5 metres (Figures 24 CC and 27 XX and Plates 8 and 95-97). It is 85 cms thick at its base.

It contains evidence for the two principal phases of construction throughout its length of 31.8 metres. There is an opening for a door towards its west end; the remains of wooden bracing in the form of ring beams at two levels; and the remains of six openings for windows. Internally it also includes a series of beam slots to carry timbers over the south ambulatory.

In the lower part of the wall, which is built of large, mostly re-used, blocks, there is a change of coursing on the external face at a distance of about 4 metres east the south door, and this corresponds to a change of fabric on the internal face, where smaller stones are used (Figures 24 CC and 26HH). The change was noted here, and less obviously in the north wall, by Kenneth Frazer in 1964, who suggested that the building was either repaired 'after an earthquake' or extended (*Unpublished 1964 – Report on Survey and Architecture*: 3). It was also noted by Gartkiewicz in the 1970s (see Chapter 3).

Plate 96: Part of the south wall where it survived to its highest level in 1992 (Photograph by Fred Aldsworth).

The lower part of the south wall is up to thirteen courses in height at its east end and, at its west end it is set on a large slab of sandstone.

Plate 98: The west end of the south wall in the 1970s (EES Photo GP553).

It is not clear whether there is sufficient evidence here to indicate two phases of construction and a later repair, or simply a change in building technique at this point. It is conceivable, however, that this represents a later rebuilding of the lowest courses of masonry at the west end of the building but the evidence is not conclusive (for further discussion see Chapter 8).

Much of the masonry in the lower part of the wall is clearly derived and re-used from a monumental temple structure or structures of Meroitic date, probably Temple 4 (*Rose 2007*). The blocks retain evidence of whitewashing and painted decoration, together with Meroitic graffiti, including the characteristic carvings of feet and hands. Many of them include vertical pilgrim scrapes on their external faces, some of which may be contemporary with the Cathedral Church. The much rougher nature of the walling below ground level, not intended to be seen, is clear on the east elevation (see below).

Plate 97: The interior face of the south wall in 1992, showing the ring beam and beam slots (Photograph by Fred Aldsworth).

The upper surface of the bedrock varies greatly in height in the vicinity of the Cathedral, due in part to previous activities, such that whilst the earliest part of the wall (Phase 1) survives to a height of 1.4 metres above the level of the internal paving throughout much of its length, it survives to a height of 5.0 metres above its footing on bedrock at its east end and to 1.2 metres above its footing on bedrock towards its west end, adjoining the door opening.

Plate 99: Pilgrim scrapes on the south wall (EES Photo GP553).

There is a door opening some 5.4 metres from the west end which is 1.05 metres wide, with rebates to take a wooden door. The opening was probably about 3 metres high. Gartkiewicz excavated several thresholds in this opening and recorded a wooden door socket on the west side (see Chapter 3 Area 9).

The interface between the original (Phase 1) wall, which for much of its length terminates with a course of relatively thin blocks, and the later (Phase 2) wall appears to be horizontal throughout the length of the south wall, except perhaps for an additional block at the south-east corner.

The later rebuild of the south wall (Phase 2) survives for a short distance to its full height of 4.8 metres above the original wall, to what appears to be the top of the parapet. It comprises twenty-six courses of smaller stone blocks, which have each been carefully tooled only on their intended external face, with a central panel of vertical tooling and marginal tooling which is diagonal. This may have been for display or to take a plaster surface. The joints are very fine on this phase of construction (Plates 100 and 101).

Plate 100: Detail of the Phase 2 stonework in the 1970s (EES Photo GP 426).

Plate 101: Samples of marginally-tooled stones from the Phase 2 reconstruction (EES Photo GP 217).

The upper part of the wall is canted out, and reaches a maximum thickness of about 90 centimetres at the level of the parapet.

The wall includes wooden bracing in the form of ring beams at two levels, which pass above and below the openings for the six windows. Immediately above the ninth course is a double frame system which has external and internal ring beams connected by tie bars, whilst immediately above the sixteenth course is a tie beam only on the external face, with some tie bars penetrating into the wall.

The system of bracing was described and illustrated by Gartkiewicz (*1990*: 149-153 Figures 77 and 78, reproduced here as Figures 20 and 21).

In 1964 the timber employed was identified by Kenneth Frazer as 'palm timber' (*Field Notes 1964 Report on Survey and Architecture*: 4) and in 1972 it was identified by Gartkiewicz as being from the 'Dom Palm'.

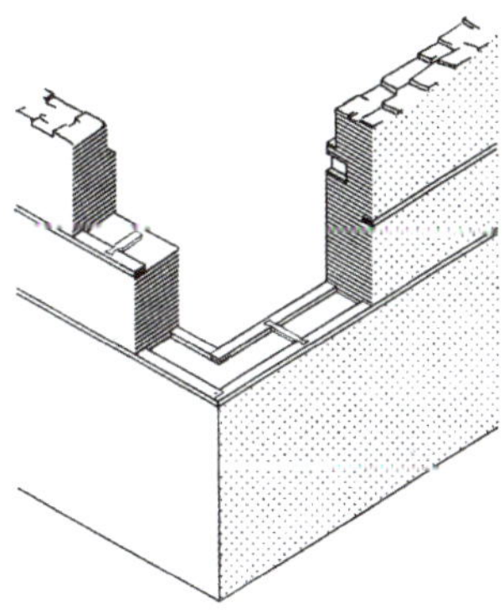

Figure 20: System of wooden bracing frames employed in the ring beams of the Cathedral during Phase 2 (after Gartkiewicz 1990: Figure 77).

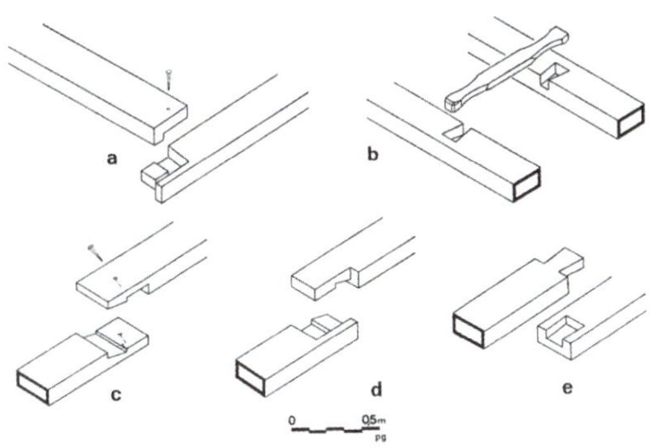

Figure 21 : Types of carpentry joint employed in the wooden bracing frames (after Gartkiewicz 1990: Figure 78):
a – corner joint of outer frame;
b – connecting bar joining bars of the inner and outer frames;
c, d and e – scarf joints.

The window openings, each 70 cms wide and 112 cms high, appear to have had stone sills with the upper ring beam forming a lintel (Plate 102). They probably contained stone grilles of which part of at least one example was found on the site (see Chapter 5 and Figure 46, No 78).

Plate 102: One of the window openings in the south wall in the 1970s (EES Photo GP 546).

The features on the internal face of the south wall are discussed with the south ambulatory

The east wall is built directly on the bedrock throughout its length (Figure 25 DD and Plate 103).

Plate 103: The east wall, looking from the north-east in the 1970s (EES Photo GP 162).

The bedrock is not visible externally but it was exposed during the excavations undertaken in the 1960s (see above Chapter 1 Trench F) and it is visible internally as the floor to the north and south crypts (Figures 27 KK & MM and 28 NN).

The original part of the wall (Phase 1) is 19.4 metres long, 105 cms thick at its base, and reduces to 75 cms in thickness above the level of the crypts (Figure 28 PP and RR). It survives to a height of a little over 4 metres throughout its length and a little higher at the north and south ends.

It is, once again, built of relatively large, mostly re-used, blocks of sandstone set in twelve courses, with the uppermost course being comprised, like the south wall, of relatively thin blocks, rising by two additional blocks at each end. Some of the blocks are scored with pilgrim scrapes and towards the north end the wall contains a re-used block inscribed with the toponym *Primis,* one of the ancient names for Qasr Ibrim (*Plumley 1971*: 11; *Priese 1984*: 488; and *Wilson 2007*: 112 Figure 18.23 CTH2). The lower courses are less-well laid than those higher up and this was presumably because they were not intended to be seen.

The upper part of the east wall comprises up to eleven courses of the smaller margin-tooled sandstone blocks of the later (Phase 2) building, which reach a height of about 6 metres above the bedrock. Above this there is some later, presumably post-Christian, rebuilding, which includes a small bowl made of granite.

There is no surviving evidence for the former existence of any openings in the east wall at any time.

Apart from its east end, the base of the north wall has not been investigated, but it is believed that for much of its length it may not have been built directly on the bedrock, but on made ground, and this is thought to be one of the reasons why only the east end of the original (Phase 1) wall and its later (Phase 2) rebuild survive. Both extend for a distance of about 15 metres from the north-east corner (Figures 24 BB and Plates 9, 10, 11, 104 and 105).

Plate 104: The north wall from the north-west in the 1970s (EES Photo GP13).

Plate 105: The east end of the north wall in the 1970s (EES Photo GP138).

The external face of both parts of the wall show signs of extensive burning, presumably caused during the Late or Post-Christian periods, and this removed the surface of the stones (Plate 106).

Plate 106: Evidence of burning on the north wall in the 1970s (EES Photo GP322).

The original (Phase 1) wall survives to a height of 1.1 metres above the level of the internal paved floor, and only four courses of stonework are visible above ground level externally, except at the north-east corner where excavations in the 1960s exposed the east wall and its north-east corner down to bedrock (see above Chapter 1 Trench F). There are the remains of an opening at the east end, but this appears to be a late insertion, perhaps connected with the residential use of the building in the post-Christian era.

The upper (Phase 2) north wall rises for a further 2.6 metres and includes the slot for a ring beam after thirteen courses of stonework and then jambs for two windows on its inner face.

The remainder of the north wall was demolished at least down to present floor level at an early date. It presumably included an original doorway to mirror that in the south wall, and the wall of a room mirroring the tower at the south-west corner. It was replaced in part by crudely-built walls, including much re-used material. This may include several phases of post-Christian reconstruction and there appears to be a blocked doorway part-way along its length.

The west wall was mostly demolished at an early post-Christian date and all that survives is the south end, which formed the west side of the south-west tower (Figure 25 FF and Plates 13 and 107).

Plate 107: The south end of the west wall in the 1970s (EES Photo GP540).

Excavations in the 1970s revealed sections of the footings of the west wall, which were found to be built on fill material within X-group houses (see above Chapter 3, Area 10).

The south-west corner of the Cathedral Church is formed of two massive sandstone blocks, set at right angles one upon the other, and adjoining them on their north side are four courses of large blocks (Figures 24CC and 25FF and Plates 98 and 107). These rise to a height of 1.8 metres and extend for a distance of 5.1 metres from the south-west corner of the building. At the north end of this is the jamb for an external west opening into the building, which is rebated for a door.

Above this, the smaller, margin-tooled stonework rises in height to a further 5.2 metres, and comprises eleven courses, a ring beam and wall tie, and then a further seven courses of stonework. These include the jambs for a window opening into the tower, but the southern part of the wall, above the level of the ring beam, evidently collapsed shortly after it had been recorded by Gartkiewicz.

The form of the west elevation between the two corner rooms is suggested by evidence surviving at its southern end. Here Gartkiewicz found the stub of a substantial foundation, implying a largely solid structure (Chapter 3 Area 2, Plates 83, 84). A projecting jamb rebated for a door survives on the corner of the stair enclosure, implying an arrangement exactly analogous to that to the east, at its junction with the west wall of the main body of the church. It is likely, therefore, that the west wall had three doorways exactly answering those immediately to the east.

In addition to the wooden door socket found by Gartkiewicz in the door in the south wall (Chapter 3 Area 9), a number of door openings along the west side and those leading into the baptistry and sacristy include a single door socket cut in stone behind one of the rebated stone jambs (Figure 15a - m). That at the north end of the west wall, which formerly gave access to the north-west room or tower from the west ambulatory, is accompanied by scrape marks on the stone threshold, and all this evidence suggests that the openings carried single wooden doors.

THE CRYPTS

The north and south crypts, the north and south antechambers, the burials contained in them, and the steps approaching them were excavated in 1964 (see Chapter 2 Figures 11, 12 and 14 Plates 45, 46 and 48 to 57).

In their basic structure the crypts belong entirely to the original (Phase 1) construction of the Cathedral Church. Later (Phase 2) modifications principally concern the entrances and the steps leading down into them.

The floors and lower parts of some side walls utilise the cut gebel sandstone bedrock. Above this the walls consist of massive roughly-laid re-used blocks (see Figure 26 GG & HH; Figure 27 JJ, KK, MM; Figure 28 NN, PP, QQ, RR; Figure 29 SS, TT, UU, VV; and Figure 31 YY).

The cross wall dividing the north and south crypts bonds into the side walls and is clearly original. The north crypt is 8.4 metres long by 2.1 metres wide and the south crypt is 8.3 metres long by 2.1 metres wide.

Offsets in the east and west walls provide the springing for skew vaults of mud brick, parts of which remained *in situ* until 2007. These consist of a half brick ring, with two courses laid flat over the crown almost to the springings (Plates 108 and 109). The side walls are 1.25 metres high and the heights to the crown of the vaulted ceilings are 2.25 metres. The haunches were then filled with fine brown debris, before laying a substantial mat of sorghum, with occasional palm fronds, evidently put in green since the desiccated leaves remained on the sorghum stems. More brown fill, containing wholly residual, late Meroitic/early X-group, material and in places covered with stone chippings, was covered sporadically with mud brick and finished as a mud floor.

The haunches were then filled with fine brown debris, before laying a substantial mat of sorghum, with occasional palm fronds, evidently put in green since the desiccated leaves remained on the sorghum stems. More brown fill, containing wholly residual, late Meroitic/early X-group, material and in places covered with stone chippings, was covered sporadically with mud brick and finished as a mud floor.

Plates 108 and 109: Remnants of mud brick vaulting in the north crypt in the 1970s (EES Photos GP 116 and 117).

A hole in the top of the south vault, about 35cms square and noted by Gartkiewicz (Figure 15a –i), survived towards the south end and appears to indicate a means of lighting the crypt, although not necessarily original since the surviving hole appears to have been cut through the vault.

Between the stairs and the crypts proper are the small antechambers, similarly vaulted in mud brick, that on south partly destroyed. The north antechamber, which has a lintelled opening to the north crypt, measures 2.1 metres by 1.25 metres internally, and is 3.3 metres high to the crown of the vaulted ceiling. The south chamber, which has an arched opening to the south crypt, measures 2.1 metres by 2.1 metres internally, and was about 3 metres high to the crown of the vaulted ceiling (Plate 110).

Plate 110: The south antechamber in the 1970s, looking east to the arched opening to the south crypt (EES Photo GP 132).

1.85 metres wide, extend virtually the whole width of the aisles and ascend to the level of the main nave floor, each step generally being formed of a single block of sandstone (Plate 111).

Plate 111: The south steps in the 1970s, looking up from the south antechamber (EES Photo GP 112).

The full width of the steps on the south side is better preserved and most visible, and it is clear that the wall representing the south nave arcade may have originally risen above floor level as a stylobate, presumably to guard the stairwell.

Slots in the main north and south walls, each about 40 cms high and up to 12 cms deep but partly obscured by later alterations, and rebates on the opposite sides of the steps appear to have been intended to take joists to support a demountable floor over the stairwells (Plates 112-114).

Plate 112: The east end of the slot in the south wall (EES Photo GP 98).

Plate 113: The west end of the slot in the south wall (EES Photo GP 99).

Plate 114: The slot and rebate on the south steps, looking west (Unreferenced EES Photo).

Whilst superficially similar, the treatment of the walls of the crypts and antechambers suggests differing functions during the early (Phase 1) life of the Cathedral Church. The following sequence can be discerned in the south crypt:

A. The mud brick vaults are plastered with a thick layer of mud identical to the material of the bricks themselves and the bonding mortar. Sporadic traces of a very thin layer (less than 2mm) of purplish lime plaster are found, which was then whitewashed. This plaster was also used to face up a cut through crumbling *gebel* at the south jamb of the doorway to south crypt. The limewashed mud was continued down the north wall of the crypt and retained for some 1.4 metres westwards, ending, so far as can be seen, in vertical joints.

B. A thin (2.3mm) layer of whitish plaster containing coarse sand, with a rough textured finish without limewash was applied over a dubbing-out layer of dark brown mud, to the stone walls, butting the mud layer A at the west. Similar distinctive plaster lined the northernmost of the graves cut through the *gebel* (Grave S4). The northern grave was first dubbed out with mud; that to the south (Grave S3) was not, and appears to be later, but perhaps only within the constructional sequence.

C. A thin layer of rather fine greyish lime plaster, with a smooth floated finish, thinly lime washed, was applied generally. This abuts, and indicates the position of a raised platform over the northernmost grave (Grave S4), which was formed by capping stones now removed. The north and east walls retain evidence for a shelf-like feature above this grave, along the north wall. This plaster also shows clear evidence of having been applied up to, and within, what must be an open, wooden, rectangular frame over the east end of the second grave from the north (Grave S3), which must have been *in situ* at the time that the plaster had been applied.

In the south antechamber, the plaster C continues, but on the walls, layers A and B are replaced by limewash over mud. This, plus the complementary use of A on the vault and B on the walls, suggests that all are in effect part of the primary scheme for the finishing of the south crypt itself; and also that the crypt itself was the more important space, being better finished. Both layers extend over the raised floor with a trapezoidal sinking on the north side of the antechamber, the purpose of which is obscure.

Layer C continues through the opening into the stairwell, covering the side of the stylobate of the outer south arcade, and is trapped by the later (Phase 2) blocking of the northern part of the stair, so is clearly part of the original (Phase 1) arrangement. It is overlain by what appears to be later (Phase 2) plaster on the south wall at the doorway into the crypt (see below).

The sequence in the north crypt is as follows:

A. Mud plaster and limewash (as A above) was applied to the whole of the interior of the crypt and antechamber except for the natural bedrock floor. This is essentially as layer A in the south crypt, but applied generally.

C. Plaster as C in the south crypt, applied to the crypt chamber only, and not extending through the doorway.

The entrance facade and soffit of the lintel, together with the north wall of the stairwell, were whitewashed directly to the stone, the joints being first filled with mud, and were then covered with designs in dark red paint. These survive only in parts, but appear to imitate ashlar jointing, roughly corresponding with the real courses, as well as a frieze above the lintel based upon pendant triangles.

The crypts and antechambers themselves remained unchanged when the Cathedral Church was refurbished (Phase 2), and indeed there is no evidence even for any redecoration after the original works. It is, however, possible that some of the burials belong to the later period of use of the building.

The major changes that did take place in Phase 2 concerned the inserted walls and arched openings over the stairs and the reduction of the widths of the staircases, to 1.05 metres, with blocking walls which contained a number of deep recesses or niches, plastered out and some clearly fitted with wooden shelves (Figures 23 and 27 JJ, KK & MM and Plates 115-117).

Plate 115: The north steps in the 1970s, looking down towards the north antechamber with the niches on the right side (EES Photo GP 77).

Plate 116: The south steps in the 1970s, looking down with the niches to the left side (EES Photo GP 149).

Plate 117: The south steps in the 1970s, looking up, with the niches to the right side (EES Photo GP 150).

THE ORIGINAL APSE

The lowest course of stonework and the footings for the original (Phase 1) apse were first encountered in 1963 (Chapter 1 Trench A1 Figure 18 and Plates 25 and 27) and, following subsequent excavations, were further recorded by Gartkiewicz (Chapter 3 Area 1 Figure 17 and Plate 61).

Part of only the lowest course of stonework survives, and this comprises the remains of a semi-circular apse, some 1.40 metres in radius and 2.6 metres deep. It has thresholds for door openings, each about 70 cms wide, to the north and south. That to the south is accompanied by a socket for a door post (Figures 22, 23 and 32 and Plates 118-120).

Plate 118: The lower courses of the two apses in the 1970s, showing the threshold on the south side of the original apse (EES Photo GP 81).

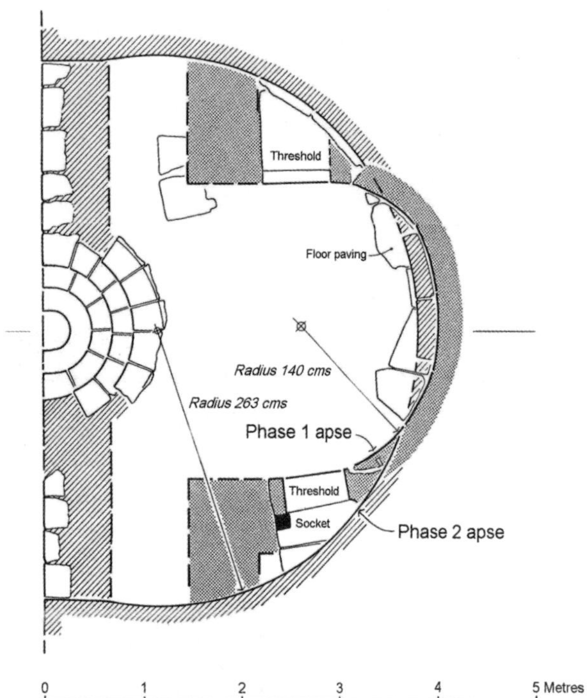

Figure 22: Simplified plan showing the relationship between the original and the later apse. North is to the top of the drawing.

The north return of the original apse, which separated the nave from a room or rooms at the north-east corner of the Cathedral, was recorded in the north sacristy in the 1970s (Chapter 3, Area 2, Figure 17 and Plate 64).

Plate 119: The threshold on the north side of the original apse (EES Photo GP 494).

Plate 120: Part of the threshold on the north side of the original apse and the return of the original apse under the later one (EES Photo GP 495).

THE LATER APSE, TRIBUNE AND ADJOINING ROOMS

The later apse, the sacristy adjoining it to the north, and the baptistry to the south were all built at the same time (Phase 2), using similar sandstone blocks to those used in the external walls. Where the walls of this phase of construction meet the original structure they are butted up to it, whereas where they meet contemporary walls they are bonded, and this is one of the primary pieces of evidence for the identification of two phases of construction. The construction of the tribune within the apse is a later piece of work.

When the new apse and the rooms to the north and south were built, the eastern *naos* wall was moved westwards, by a distance of about 1.5 metres, and set at right angles to the north and south walls. The new arrangement provided for a larger apse of more than a half circle in plan, 2.63 metres in radius, 3.75 metres deep, and 5.2 metres wide at its opening into the naos (Figures 19, 20, 26GG and HH, 27JJ and 31YY). Its construction necessitated encroaching southwards on the baptismal tank, the new wall being carried on an arch over its northern end (see below).

The later apse is built directly on the remains of the original one and stands to a height of 5 metres at its highest point above this (Plates 121 and 122).

Voussoirs, probably for two arches spanning openings about 5 metres wide and incised with interlace and Greek fret decoration, lie amongst the collapsed masonry on the site (Chapter 5 Groups 5 and 6 Figure 44 Nos 57-60 and 61-71). One of these two groups of *voussoirs* may have formed the arch over the opening into the later apse.

Plate 122: The later apse in the 1970s, from the south-west (EES Photos GP 468).

The robbing of the part of the crypt wall in the sacristy produced a piece of green marble *opus sectile* paving from a large circular or semi-circular pavement, which seems likely to have been displaced from the apse when the tribune was constructed.

The tribune survives, in part at least, five courses or steps high, and it is clear from the sinking on the topmost surviving course that at least another one was present.

In fact six courses probably represents its maximum height. The stonework is precisely cut in a fine sandstone with very tight joints. There would have been a throne on the top platform, quite possibly covered by a *baldachino*, or more properly a *ciborium*.

Plate 121: The later apse in the 1970s, from the west (EES Photos GP 448a).

Two fragments of small red sandstone columns found in the robbing fill behind the surviving section of the tribune could have been part of such a structure, but this was evidently sealed by a hard white plaster floor which should relate to the tribune steps (Chapter 1 Trench A1 and Figures 5, 19, 23, 27JJ, 31YY and 32ZZ and Plates 121-124).

Plates 123 and 124: The tribune from the west and south sides (EES Photos GP 327 and 329).

The sacristy is partly built over the north antechamber. It is entered at the south-west corner from the naos by an opening, 1.0 metres wide and rebated for a door. There is a door socket on its south-east side (Figure 16 – m). It is L-shaped in plan. The first part is 5.2 metres by 2.7 metres and then it returns over the north crypt for a distance of 8.8 metres at a width of 2.5 metres.

Two vertical slots in the east wall and holes in the paved floor may indicate the former positions of screens (Figure 16 – j). Different patterns of paving in the floor also suggest that it may have been subdivided (Figures 26GG, 28NN and QQ, and 29UU and VV).

The rear of the apse is parallel to the east wall of the building and terminates at either end in large pilasters, which are mirrored by smaller pilasters in the north and south walls.

Also at the rear of the apse are the remains of a doorway between the sacristy and the baptistry (Figure 28PP and RR).

The baptistry is partly built over the south antechamber. It is entered at the north-west corner from the naos by an opening, 1.0 metres wide and rebated for a door. There are two door sockets on its south-east side (Figure 16 – m). It is L-shaped in plan. The larger part measures 5.2 metres by up to 3.6 metres and then it returns over the south crypt for a distance of 8.5 metres at a width of 2.5 metres (Figures 26HH, 28NN, 29SS and TT).

The shallow pilaster on the south wall contains a semi-circular recess, presumably for a lamp (Figure 26 HH and Plate 125).

Plate 125: The pilaster and recess for a lamp, on the south side of the baptistry (EES Photo GP 414).

The original baptismal tank on the north side was uncovered in 1964 and survives, though the re-used Meroitic stele has been broken (Chapter 2 Plates 59 & 60, Figure 29SS andTT).

During the excavations in 1964, a small column base was found *in situ* midway between the pilaster buttresses on the north and south sides of the baptistry, and this evidently supported a small collapsed column which was found alongside it (Chapter 2 Figure 8, Figure 23, and Plates 126 and 127, and Chapter 5 Figure 35 Nos 6 and 10).

The base had slots in either side and when discovered these appear to have been on the sides which faced north and south. The pilaster and column evidently subdivided the baptistry into two parts and helped to support the roof. A similar arrangement probably existed in the sacristy.

Plate 126: The small column base in the baptistry in the 1970s, from the east (EES Photo GP 382).

Plate 127: The small column base in the baptistry in the 1970s, from the south (EES Photo GP 383).

The sacristy, the baptistry, and the north and south walls of the *naos* were clearly intended to be plastered, and some of this remains. It is a fine purplish grey lime plaster on a mud dubbing-out layer. On the south naos wall slight traces of painted decoration were evidently still visible in the 1970s, but no further details are known.

Entry to the crypts is now via small round-headed openings, 1.05 metres wide - the width of the reduced stairs. Their arched heads have a square hood mould and a keystone ornamented with an inscribed Christian cross.

The outer imposts of the arched openings are set into the slots originally designed to support the timber floor over the steps (Figure 27JJ, Plates 128-130 and Chapter 5 Figure Nos 29 and 30).

Plate 128: The north entrance into the crypts in 1992 (Photograph by Fred Aldsworth).

Plate 129: The south entrance into the crypts in 1992 (Photograph by Fred Aldsworth).

Plate 130: The north side of the north arch, seated in the earlier beam slot (EES Photo GP 525).

Plate 131: Some of the column bases on the south side of the nave, looking west in the 1970s (EES Photo GP 90).

THE NAVE

The main body of the Cathedral, or naos, is square in plan, measuring close to 18.0 metres in each direction. It is divided into five parts by a series of column bases and arcade bases. There are the remains of seven entrances into the enclosed space at its west end, one each in the north and south walls, three through the west wall from the narthex, and lesser entrances in the west wall from north-west and the south-west towers (Figure 20).

All the entrances give access into the west ambulatory, which extends the full width of the naos at its west end and is 2.4 metres wide. The remainder of the naos is divided east-west into five elements – the nave, the south aisle, the south ambulatory, the north aisle and the north ambulatory.

The nave is contained by the apse and tribune at its east end, by the arcade of the west ambulatory at its west end, and by rows of column bases on its north and south sides. It is 15.1 metres long. The six large granite column bases on either side of the nave have their centres at 2.15 metres apart along the line of the nave and are between 6.60 and 6.70 metres apart across its width (Plate 131).

The column bases are each square at the bottom, measuring an average of 64 cms along each side, and then reduce to circular form, between 48 and 54 cms in diameter at the top (Chapter 5 Figure 35, No 9 and Plate 132).

Plate 132: One of the large column bases (EES Photo GP 25).

The overall height of each column base cannot be ascertained, as the paved floor is laid up to them, but it is in excess of 50 cms. The upper, circular, sections vary between 25 and 36 cms in height.

At least seven of the twelve bases are marked with a mason's letter. The two bases at either end of the row of six on the south side of the nave are marked with the Greek letter *alpha* on the upper surface (Plate 133), whilst at least five of the six on the north side of the nave carry the Greek letter *pi* at one corner, on the top of the offset between the square lower section and the circular section above. That at the east end is obscured by paving.

Plate 133: The Greek letter alpha *inscribed on one of the column bases (Photograph by Fred Aldsworth).*

The levels of the tops of the bases, as presently located, varies by as much as 26 cms, between about 183.60 and 183.86 metres above sea level.

It is not possible to determine how much or if any of the existing paving in the Cathedral Church formed part of the original (Phase 1) arrangement. Parts of it have certainly been re-laid on at least one occasion and alongside the piers of the south arcade this may have occurred several times. Much of what survives can probably best be attributed to the major (Phase 2) reconstruction of the building.

The paving consists of rectangular blocks, mostly of a whitish sandstone, laid in courses running approximately north-south, although the course lines are not straight (Figures 16 and 23 and Plate 127).

Plate 134: Some of the paving in the nave (EES Photo GP 123).

The direction of the courses is reversed in the surviving paving of the north and south ends of the west ambulatory, relating to the principal north and south doors. A discontinuity along the line of the inner north arcade may suggest replacement, or a construction joint; the latter is more likely since the paving is otherwise identical. Paving in the eastern part of the sacristy, which no longer existed in the 1990s, may have been part of the same scheme, but the remainder of this, and that in the baptistry, were replacements.

A broad strip of paving runs along the long axis of the nave, and another forms a cross with it, with a circular stone at the intersection having a central sinking about 30 mm in diameter. The long arm of this cross continues through the paving of the *haikal*, where the floor is otherwise laid in a less-regular manner then elsewhere in the naos.

The *haikal* is raised about 15 cms above the general level of the surrounding floors and is defined by a kerb of the same stone as the paving. The layout of the *haikal* is clear from mortices for timber uprights cut in the paving and kerbs (Figure 23 and Plates 135, 136).

Plate 135: The east end of the nave in the 1970s, showing the haikal *to the left (EES Photo GP227).*

Not all the features which survive here necessarily belong to the same phase of construction, but there is no way of distinguishing between them.

Plate 136: The haikal *from the west in the 1970s (EES Photo GP 226).*

There are mortices for the uprights supporting a timber rail separating the *haikal* from the nave and aisles, between the second and third nave arcade bays, the first forming an entrance on both sides, and on the west, the axial entrance is defined by more substantial posts than the intermediates (Figure 16-d and Figure 23). Within the space, which encloses an area measuring a little over 6 metres square and just outside the apse, are four post sockets for the uprights supporting an altar, set in a square measuring 1.0 metres across, with small holes for timber rods between them on the east, north and south sides. These suggest a screen, the rods serving perhaps to support or tension a cloth covering (Figure 16-a, Figure 23 and Plate 137). Outside this, four post sockets, set in a rectangle measuring 2.0 metres by 1.8 metres around the altar, appear to have supported a *ciborium* or similar structure over the altar.

Plate 137: The post sockets and rod holes for the altar (EES Photo GP 475).

Outside this again, but still within the *haikal*, there is a further series of post sockets, set in a square measuring 3.5 metres across, which may have supported another screen around the area occupied by the altar (Figure 16-b and Figure 26).

On the north side of the nave, about 3 metres west of the *haikal*, is a setting of four small post sockets, set in a square about 90 cms across, and several others, which may be the remains of a pulpit and stairs (Figure 13a – k, Figure 23 and Plate 138).

Plate 138: The setting of post sockets believed to have supported a pulpit.

THE SOUTH AISLE AND AMBULATORY

These extend from the west ambulatory to the west wall of the baptistry and are both 15.8 metres in length. The remains are more complete and informative than those on the north side of the naos and include part of the south wall standing to its full height as well as two complete openings of the south arcade (Figures 23, 26HH, and 30WW and XX and Plate 139).

The south wall survives to its full height, with parapet, of 6.2 metres above the paved floor level for part of its length. The lower 1.4 metres being mostly part of the original (Phase 1) Cathedral Church, but is partly rebuilt or refaced for a distance of about 4 metres from the south door. The remainder is the later (Phase 2) reconstruction.

At a height of 5.6 metres above floor level the wall reduces in thickness to form the parapet and just below the offset are remnants of ten beam pockets for timbers supporting a roof over the south ambulatory.

The bottoms of the beam pockets are at a height of 5.1 metres above the floor level, and they are each about 35 cms deep, 20 cms wide, and between 100 and 115 cms apart.

The *mihrab* is set at a height of 100 cms above the paved floor level of the Cathedral, the floor of the building having been raised to this level when it was used as a mosque.

Plate 139: The south-east corner of the naos *in the 1960s, showing parts of the south arcade and the south wall (EES Photo WF 129).*

The upper part of the wall is less well-built on the internal face and was plastered. In the wall are the remains of window openings, the lower of the two wooden ring beams, and the *mihrab*, inserted when the building was adapted as a mosque (Period 4) (Plate 140).

It is 230 cms high and 85 cms wide and was described in some detail in 1963 (see Chapter 3).

It is constructed with what would have been a stone threshold and stepped brick jambs, and is in the form of a pointed arch containing a semi-circular recess of brick, which is 55 cms deep. In its original form the *mihrab* appears to have been plastered externally and internally.

The south ambulatory is 2.3 metres wide, and contains the steps to the south crypt at its east end (Plate 141).

Two openings of the south arcade survive complete and there are now only fragmentary remains of a third (Figure 30WW and Plates 139 and 142).

Plate 140: The part of the south wall containing the inserted mihrab *(EES Photo GP 235).*

Plate 141: The south ambulatory, looking east towards the steps to the crypt (EES Photo GP 129).

Plate 143: The base of one of the piers in the south arcade and its smaller footing (EES Photo GP 109).

Plate 142: Composite photograph of the south arcade, taken in the 1970s after the third pier had been dismantled (EES Photo GP 222).

The arcade was supported on a pilaster buttress at the east end, three intermediate piers, and then one L-shaped pier at its west end where it abutted the west ambulatory. When constructed, probably in Phase 2, the piers were originally square in plan, measuring 70 cms in each direction and were 3.02 and 3.15 metres apart. The footings of all three are visible at the base of the existing piers (Figure 30WW and Plate 143).

The paving slabs in the south aisle and ambulatory were laid up against the earlier footings, but the piers have subsequently been demolished down to the footings and rebuilt on a larger scale, such that they now extend beyond the original footings and over some of the earlier paving.

The remains of two pier bases survive in their original form on square bases in the north arcade (see below).

If the south arcade was rebuilt with square footings to the piers at the same time as the external walls were reconstructed and the larger apse, baptistry, and sacristy were added (Phase 2), the south arcade must have been reconstructed, again, at a later (Phase 3) date.

The three existing piers are rectangular in plan, measuring 70 cms by close to 100 cms. The two at the east end rise to a height of 2.7 metres above the level of the paved floor and incorporate timber lacing beams at the top and at a height of about 1.0 metres above floor level (Figure 30WW and XX, Plates 144-146).

The third pier, to the west of the remaining two, survived to its full height and with part of the springing for the arch to the east until the 1970s. It was photographed in 1963 (Plates 139 and 147) and drawn by Gartkiewicz in the 1970s immediately prior to dismantling down to a height of 85 cms.

Plate 144: One of the piers in the south arcade in the 1970s (EES Photo GP 541).

Plate 145: A timber lacing beam in the south arcade (EES Photo GP 102).

Plate 146: A timber lacing beam joint in the south arcade (EES Photo GP 549).

The two complete and the one incomplete arcade arches that survive are mostly built from re-used carved stones, and there are other pieces which also derive from these openings, or similar ones in the north arcade, amongst the material lying on the site (Figure 27WW, Plates 148-152 and Chapter 5 Group 4, Figure 42 Nos 38-56 and Figure 43 Nos 72-77). The re-used elements were evidently originally designed to be supported on square piers, measuring 70 cms across and set a little over 3.0 metres apart, and which have been adapted for the latest arrangement in the standing section of the south arcade. The upper level of timber lacing in the stone piers is capped by stone imposts, with a half-round moulding surmounted by a concave section finishing with a flat band, originally decorated with an incised chevron pattern (Figure 45 Nos 72-77).

A drawing of one of the piers by George Dales, shows the lacing timber in one of the piers to be decorated, and Somers Clarke, who visited the site in 1899, described the decoration on the lacing timbers in the south arcade as in the form of a leaf-pattern and also a pattern in circles and flowers (see Introduction).

In 1972 Gartkiewicz identified the timber used in the piers as being from the tamarisk tree (*Plumley notes in the archives QI 1972*).

Plate 147: The south arcade in 1963. Note the pier at the right (west) end of the south arcade surviving to its full height, but with alterations to its west (right) side at the top (EES Photo 63-116).

Plates 148 and 149: Parts of the east end of the south arcade in the 1970s (EES Photos GP 220 and 221).

Plates 150 and 151: Details of the south arcade in the 1970s (EES Photos GP 320 and 325).

Plate 152: Detail of the south arcade in 1992 (Photograph by Fred Aldsworth).

The imposts support *voussoirs*, now forming openings which are 2.8 and 3.0 metres in diameter, and hood mouldings decorated in a similar fashion to the imposts. The *voussoirs* are each 58 cms in length and pass through the full thickness of the arches. Four of these are decorated with carved Christian symbols on their north face (Chapter 5 Group 4 Figure 43 Nos 43-46). A number of *voussoirs* similar in size and length occur amongst the debris on the site and of these at least five are decorated with carved Christian symbols at both ends (Chapter 5 Group 4 Figure 42 Nos 38-42). A further ten are now decorated with carved Christian symbols at one end only (Chapter 5 Group 4, Figure 43 Nos 47-56).

The employment of re-used stones with carved Christian symbols suggests that the south arcade was rebuilt during the Christian era (i.e. Period 1), but sometime after the external walls had been restored and the larger apse, baptistry and sacristy had been added (Phase 2).

Fragmentary remains of two timbers set between two of the arches in the south arcade may be the remains of scaffolding (Figure 30WW).

The fourth, or westernmost, arch in the south arcade appears to have been abandoned as part of the arcade at a late stage in the use of the building, perhaps when it was adapted as a mosque. There were no surviving traces of the springing for the opening and the top of the pier appears to have been rebuilt on its west side, a feature noted by Somers Clarke in 1899 (see Introduction) and recorded by Gartkiewicz (Figure 30WW and Plate 147).

The south aisle terminates at its east end in the opening into the baptistry. It is 2.4 metres wide from the column bases to the south arcade.

The paving in the south aisle and ambulatory appears to immediately post-date the construction of the square piers for the south arcade (Phase 2) and pre-date the reconstruction of the south arcade (Phase 3). It probably dates to the phase of restoration of the Cathedral Church which included the rebuilding of the external walls and the insertion of the larger apse, the baptistry, and the sacristy (ie Phase 2), but may have been subject to some later repair.

The paving appears, at least in part, to conform to the pattern in the western part of the nave and may be contemporary with it.

THE NORTH AISLE AND AMBULATORY

The evidence is less well preserved here than on the south side, but what survives suggests that the features here mirrored those in the south aisle and ambulatory, except perhaps for the late reconstruction of the arcade.

The north wall survives for only part of its length. It preserves evidence for the two phases of construction seen in the south wall, as well as the slot for the lower of the two ring beams and the jambs of two windows set 2.8 metres apart (Figures 20, 26GG, Plates 153, 154).

Plate 153: The north wall in the 1970s, looking east from near the west end (EES Photo GP 133).

Plate 154: The east end of the north wall in the 1970s, showing the two phases of construction, the ring beam, and the jambs of two windows (EES Photo GP 219).

The north ambulatory extends from the west ambulatory to the sacristy. It is 15.75 metres long by 2.25 metres wide and includes the steps to the north crypt at its east end.

The north arcade is represented by a pilaster buttress at its east end, a large pier base forming its junction with the west ambulatory at its west end, and the remains of three intermediate piers or pier bases.

The two intermediate piers towards the east end are in their original (Phase 2) form and are both square, measuring a little over 60 cms across, up to 90 cms in height, and are 3.2 metres apart (Plates 153 and 155). They are both built of finely cut blocks, tooled in a manner identical to that employed on the reconstructed sections of the external walls (i.e. Phase 2) and they are both set on square footings up to about 6 cms high. These appear to be cut out of the tops of larger blocks of stone, up to 1.0 metres across, which otherwise have their upper surfaces at floor level. The pier at the east end is 3.18 metres from the pilaster buttress built into the west wall of the sacristy.

Plate 155: The most easterly of the intermediate pier bases of the north arcade, from the south (EES Photo GP 122).

The footing for a third pier can be seen as a large block of stone, measuring about 80cms across in each direction, set at floor level between the most westerly of the two piers and that forming the corner with the west ambulatory (Figure 23).

The north aisle terminates at its east end in the opening into the sacristy. It is 2.4 metres wide from the column bases to the north arcade.

The paving is generally of smaller slabs than that in the south aisle and parts of the nave, and unlike the paving in the south aisle, the lines of paving in the north aisle do not align with those in the nave, although they are laid up against the larger footings of the piers (Figures 16 and 23).

THE WEST AMBULATORY

This forms the west end of the *naos*, and extends along the interior of the west wall from the doorway in the south wall to that which originally existed in the north wall. It is 17.7 metres long by 2.4 metres wide.

The west wall of the *naos*, which also forms the west side of the west ambulatory, contains three principal openings from the *narthex* and two smaller openings from the north-west and the south-west towers, and each one is rebated for a door (Figures 23, 25EE, 27LL, Plate 156). Several openings include door sockets and slots for horizontal timbers (Figure 16 – m and v).

The two principal forms of construction seen in the external walls are also present here. The courses of large blocks survive, as elsewhere in the building, to 1.4 metres above the internal floor level on both faces (Plates 156 and 157). Above there are the finer, marginally-tooled blocks associated with the later (Phase 2) reconstruction, though the ring beams are not present, and the masonry inside the west towers was not to the same quality as that on the exterior elevations.

Plate 156: The west wall of the naos, looking north-west (EES Photo GP 130).

Plate 157: The two forms of construction seen on the external face of the west wall of the naos *(EES Photo GP 310).*

The east side of the west ambulatory is defined by a series of four pier bases. The two at either end are L-shaped in plan, reflecting their role at the corners of the three ambulatories. The two forming the west ends of the north and south aisles, approximately answering the inner arcades, appear at first sight also to have been originally square, because of the use of monolithic stone blocks to form the northern and southern base courses of the northern and southern piers respectively. However, the paving was laid around rectangular, not square, piers, each measuring 1.3 metres by 0.6 metres, and it is clear on close examination that these piers have always been rectangular, the large blocks seemingly used to give strength to the crucial corners of the arcade (Figures 16, 23, Plate 150). The space between them is 4.55 metres across.

Plate 158: The rectangular pier base at the south-west corner of the nave, looking west (EES Photo GP40).

Voussoirs for arches spanning openings about 5 metres wide, and incised with interlace and Greek fret decoration, lie amongst the collapsed masonry on the site. (Chapter 5 Groups 5 and 6, Figure 44 Nos 57-60 and 61-71). One of these two groups of *voussoirs* may have formed an arch at the west end of the nave, in front of the west ambulatory.

THE SOUTH-WEST TOWER

This structure is contained within the south-west corner of the Cathedral Church and its two external walls, both 85 cms thick, form parts of the south and west walls of the main building (Figures 23, 24CC and 25FF).

There is a rebate for a door at the north end of the west wall of the tower which evidently mirrored the opening in the west wall of the *naos*.

The north wall of the tower is 72 cms thick and has an opening at its east end, giving access into the base of the tower from the *narthex*, but it is not rebated for a door. (Figure 24BB and Plate 159).

Plate 159: The north wall of the south-west tower, looking south in the 1970s (EES Photo GP 255).

The first few courses of the external walls of the south-west tower, as in the west wall of the *naos*, are formed from large blocks, whereas above this smaller, margin-tooled blocks are employed, as elsewhere in the building. The significance of the employment of these two forms of construction in the west end of the Cathedral Church are discussed later (Chapter 8).

Within the enclosed space there is a central block of masonry, 1.9 metres square, which is partly plastered, supporting two flights of a stone staircase over a vaulted chamber (Figures 23, 25EE, 26HH, Plates 160 and 161).

Scars on the north side of the central block of masonry indicates that the stairs rose to at least 5 metres above the floor level in the Cathedral Church and may have comprised three flights of steps giving access to the roof level, some 5.5 metres above the level of the floor (Figure 26HH).

Plate 160: The first flight of stone steps in the south-west tower (EES Photo GP128).

Plate 161: Part of the stone-vaulted chamber under the stairs in the south-west tower (EES Photo GP 91).

THE *NARTHEX* AND NORTH-WEST TOWER

All that survives of these are the east wall of the *narthex* and tower, which also forms the west wall of the *naos* and west ambulatory, and the south wall of the narthex, which also forms the north wall of the south-west tower.

Excavations in the 1970s revealed foundations which appear to be those of the west wall of the *narthex* and the south wall of the north-west tower (Chapter 3 Area 10). This evidence, together with the surviving evidence for doors, suggest a room or tower at the north-west corner, and a *narthex*, some 9.3 metres long and 3.5 metres wide, between the two towers, probably entered from the west by three doors mirroring those in the west wall of the *naos*.

FIGURES 23-32

The material which formed the basis for this set of record drawings of the standing remains of the Cathedral Church was first prepared by Gartkiewicz in the 1972, 1976 and 1978 seasons (Chapter 3). The results of his drawn surveys of the building were copied, revised, extended to include all the elevations accessible in 1992, and then prepared for publication by Fred Aldsworth.

It is evident from the photographs and drawings produced in the 1970s that some elements of the building had either been demolished for reasons of safety or had collapsed during the period when Gartkiewicz was working, but seemingly not before most of them had been drawn and photographed.

Hence some of detail shown on the drawings appears in photographs taken during the early 1970s but not in photographs taken in the later 1970s and, of course, this and material and other fabric which had subsequently been removed was not available for study in the 1990s.

For these reasons the drawings originally produced by Gartkiewicz show the extent of fabric surviving in the early 1970s, whereas the drawings added in 1992 show only the fabric that existed at that time.

A horizontal datum was established on the Cathedral by Gartkiewicz and given an arbitrary value of 25. By extrapolation with the site datum, which is based on the water level in Lake Nasser as measured at Aswan, this was found to be at approximately 184.31 metres above sea level. The datum on the drawings has a value of about 185 metres above sea level.

(For an index to the positions of the elevation and section drawings see Figure 18 on p. 56).

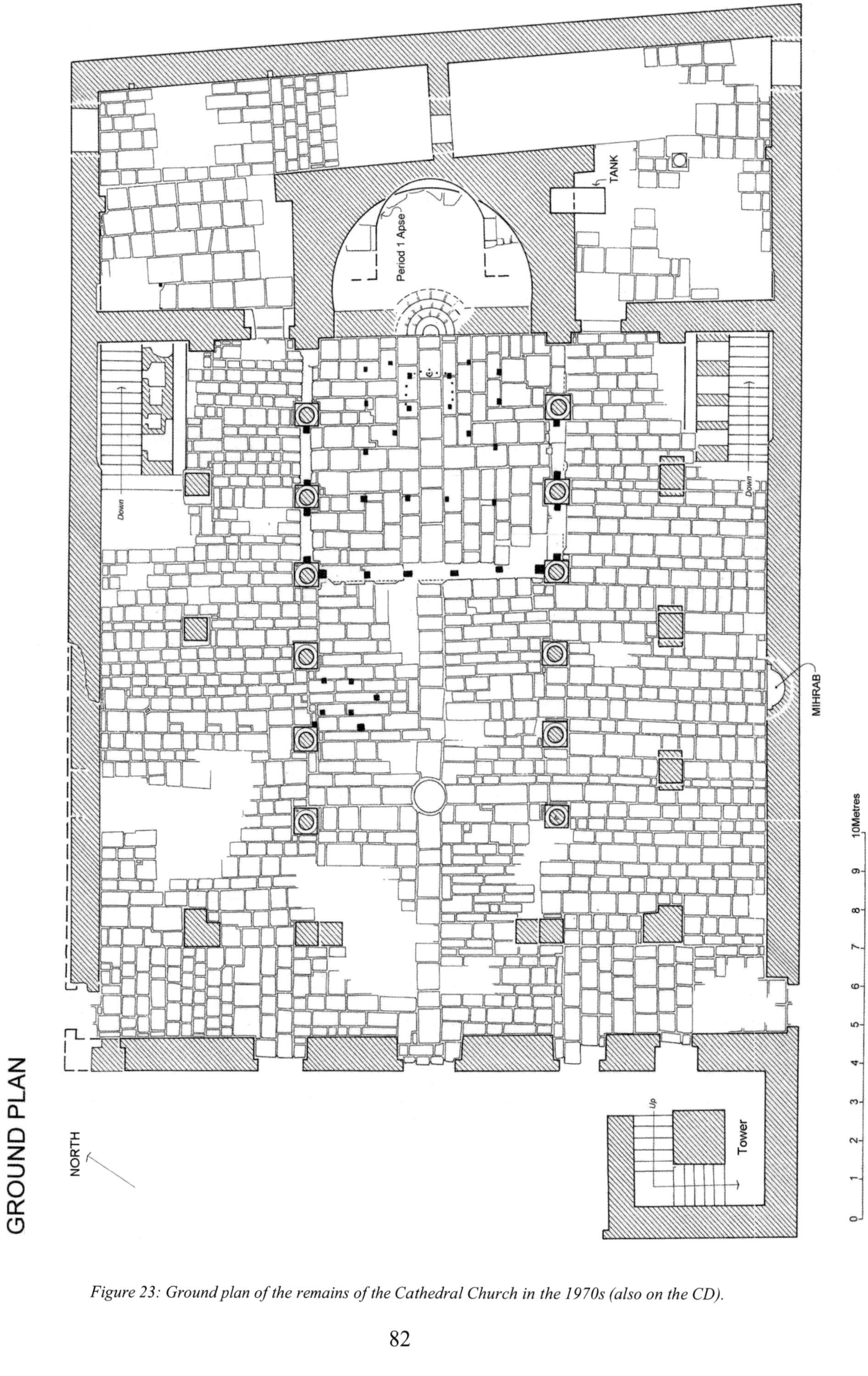

Figure 23: Ground plan of the remains of the Cathedral Church in the 1970s (also on the CD).

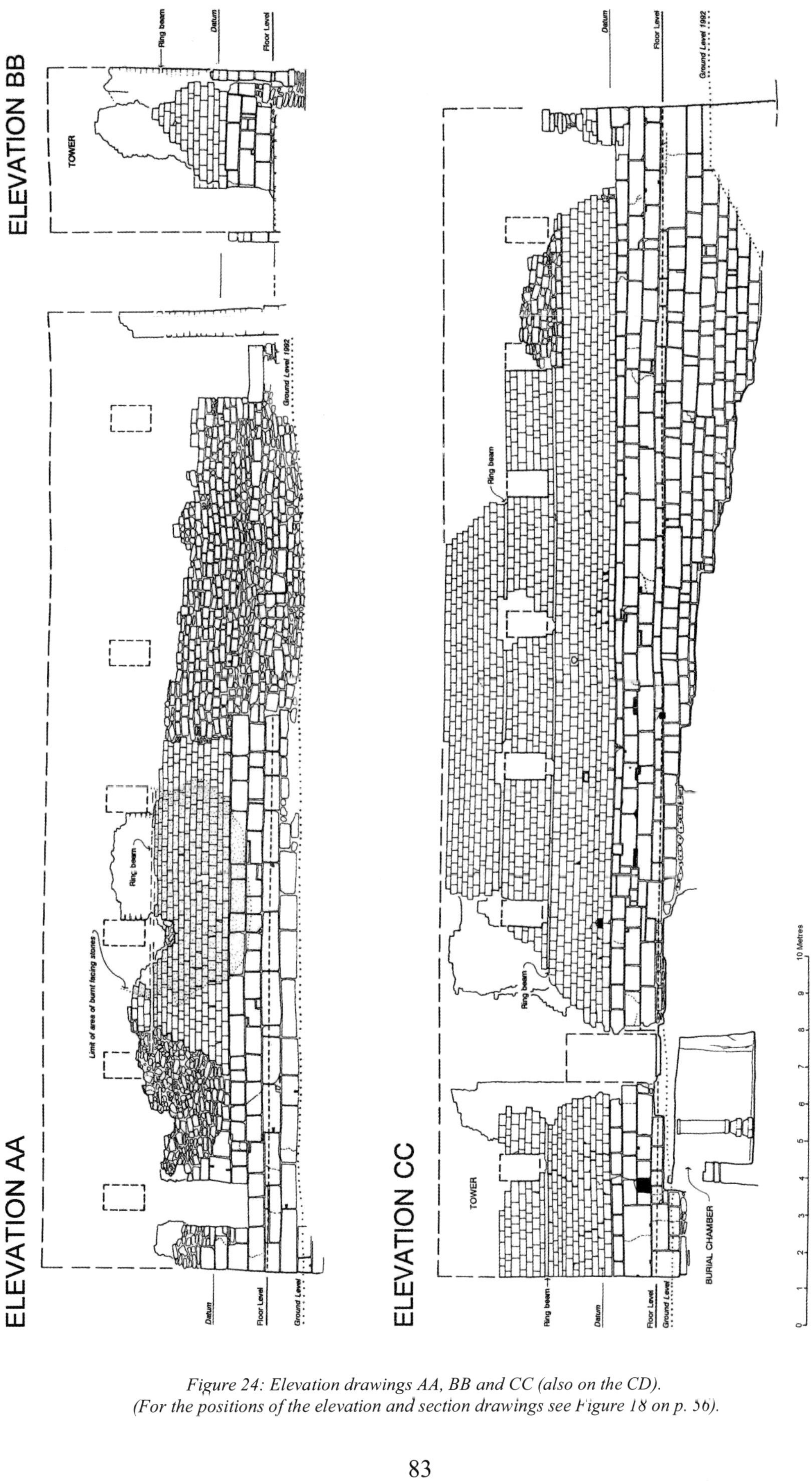

Figure 24: Elevation drawings AA, BB and CC (also on the CD).
(For the positions of the elevation and section drawings see Figure 18 on p. 56).

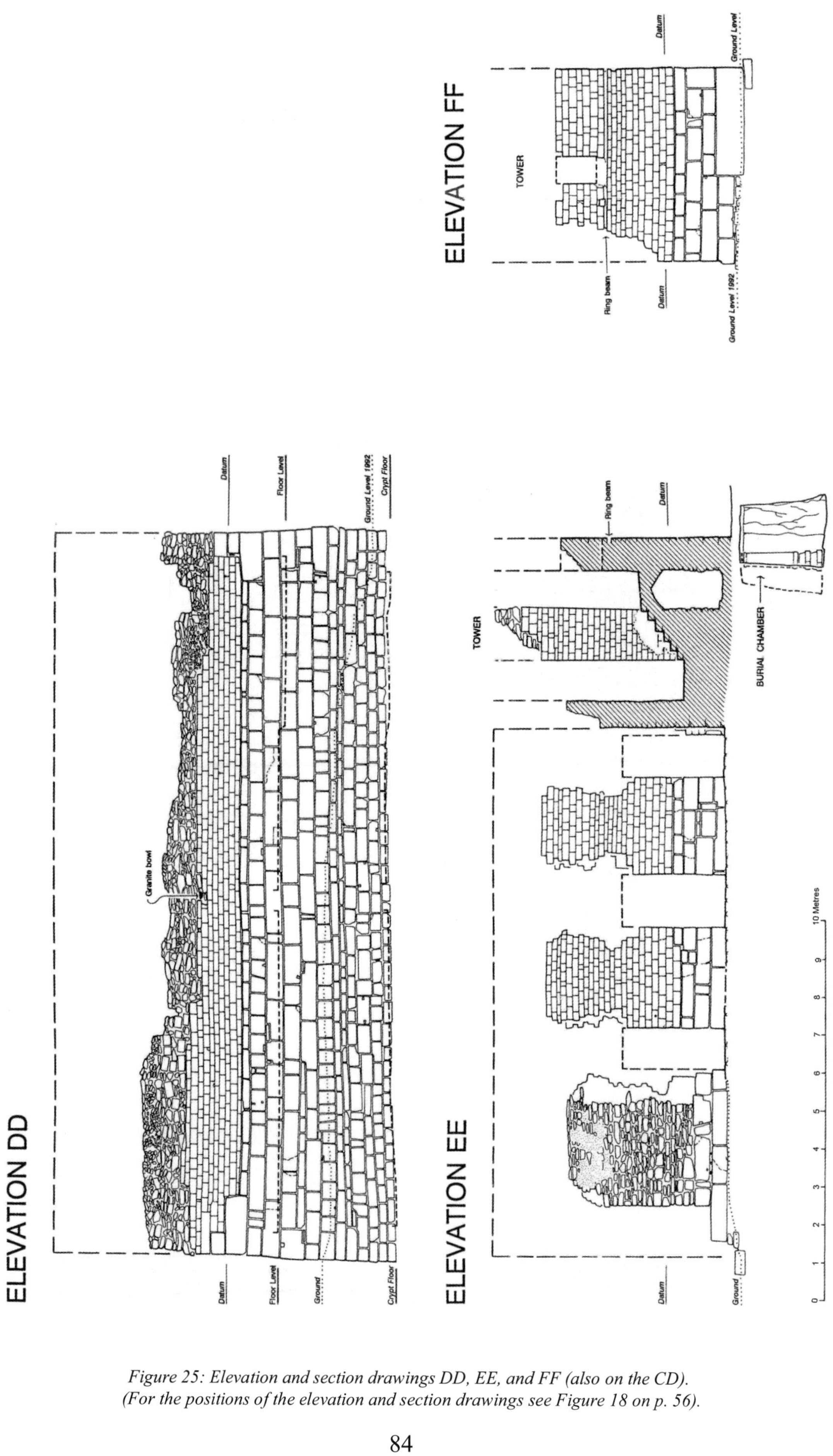

Figure 25: Elevation and section drawings DD, EE, and FF (also on the CD). (For the positions of the elevation and section drawings see Figure 18 on p. 56).

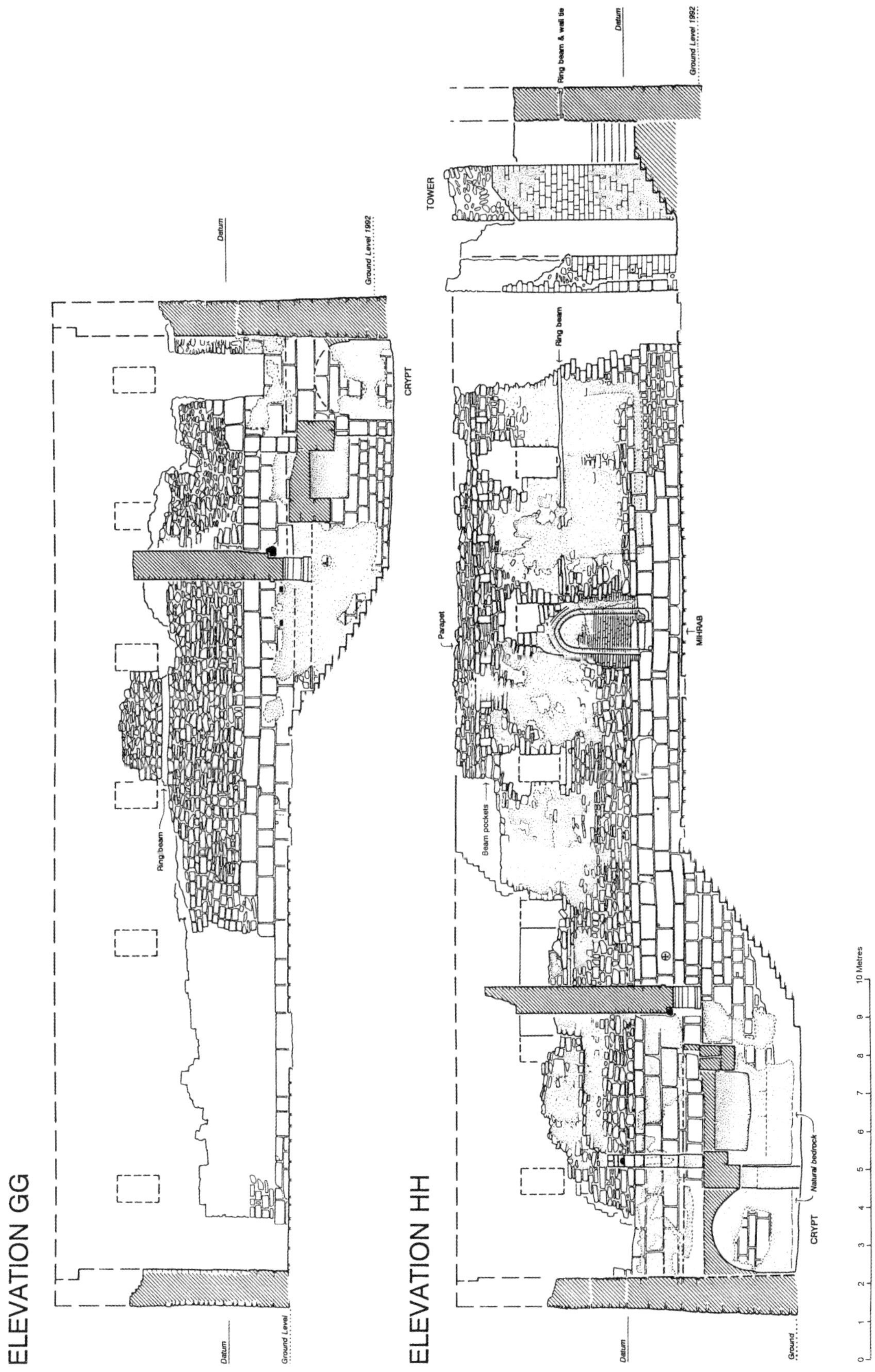

Figure 26: Elevation and section drawings GG and HH (also on the CD).
(For the positions of the elevation and section drawings see Figure 18 on p. 56)

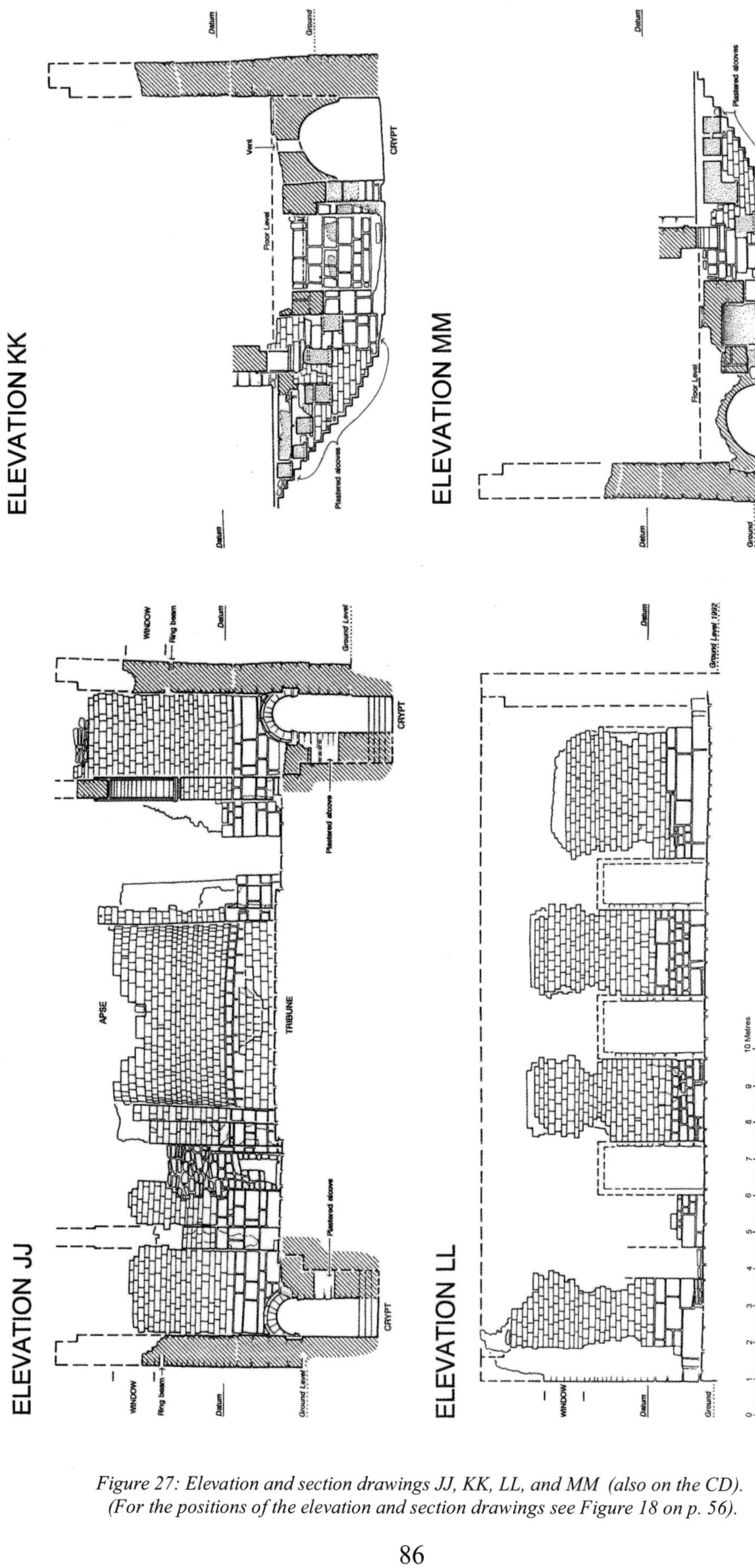

Figure 27: Elevation and section drawings JJ, KK, LL, and MM (also on the CD). (For the positions of the elevation and section drawings see Figure 18 on p. 56).

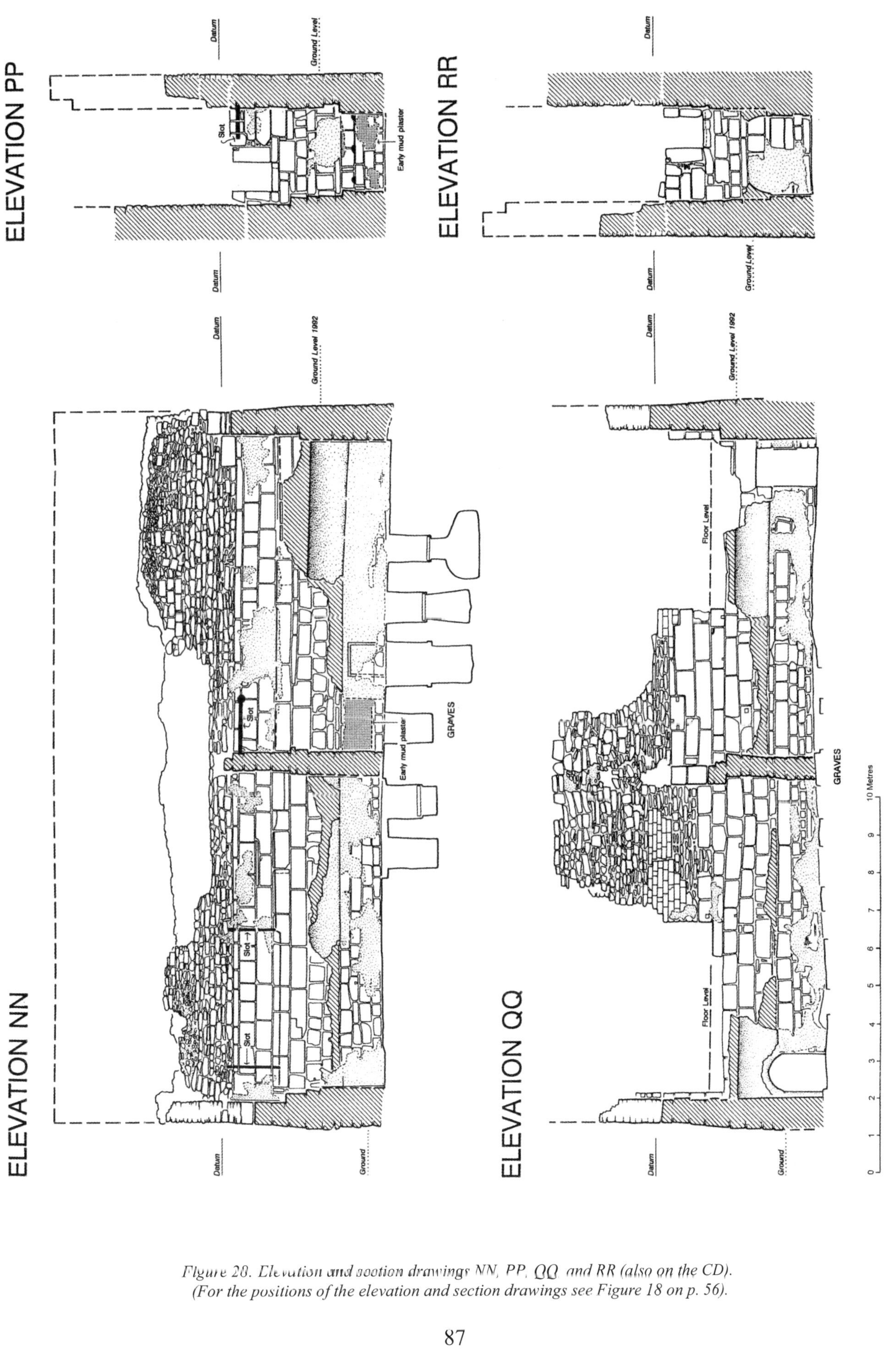

Figure 28. Elevation and section drawings NN, PP, QQ and RR (also on the CD). (For the positions of the elevation and section drawings see Figure 18 on p. 56).

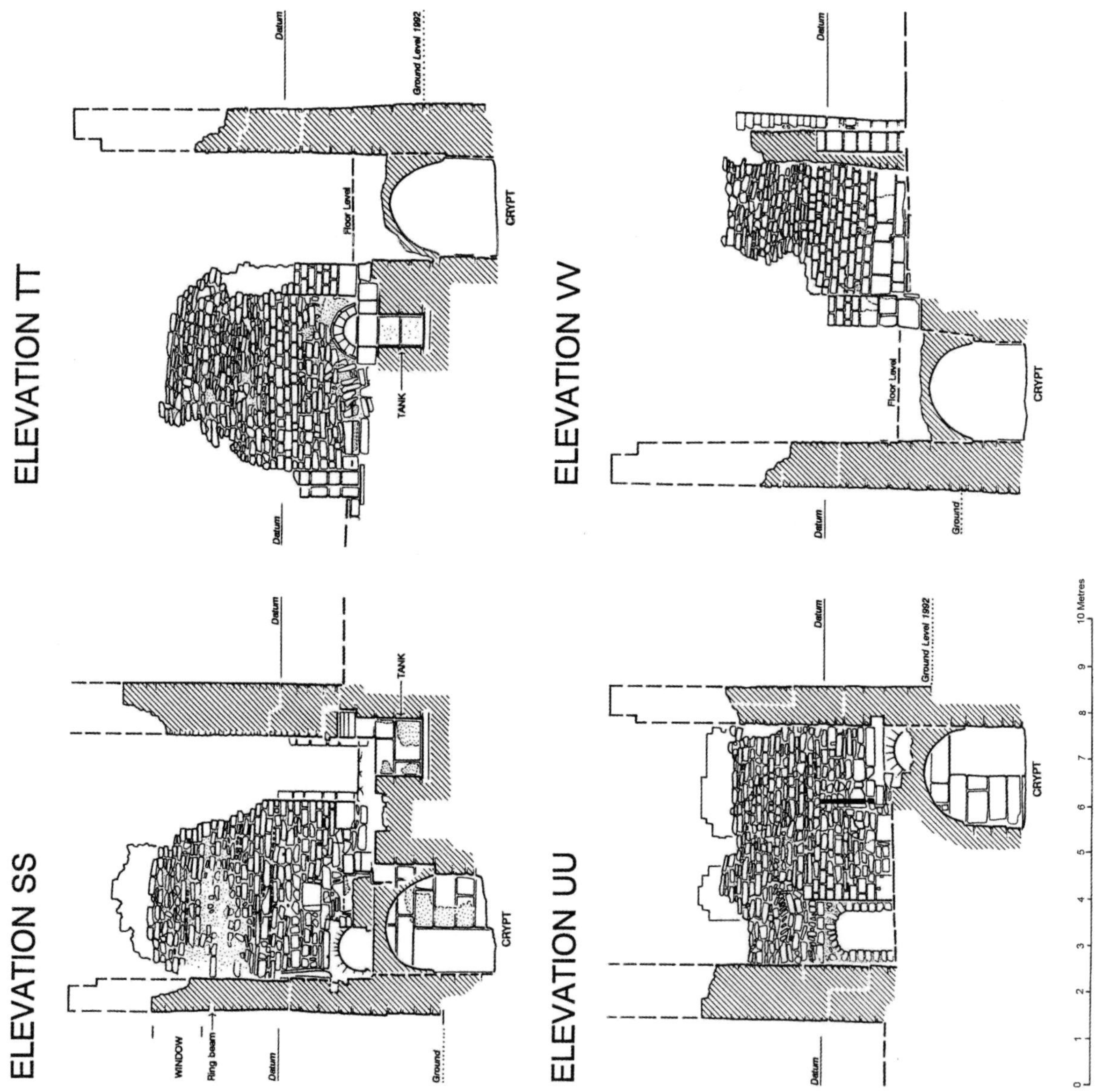

Figure 29: Elevation and section drawings SS, TT, UU and VV (also on the CD). (For the positions of the elevation and section drawings see Figure 18 on p. 56).

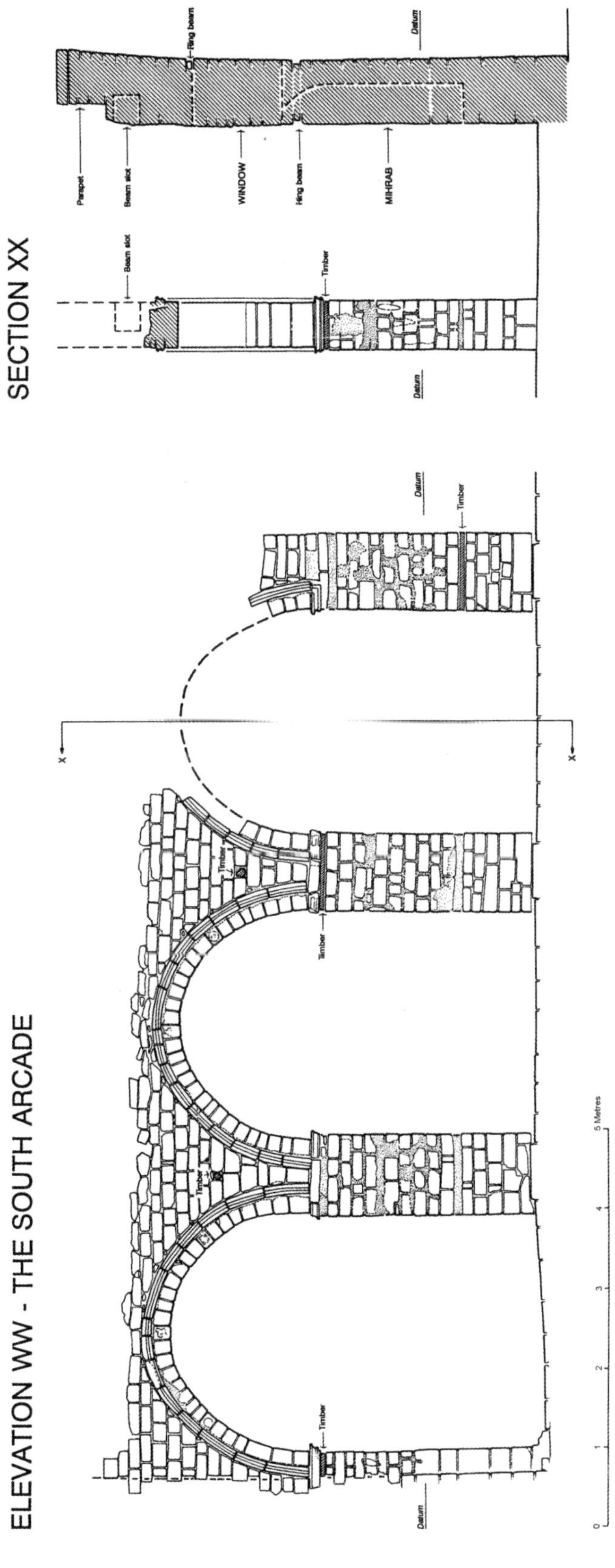

Figure 30: Elevation and section drawings WW and XX (also on the CD).
(For the positions of the elevation and section drawings see Figure 18 on p. 56)

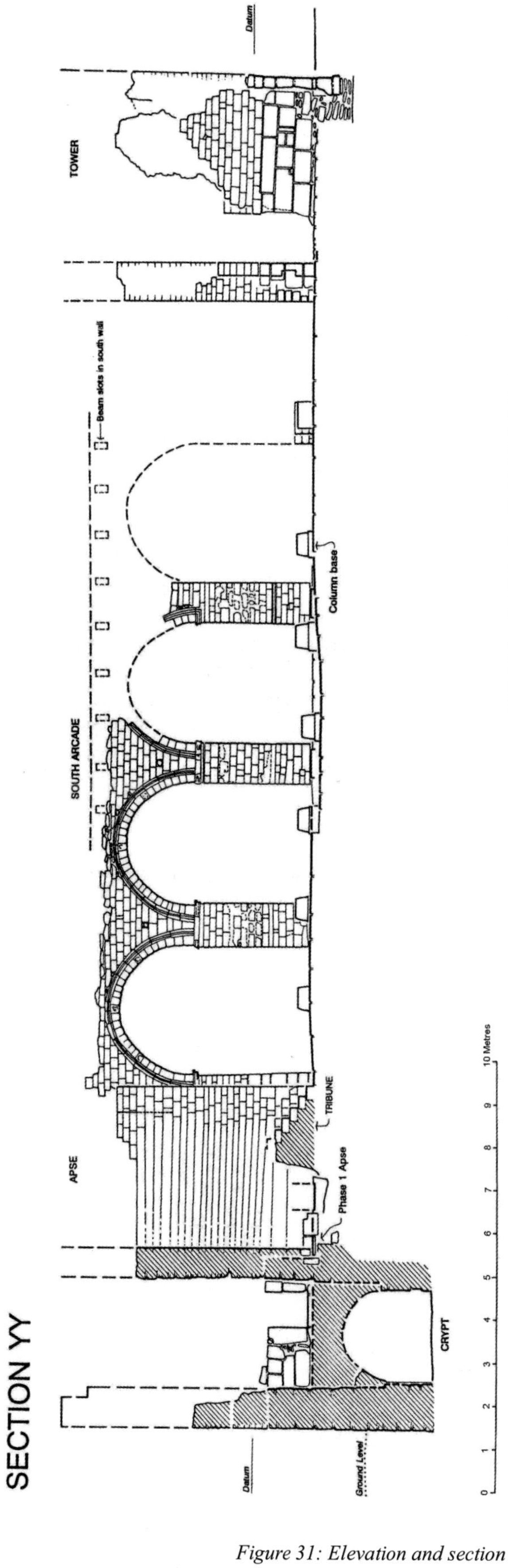

Figure 31: Elevation and section drawing YY (also on the CD).
(For the positions of the elevation and section drawings see Figure 18 on p. 56).

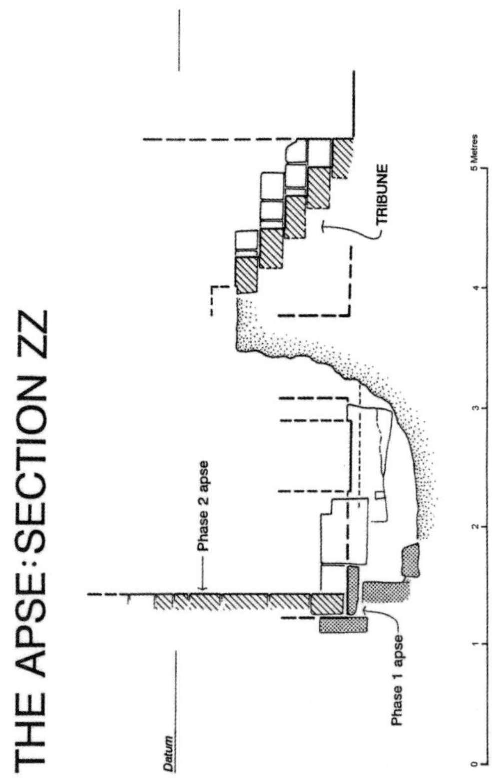

Figure 32: Section drawing (also on the CD).
(For the positions of the elevation and section drawing. see Figure 18 on p. 56).

Chapter 5: THE ARCHITECTURAL COMPONENTS

In January 1992, a number of architectural components from the Cathedral Church were still lying in and around the building, where they had be left after the investigations in the 1960s and 1970s. Although a number of these had been photographed by Gartkiewicz, and some carried find numbers ascribed to them by him, they had not been listed, drawn nor described.

The following catalogue of this material was prepared by Fred Aldsworth. It does not include all the material existing at that time but concentrates on those items most likely to assist in determining the previous forms and some of the decoration of the building. It is described under the following categories :

Capitals, shafts and bases
Granite capitals
Granite shafts
Granite bases
Red sandstone capitals
Red sandstone shafts and bases
Imposts
Decorated *voussoir* stones
Arcade mouldings
Window grille

Subsequent to 1992 it was noted that some of the photographs held by the Egypt Exploration Society recording excavations in the 1960s, included images of column capitals which did not survive on the site. A photograph of four further stone capitals, allegedly from Qasr Ibrim which had at some earlier date found their way to the Cairo Museum, was published in 1935 and two of these, along with three other stone capitals also said to be from Ibrim, were found to be on display at the Nubia Museum in Aswan in 1998. Since there are doubts as to whether any of these items derive from the Cathedral Church they are dealt with after the material which is still located on site, under the heading 'other stone capitals'.

In the following list, the excavator's find number is given where known and prefixed by the letters QI and the year (eg *QI 78/C74*), whilst the numbers of the photographs in the Gartkiewicz collection are prefixed by the letters GP (eg *GP 257*). The items in the new Nubia Museum, in Aswan, have been given a different series of numbers to identify them (i.e. NM1 – NM5).

CAPITALS, SHAFTS AND BASES

In an attempt to determine the forms of the Phase 1 and the Phase 2 Cathedral Church, the surviving remains of capitals, shafts and bases were measured and drawn. They are all manufactured from either pink granite, presumably from Aswan, or sandstone. The granite items are all listed before those that are of sandstone.

Granite Capitals

Gartkiewicz classified the forms of granite capitals employed in the Nubian buildings at Dongola, Faras, Estebel near Gebel el-Grein, and Qasr Ibrim into two forms, Type I and Type II, according to the variability in the shape of the lower part (Figure 33 *Gartkiewicz 1990*: 189-197 Figures 105 – 110). Both types have an upper element which is square in plan, but differ in the way that the distance across the top is reduced in size and converted to a circle in order to sit on a round column. In his Type I capitals the lower part is in the form of a cylinder which has the same, or a very similar, diameter to the width of the upper square section, until at its lower end it suddenly reduces in size, in a shape which he described as an inverted cone, to fit the top of a capital. In his Type II the lower part narrows sharply downwards to fit the top of a column.

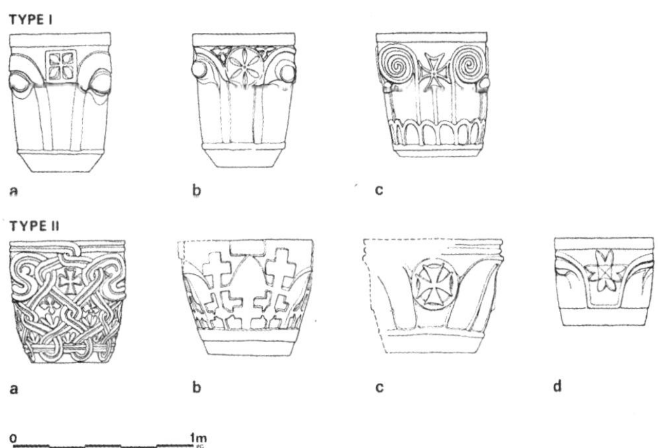

Figure 33: The classification of granite capitals in Nubian churches. The examples shown are:
Type I :
a and b from Faras;
c from Qasr Ibrim (see below No.1);
Type II :
a from Qasr Ibrim (see below No.2);
b from Dongola;
c from Estebel;
d from Faras (after Gartkiewicz 1990: Figure 107).

Gartkiewicz also identified a series of motifs which appear in the centre fields of capitals from Christian Nubia (Figure 34).

Figure 34: Motifs employed on granite capitals in Christian Nubia (after Gartkiewicz 1990: Figure 111).

Three granite capitals were located within the Cathedral in 1992.

1. Complete granite capital of Gartkiewicz Type I, 63 cms square at the top, 43 cms in diameter at the bottom, and 64 cms high (*QI 78/C71; GPs 376 and 377*; *Gartkiewicz 1990* Figs 107c and 108c; Figure 35, No 1, Plates 162 and 163).

   According to the record plan produced in 1964 and photographs taken at the time, it was found during excavations in the south ambulatory, close to the *mihrab* (Chapter 2 Figure 8, Cap 1 and Plate 44 and here, Figure 36 Cap 1).

2. Complete granite capital of Gartkiewicz Type II, 63 cms square at the top, 43 cms in diameter at the bottom, and 64 cms high (*QI 78/C72; GPs 365-370*; *Gartkiewicz 1990* Fig 107a; and here Figure 35 No 2, Plates 164 and 165).

   According to the record plan produced in 1964 and photographs taken at the time, this was found in the nave about midway down its length (Chapter 2 Figure 8, Cap 2 and Plate 44 and here, Figure 36 Cap 2).

Plates 164 and 165: Granite capital No 2 (EES Photos GP 365 & 369).

Plates 162 and 163: Granite capital No 1 (EES Photos GP 376 & 377).

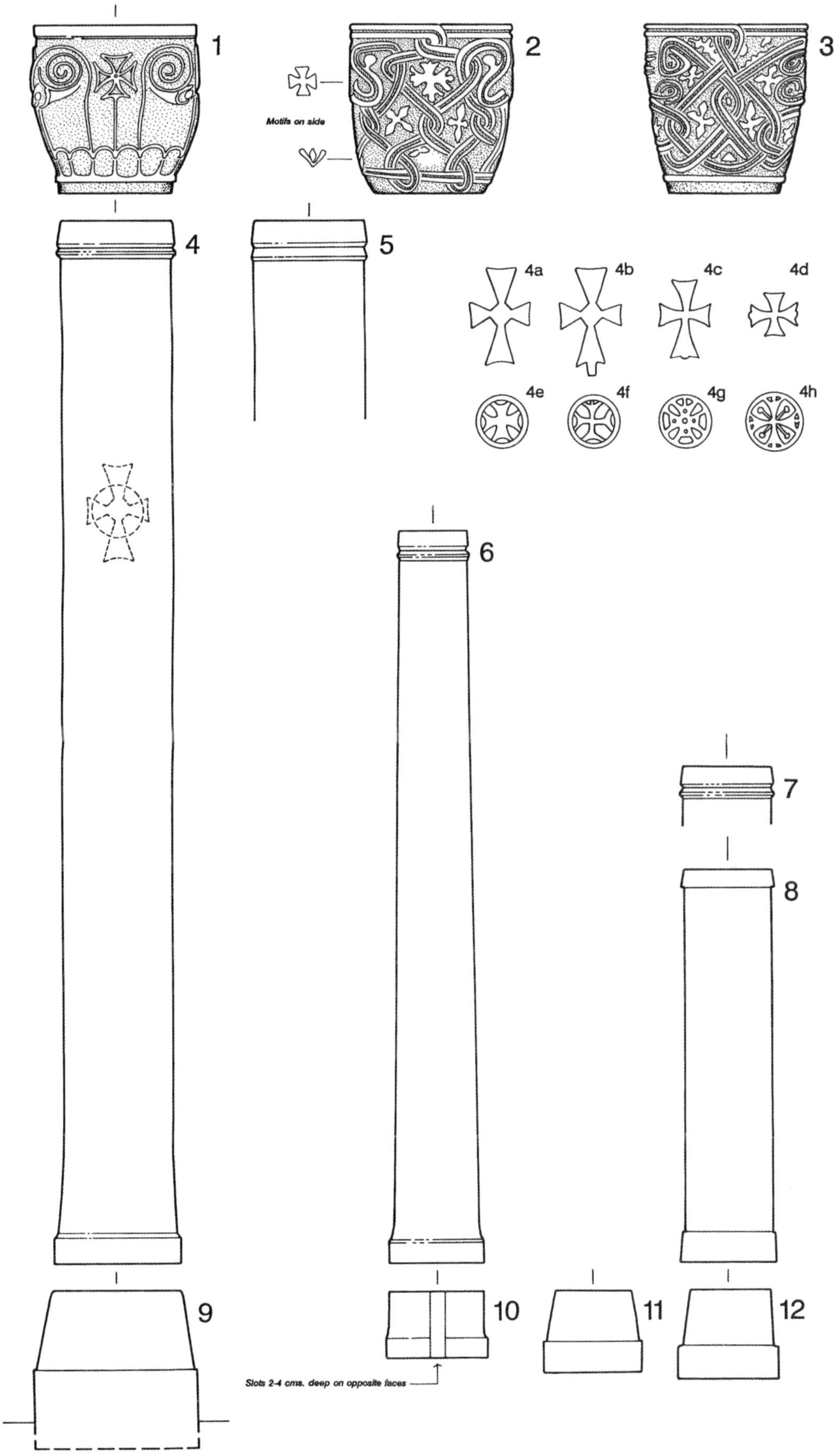

Figure 35. Granite capitals, shafts and bases, with the eight types of motif employed on the shafts.

3. Complete capital, probably of Gartkiewicz's Type II, 63 cms square at the top, 43 cms in diameter at the bottom, and 64 cms high (*QI 78/C73; GPs 371, 372 and 375*; and here Figure 35 No 3 and Plates 166 & 167).

   According to the record plan produced in 1964 and photographs taken in the 1970s, this was found in the north aisle near its east end (Chapter 2 Figure 8, Cap 3, and Plate 44 and here, Figure 36 as Cap 3).

Plates 166 and 167: Granite capital No 3 (EES Photos GP 371 and 372).

Granite Shafts

The positions of the three complete and twenty-five fragments of other granite shafts as found in the Cathedral in 1964 were shown on the record plan and photographs taken at the time. One of the complete shafts was still standing on its base in the nave (Figure 36 C1), whilst an example of a smaller type was found next to a smaller base in the baptistry (Figure 36 C13, Chapter 4 Figure 8 and Plates 28, 42- 44 and 168).

The two complete columns and the fragments of the others all appear to have been found adjacent to the bases from which they had fallen, although part of that at the east end of the north arcade appears to have been first discovered in the previous year within the apse (Chapter 1 Trench A1). The pieces recorded within the nave in 1964 clearly represented the twelve complete large shafts required to be accommodated on the twelve granite bases (Figure 36 B1-B12 and C1 –C12).

Plate 168: The granite shaft (C1) still standing on its granite base (B1) at the east end of the south aisle in 1963 (EES Photo GD 208).

By January 1992 there were two complete shafts and thirty-one fragments lying within the Cathedral, all from the larger type of shaft employed in the nave, except for the smaller example (C13) which had been moved from the baptistry. All the pieces in the nave had been moved from their original locations to the west end of the *naos* and some further breakages had occurred, increasing the number of fragments.

A search throughout the remainder of the Qasr Ibrim site, above water level, revealed a further four complete examples and thirty-five fragments, giving a total of seventy-two pieces of granite shafts in all. Some of them were clearly of the larger type used in the nave and this came as something of a surprise as it clearly indicated that a greater number of these large shafts had existed on the site than was required to be accommodated on the twelve granite bases in the nave.

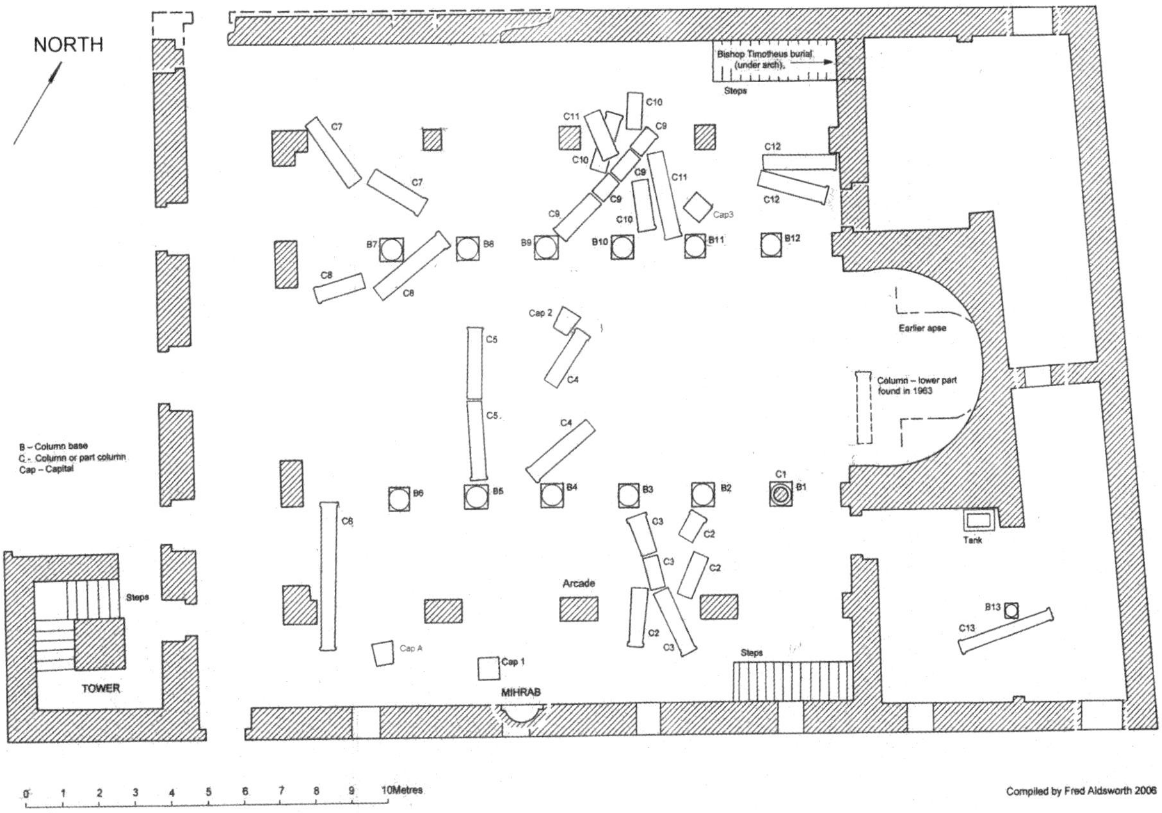

Figure 36: A revised version of the record plan produced in 1964, showing the locations of the collapsed shafts and capitals.

It was decided, therefore, to measure and describe all the surviving fragments in order to determine the minimum number of complete shafts represented, although it is acknowledged that some pieces may no longer be visible whilst others could have been re-worked and re-used, as, for example, with the granite bowl built into the later phases of the east wall of the Cathedral (Figure 25). The diameter and length of each piece, or approximate length in the case of the broken pieces, were measured and notes were taken of the form of their terminal mouldings and of any decoration on them.

Three distinct sizes of shaft are represented by the surviving pieces:

> Type A – of which the only complete example is 396 cms long.
>
> Type B – of which the only complete example is 278 cms long.
>
> Type C – of which the four complete examples are between 136 and 150 cms long.

Type A Granite Shafts

This is the largest type of shaft used at Ibrim (Figure 35 No 4). The only complete example is 3.96 metres long, 0.43 metres in diameter at the top and throughout its length expanding to 0.50 metres in diameter at the bottom (Plate 169).

Plate 169: The complete Type A granite shaft, presumably C6, during excavation in 1964. This is now broken (EES Photo GP 409).

Of the certain examples of this type, the diameters range from 0.37 to 0.50 metre at the top and from 0.48 to 0.57 metres at the base. The mouldings at the lower end are fairly consistent, but at the top the mouldings vary a little in detail (Figure 35 Nos 4 and 5, Plates 170 and 171).

Plates 170 and 171: Variations in the mouldings on the tops of the Type A granite shafts (EES Photos GP 393 and 394).

At a point usually a little over 1.0 metre from the top end, the shafts each carries a motif carved in relief representing a cross either enclosed in a circle or unenclosed. These are similar to some of the motifs identified by Gartkiewicz on granite capitals in Christian Nubia (see above Figure 34, Figure 35 Nos 4a-4h, Plate 172).

Plate 172: Some of the designs of the carved crosses on Type A granite shafts (EES Photos GP 387, 388, 392, 401, and 402).

Setting aside the smaller example from the baptistry, the complete shaft and the thirty-one fragments lying in the Cathedral are certainly of this type. Including the complete example, twelve mouldings from the upper ends of shafts and twelve mouldings from the lower ends of shafts are present, and there are also twelve pieces decorated with a cross - six enclosed in a circle and six unenclosed. There is a slight variation in design within these two groups and the number of examples to each design is as follows –

Type 4a - one	Type 4e - three
Type 4b - three	Type 4f - one
Type 4c - one	Type 4g - one
Type 4d - one	Type 4h - one

Given that the shaft fragments have diagonal breaks, it is difficult to be precise about the overall lengths represented by the pieces without re-engaging, but an approximate total length of 47.15 metres appears to be indicated. If this figure is divided by twelve an average length of about 3.92 metres results and this figure is very close to the length of the one surviving complete example.

It can be deduced, therefore, that the one complete and thirty-one fragments of Type A granite shaft lying in the Cathedral in 1992 are sufficient to reconstruct the twelve large shafts which would have been mounted on the six pairs of granite bases in the later phases of construction of the building.

Without re-engaging the pieces it is difficult to determine precisely which pieces fit together and which fragments belong to which base. Using original photographs it is possible, however, to determine to which bases some of the cross-types belonged. Thus the shaft standing on the base at the east end of the south aisle (B1), for example, was certainly the complete shaft that survives, and this carries the only example of a Type 4f cross amongst the group of pieces.

Of the thirty-nine pieces of shaft located elsewhere on the site, eleven are probably from the large Type A shafts and of these two fit together to make a complete example 3.96 metres long. Four have mouldings from the top of a shaft and four have mouldings from the bottom of a shaft. Three fragments are decorated with an enclosed cross motif of Type 4e and one is decorated with an unenclosed cross motif of Type 4b. It is safe to assume, therefore, that at least four shafts are represented by these fragments but there may have been more.

The total length of shaft represented by the eleven pieces is about 17.15 metres, suggesting perhaps 4.3 shafts averaging 3.96 metres in length. There are two further shaft fragments which may also be of this type, but equally well may fall into the smaller, Type C, category. One piece is from the bottom of a shaft and is 0.42 metre, in diameter and 0.44 metre long. The other is from the top of a shaft and is 0.41 metre in diameter and 0.65 metre long. Their diameters suggest that they would best fit Type A and if added to the eleven pieces already noted, this makes a total of five shaft tops, five shaft bottoms, and a total length of 18.24 metres giving 4.6 shafts averaging 3.96 metres in length.

If the fragments of shaft currently outside the Cathedral are added to those lying inside then there is evidence for at least sixteen shafts existed, and possibly seventeen or more. They include at least sixteen pieces carrying a carved cross either enclosed or unenclosed; and an approximate total length of between 64.30 metres and 65.39 metres giving a total of between 16.2 and 16.5 shafts each 3.96 metres long.

It is safe to conclude, therefore, that there were at least eight pairs of the larger Type A shafts on the site at one time. If this figure is accepted as indicative of the original or intended number in the Cathedral Church, allowing for the remote possibility that there were more on the site than were actually needed in the building, then all the top and bottom ends survive; all the pieces with cross motifs survive; and the total length of the original number of shafts is represented by the surviving pieces. If the two doubtful pieces are brought into reckoning then a greater number of shafts of the type are represented by the survivals and, of course, all the calculations assume that there are no other pieces have been lost or still lie buried on the site.

Type B Granite Shafts

This is the second largest type of granite shaft (Figure 35 No 6). The only complete example is 2.78 metres long, 0.29 metre in diameter at the top, and 0.38 metre in diameter at the bottom. This example was found in 1963-64 adjacent to a base in the baptistry and in 1992 it lay in the nave (Chapter 2 and Figure 36). A further three pieces, distinguished by a diameter of less than 0.30 metre, have been found elsewhere on the site. They have a total length of 1.95 metres and presumably formed part of a second Type B column in the sacristy.

Type C Granite Shafts

This is the smallest type of shaft (Figure 35 Nos 7 and 8). The four surviving complete examples are between 1.36 and 1.50 metres long, between 0.32 and 0.40 metre in diameter at the top and between 0.30 and 0.40 metre in diameter at the bottom. Of these, one is built into the burial chamber under the south-west corner of the Cathedral (Figures 24CC, 25EE and Plate 164) and the other three lie elsewhere on the site.

Plate 173: The Type C shaft re-used in the burial chamber under the south-west corner of the Cathedral in 1992 (Photograph by Fred Aldsworth).

The mouldings at the lower end of this type are fairly consistent but at the top they vary a little in detail (Figure 35 Nos 7 and 8). Of the eighteen other fragments of shafts of this type so far identified, five are from the tops of shafts; six are from the bottoms of shafts; and the total length represented is about 13.10 metres or 8.7 columns each 1.50 metres in length. If two pieces with slightly larger diameters are accepted as belonging to this type this type, rather than Type A, then six are from the tops of shafts; seven are from the bottoms of shafts; and the total length represented is about 14.19 metres or 9.46 shafts each 1.50 metres long.

Taking into account the four complete examples, the minimum number of Type C shafts represented by the surviving fragments is 12.7 (i.e. 13) but there may be as many as 13.46 (i.e. 14). Whichever of the two figures is correct it is probably safe to assume that there were at least seven pairs of columns made for, and presumably used in, the building at some time, but they were all discarded at a later stage of rebuilding.

Bases in Granite

Three distinct sizes of column base in pink granite are represented by the surviving examples. These were presumably manufactured to take the three different sizes of shaft.

Type A Granite Bases

The largest type is represented by the twelve examples which survive *in situ* in the Cathedral Church (Figures 23, 31YY and 36 B1 – B12). To accommodate the sixteen or more shafts identified on the site there should originally have been a greater number than this, and it is, perhaps, surprising that no other intact or broken examples have been found.

The surviving examples are square at the bottom, measuring on average 64 cms along each side, and then reduce to a circular form, between 48 and 54 cms in diameter at the top (Figure 35 No 9 and Plates 131 and 132). The overall height of each piece cannot at present be ascertained, as the paved floor is laid up to them, but it is in excess of 50 cms. The upper, circular, sections vary between 25 and 36 cms in height.

At least seven of the bases are marked with a mason's letter (see Chapter 4).

Type B Granite Base

The second largest type is represented by a single example, which was located in 1992 outside the north-west corner of the Cathedral Church (Figure 35 No 10). It was found during the 1963-64 excavations in the baptistry where it was presumably used to support the only surviving complete Type B granite shaft (*QI 78/C74* and Plates 126, 127 and 174).

Plate 174: The Type B granite base from the baptistry (EES Photo GP 56).

The Type B granite base is 40 cms square at the bottom, reducing to a circular top, 38 cms in diameter, and its full height is 26 cms. It has vertical slots between 2 and 4 cms deep on two opposite faces and when discovered these appear to have been on the sides which faced north and south.

Type C Granite Bases

The smallest type of base is represented by only two examples which are re-used in the burial chamber under the south-east corner of the Cathedral (Figure 35 Nos 11 and 12 and Plates 173 and 175). They are similar in size and design but differ a little in detail. The smaller of the two (Figure 35 No 11) is 38 cms square at the base and reduces to a circular top, 34 cms in diameter. It is 31 cms in height. The larger one (Figure 35 No 12) is 40 cms square at the base and reduces to a circular top, 34 cms in diameter. It is 34 cms in height.

Plate 175: The Type C granite bases re-used in the burial chamber under the south-east corner of the Cathedral (EES Photo GP 257).

Given that the Type C granite bases probably supported the Type C granite shafts, of which at least fourteen examples are represented on the site and at least sixteen probably existed in the original building, a much larger number of bases of this type must have existed, but their size and shape would have rendered them ideal for conversion, especially into large *mortaria* or bowls, once they were removed from the building.

SANDSTONE ELEMENTS

Amongst the material recovered during excavations are a number of pieces carved in red sandstone. It is difficult to be precise about the number of complete items represented by the pieces, and to some extent their precise form, but they appear to include fragments of capitals, probably one shaft, and at least one base.

Large Capitals in Red Sandstone

There appear to be pieces of at least five large capitals of red sandstone on the site (Figure 37 Nos 13-17). Apart from the complete example (No 13), there is no record of where these pieces were found on the 1964 record plan and the find numbers marked on them were added in 1978 and 1981.

13. Complete capital in red sandstone, partly damaged, 56 cms square at the top, 41 cms in diameter at the bottom, and 60 cms high (Figure 37 No 13; *QI 78/C70 and C91 GPs 373, 378, 380 and 381*, and Plates 176 and 177).

    According to the 1964 record plan and photographs, this was found in the south ambulatory, close to the *mihrab* (Figure 36 Cap A).

14. Four pieces in red sandstone which together make the upper part of a capital measuring 52 cms square at the top and now 35 cms high (*GPs 196 and 203,* Figure 37 No 14 and Plates 178 and 179). The lower face has been re-worked flat and is worn smooth, presumably having been re-used.

Plates 178 and 179 (above): The sandstone capital No.14 (EES Photos GP 196 and 203).

15. One piece from the lower part of a capital in red sandstone, about 44 cms across and now 34 cms high (Figure 37 No15; *QI 78/64; GP 52*, and Plate 180).

Plate 180: Fragment from red sandstone capital No 15 (EES Photo GP 52)

Left. Plate 176 and 177: The large sandstone capital No.13 (EES Photos GP 373 and 378).

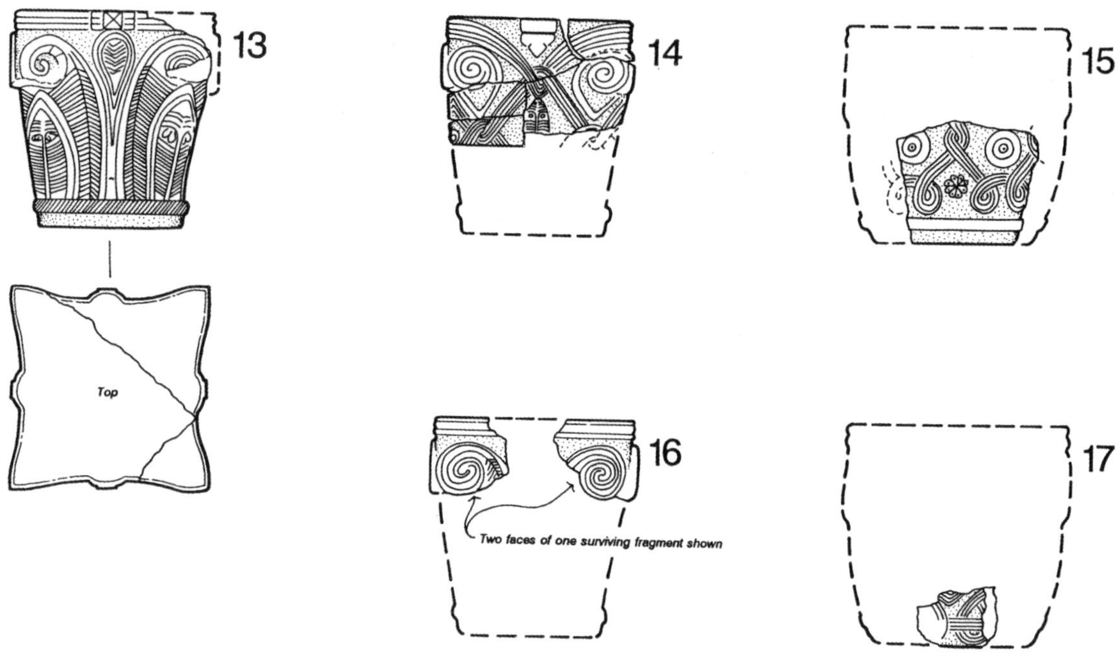

Figure 37: Large capitals in red sandstone.

16. One piece from the top corner of a capital in red sandstone, perhaps of similar size to 13 (Figure 37 No 16; QI 81/C84; GP 181, and Plate 181).

17. One small piece from the bottom of a red sandstone capital (Figure 37 No 17; *QI 78/C85; GP 181*, and Plate 181).

Plate 181: Fragments from red sandstone capitals (EES Photo GP 181).

Small Capitals in Red Sandstone

There are pieces of at least four or perhaps five small capitals in red sandstone on the site (Figure 38 Nos 18-22)

18, 19. Two pieces, probably from the same capital, 42 cms square at the top and now up to about 22 cms high (Figure 38 Nos 18 and 19; *QI 78/C46 and C46A; GPs 179 and 379*, and Plates 182 and 183).

Plates 182 and 183: Fragments of red sandstone capital Nos 18 and 19 (EES Photos GP 179 and 379).

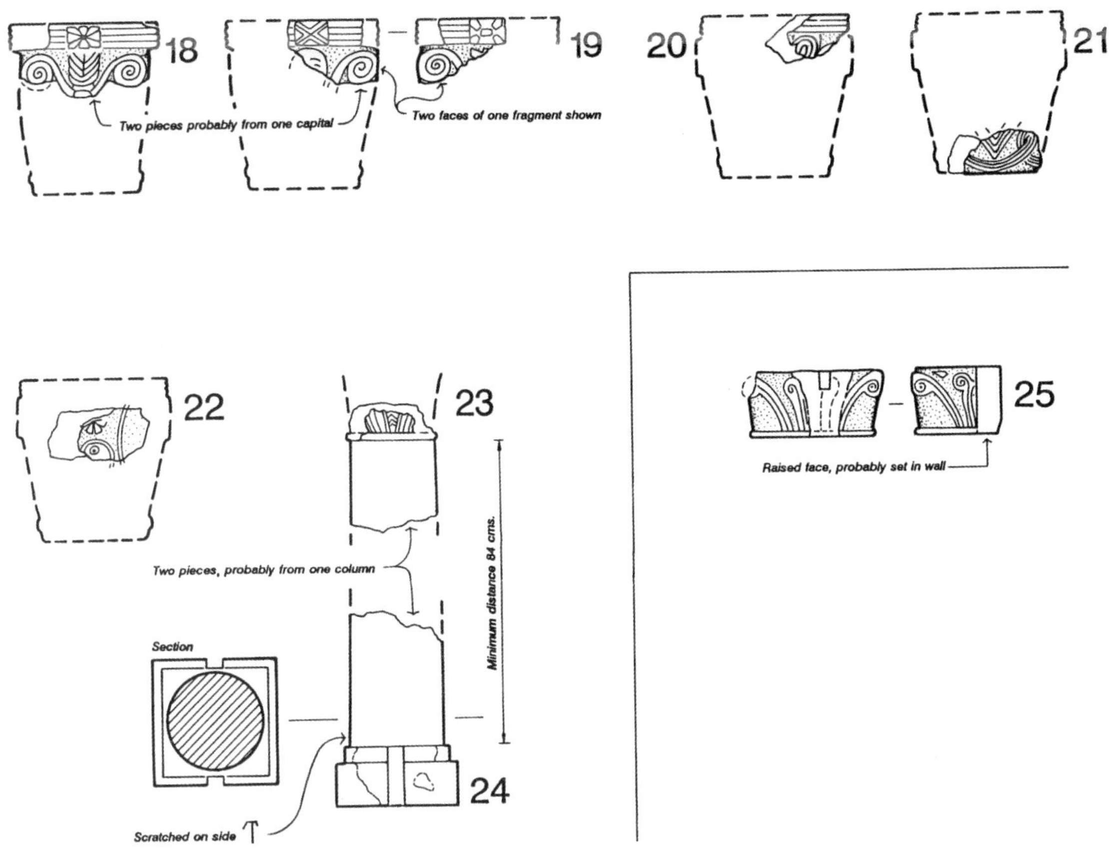

Figure 38: Small capitals, a column, a column base, and an impost in sandstone.

20. One small piece from the top corner of a red sandstone capital (Figure 38 No 20; *QI 78/C88; GP 181*, and Plate 181).

21. One piece from the bottom of a capital, about 36 cms in diameter (Figure 38 No 21; *QI 78/87 GP 181,* and Plate 181).

22. Two pieces from the side of a capital of indeterminate size (Only one piece seen in 1992 - Figure 38 No 22; *QI 78/68 & 69 GP 54,* and Plate 184).

Plate 184: Fragments of red sandstone capital No 22 (EES GP 54).

Shafts and Bases in Red Sandstone

23. A broken piece of shaft, 25 cms in diameter and up to 25 cms in length, ith a small part of an integral capital attached (Figure 38 No 23), which may originally have been part of 24.

24. A base with an integral piece of shaft which is broken (Figure 38 No 24). The base is 24 cms square, reducing to 30 cms square, and in all 17 cms high. It has a shallow slot cut into each of two opposed faces. The shaft is 27 cms in diameter and survives up to 37 cms in length. It has graffiti scratched on one side. There is a strong possibility that it originally formed part of a complete one-piece capital, shaft and base with 23. It is not possible to determine the full length of the original piece from the two fragments but it must have been in excess of 84 cms.

IMPOST

25. A probable sandstone impost, 34 cms long, 23 cms wide and 19 cms high (Figure 38 No 25; *QI 78/C125*). It is decorated on one face and includes a round bead on the lower edge, which extends for a distance of 16 cms down each side, terminating in a flat raised section, which was probably set within the line of the wall.

    The only obvious location for this within the structure is on the top of one of the pilaster buttresses in the baptistry or sacristy of the later (Phase 2) building.

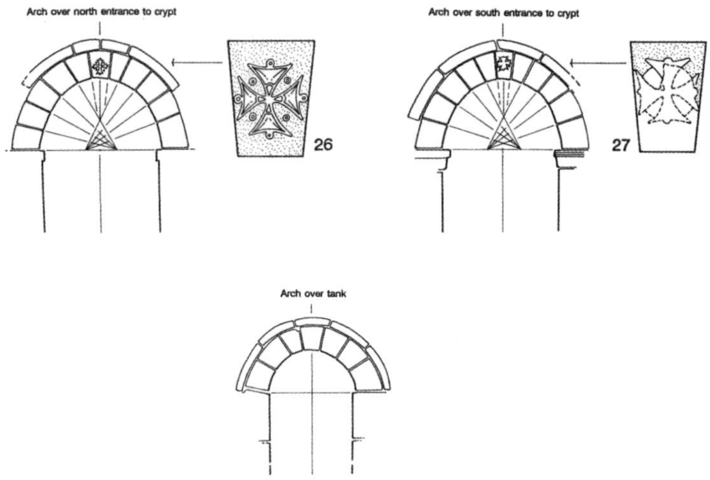

Figure 39: Arches and voussoir*s over the doors to the crypts and the baptistry tank.*

DECORATED *VOUSSOIR* STONES

In 1992, there were six decorated *voussoir* stones incorporated in the standing structure and a number of others, recovered during excavations, were on the ground outside the west end of the Cathedral Church. Since these throw light on the form and detailing of the building, some forty-six examples are described and illustrated here, and, where they are not *in situ,* attempts are made to suggest the size and position of the openings in which they were originally located.

The decoration includes a range of individual motifs (Groups 1- 4) as well as painted interlace and Greek fret linking between adjoining stones (Groups 5 and 6).

***Voussoir*s from Small Openings**

There are three small arches in the surviving building. These are over the north door to the crypt, over the south door to the crypt, and over the baptistry tank (Figures 27JJ, 29TT and 39). They are all built of *voussoir* stones, the first two include a decorated keystone but the third is plain. There is no reason to believe that any of them have been reconstructed.

The two arches over the doors to the crypt are similar in size and form, and each has a plain hood mould over the top. The openings are both 104 cms wide and 60 cms high. The *voussoir* stones are 24 cms high and are made from red sandstone, whereas the imposts on which they are seated are of yellow sandstone. By careful measurement it can be shown that the openings were not intended to be semi-circular, with *voussoir*s cut on the radius, but are each three-centred with a radius at the top of about 36 cms and lower down of about 64 cms (Figure 39 Nos 26 and 27 and Plates 185 and 186).

The arch over the baptistry tank is, however, semi-circular with a radius of 36 cms. The stones are cut on the radius and are each 20 cms long (Figures 29TT and 39).

If the method of construction seen in the arches to the crypt was used throughout the building it might not be possible to infer opening sizes from individual *voussoir* stones, so wherever possible they were re-assembled on the ground prior to measurement and inclusion in the following lists.

The stones are grouped by size, shape, material and, sometimes, by their decoration. The length dimension given is the depth to which the stone penetrated into the thickness of the opening in which it was set.

Group 1: Small *Voussoir*s

The first two of these survive *in situ,* over the north and south doors to the crypt. They are both set as keystones in three-centred openings, as already described, 104 cms wide and 60 cms high, and they are both 56 cms long and cut from red sandstone.

26. *Voussoir* stone *in situ* in head of north door to crypt, 24 cms high, 19 cms wide at the top tapering to 14 cms wide, and 56 cms long, of red sandstone (Figure 39 No 26; *GP 195,* and Plate 185).

27. *Voussoir* stone *in situ* in head of south door to crypt, 24 cms high, 19 cmswide at the top tapering to 14 cms wide, and 56 cms long, of red sandstone (Figure 39 No 27; *GP 194,* and Plate 186). The motif on this *voussoir* had been badly defaced between the 1970s and 1992.

Plates 185 and 186: Group 1 voussoir *stones over the south and north doors to the crypt (EES Photos GP 194 and 195).*

Group 2: Small *Voussoirs*

The next group of four or five pieces when assembled together produce an arch with an internal radius of about 36 cms. The first four are cut from either pink or purple sandstone and are each 17 cms high, 31 cms long, and decorated at one end. When in place the soffit of the arch and the undecorated ends were painted white.

28. *Voussoir* stone 17 cms high, 23.5 cms wide tapering to 15.5 cms, and 31 cms long, of purple sandstone (Figure 40 No 28; *QI 78/C1; GP 358,* and Plate 187).

29. *Voussoir* stone 17 cms high, 26 cms wide tapering to 19 cms, and 31 cms long, of pink sandstone (Figure 40 No 29; *QI 78/C1; GP 358,* and Plate 187).

30. *Voussoir* stone 17 cms high, 25.5 cms wide tapering to 18.5 cms, and 31 cms long, of purple sandstone (Figure 40 No 30; QI 78/C13; GP 359, and Plate 188)

31. *Voussoir* stone 17 cms high, 20 cms wide tapering to 14 cms, and 31 cms long, of purple sandstone (Figure 40 No 31; QI 78/C4; GP 359, and Plate 188).

A fifth piece (No 32) may be from the same or a similar opening to the other four. It is of the same height and length as the others and also decorated only at one end. Although it has a much smaller internal radius, the overall radius represented by the pieces differs little when this one is added or omitted. It is, however, of a different coloured sandstone and it bears no sign of having been painted white.

Plate 187: Group 2 voussoirs *Nos 28 and 29 (EES Photo GP 358).*

Plate 188: Group 2 voussoirs *Nos 30 and 31.*

32. *Voussoir* stone 17 cms high, 15 cms wide tapering to 10 cms, and 31 cms long, of white sandstone (Figure 40 No 32). The internal radius is about 18 cms.

When all five pieces in this group are placed together they form a substantial part of an arch with perhaps only two pieces missing. If used together they would have provided the head of an opening about 72 cms wide, which is the size of that over the baptismal tank, although this survives complete and is undecorated.

The only other openings of about this size identified in the Cathedral Church are the windows in the external walls, which had flat heads. No location for this group of *voussoir*s has been identified in the Phase 2 building.

The only openings of about this size in the Cathedral Church are the external and internal door openings, which had flat heads, and no location for this group of *voussoir*s has been identified in the building.

Figure 40: Voussoir*s of Group 2.*

Group 3 : Small *Voussoirs*

This group of five pieces when assembled together produce an arch of about 58 cms internal radius. They are all 13.5 cms high, 40 cms long, made from white or grey sandstone, and decorated at only one end.

33. *Voussoir* stone 13.5 cms high, 20 cms wide tapering to 15 cms, and 40 cms long, of white sandstone (Figure 41 No 33; *QI 78/C12; GP 484,* and Plate 189). The internal radius is about 50 cms.

34. *Voussoir* stone 13.5 cms high, 19.5 cms wide tapering to 16 cms, and 40 cms long, of grey sandstone (Figure 41 No 34; *QI 78/C38*). The internal radius is about 70 cms.

Plate 189 (above): Group 3 voussoir*s Nos 33, 36 and 37 (EES Photo GP 202).*

Plate 190 (right): Group 3 voussoir *No 35 (EES Photo GP 484).*

Figure 40: Voussoir*s of Group 3.*

35. *Voussoir* stone 13.5 cms high, 16 cms wide tapering to 12.5 cms, and 40 cms long, of white sandstone (Figure 41 No 35; *QI 78/C38; GP 202,* and Plate 190). The internal radius is about 70 cms.

36. *Voussoir* stone 13.5 cms high, 17.5 cms wide tapering to 14 cms, and 40 cms long, of white sandstone (Figure 41 No 36; *QI 78/C33; GP 484,* and Plate 189). The internal radius is about 60 cms.

37. *Voussoir* stone 13.5 cms high, 16.5 cms wide tapering to 14 cms, and cms long (Figure 41 No 37; *GP 484,* and Plate 189).

When all five pieces in this group are placed together they form a little less than half an arch, with perhaps eight pieces missing. If used together they would have provided the head of an opening about 116 cms wide.

***Voussoirs* from Large Openings**

There are a number of decorated *voussoir*s which derive from larger openings than those already described.

In January 1992, four were located where they had been re-used in the outer south arcade (Figure 30WW and Nos 43-46) and the others were on the ground at the west end of the Cathedral.

No attempt has been made to re-assemble these *voussoir*s in order to determine the size of the openings they represent, but there is a strong likelihood that those in Group 4 derive from outer arcades of the Phases 2 and 3 building and those in Groups 5 and 6 derive from openings across the full width of the nave, in front of the Phase 2 apse and at the west end of the building.

Group 4: Large *Voussoirs*

There is a strong possibility that in their original form the pieces in this group were all decorated at both ends. Five surviving examples are in this form (Nos 38-42), though two are now defaced at one end. The complete examples are 58 cms long; the four examples re-used in the south arcade (Nos. 43-46) have been defaced at one end and reduced to 54 cms in length; whilst the remainder are all broken. The height of the pieces in this group is normally between 19 and 21 cms, but there is a single example (No 54) which is 26 cms high and it is not certain that this is sufficiently tapered to be considered as a *voussoir*.

The arches in the outer arcade, from which they probably derive, were originally built to a radius of about 1.50 metres (Phase 2) and then were rebuilt to a radius of about 1.40 metres (Phase 3). Alternative locations, which were perhaps too small to accommodate these pieces, include the openings between the pilaster buttresses and intermediate columns of the rebuilt (Phase 2) baptistry and sacristy, which are about 2.20 metres across, and the original (Phase 1) arches linking the columns of the inner and outer arcade, which were about 1.80–1.90 metres across.

38. *Voussoir* stone 21 cms high, 19.5 cms wide tapering to 17.5 cms, and 58 cms long, of grey sandstone (Figure 42 No 38; *QI 78/C25; GP 411* and Plate 191). It is decorated at both ends and has traces of red paint.

39. *Voussoir* stone 21 cms high, 20 cms wide tapering to 19 cms, and 58 cms long, of white sandstone (Figure 42 No 39; *QI 78/C25; GP 411* and Plate 191). It is decorated at both ends.

40. *Voussoir* stone 21 cms high, 19.5 cms wide tapering to 19 cms and 58 cms long, of red sandstone (Figure 42 No 40; *QI 78/C136*; *GP 209* and Plate 192). It is decorated at both ends.

Plates 191 and 192: Group 4 voussoirs *Nos 38, 39 and 40 (EES Photos GP 209 and 411)*

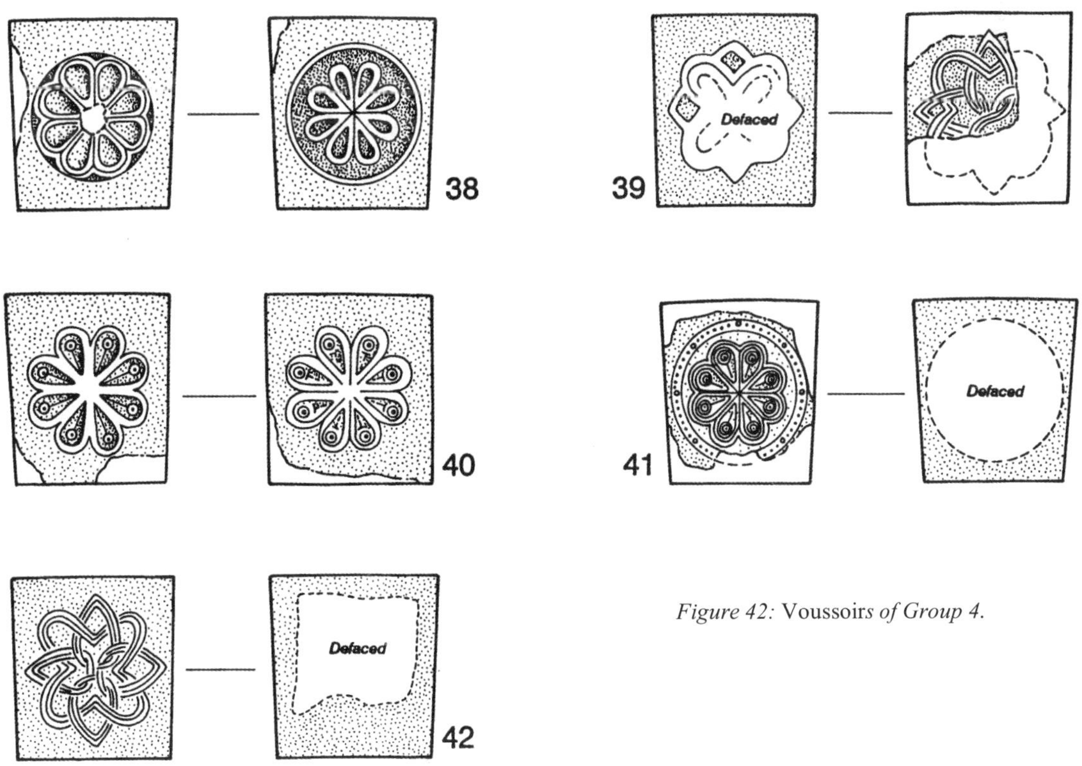

Figure 42: Voussoirs *of Group 4.*

41. *Voussoir* stone 20 cms high, 19 cms wide tapering to 17 cms, and 58 cms long, of red sandstone (Figure 42 No 41; *QI 78/C134*). Originally decorated at both ends but one end has been defaced.

42. *Voussoir* stone 20 cms high, 19 cms wide tapering to 18 cms, and 58 cms long, of white sandstone (Figure 42 No 42; *QI 78/C134; GP200,* and Plate 193). Originally decorated at both ends but one end has been defaced.

The following four pieces have been reduced in length and incorporated into the outer south arcade, which was re-built in Phase 3 (Figures 30WW & 43 and Plate 142).

43. *Voussoir* stone 21 cms high, 17 cms wide tapering to 15 cms, and 54 cms long (Figure 43 No 43). It is now decorated only at one end.

44. *Voussoir* stone 19 cms high, 16 cms wide tapering to 14 cms, and 54 cms long (Figure 43 No 44). It is now decorated only at one end.

45. *Voussoir* stone 19 cms high, 16cms wide tapering to 14 cms, and 54 cms long (Figure 43 No 45). It is now decorated only at one end.

46. *Voussoir* stone 20 cms high, 18 cms wide tapering to 16 cms, and 54 cms long (Figure 43 No 46). It is now decorated only at one end but this has been partially defaced.

The remainder of the pieces in this group are broken.

47. *Voussoir* stone 20 cms high, 20.5 cms wide tapering to 17 cms, and now 30 cms long, in yellow sandstone (Figure 43 No 47; *QI 78/C135*).

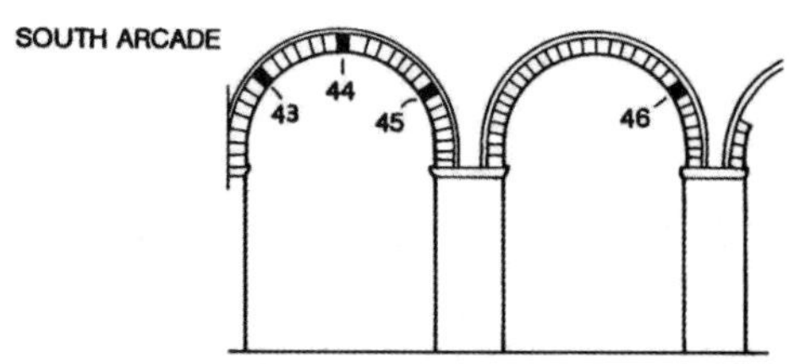

Figure 43: Voussoir*s of Group 4.*

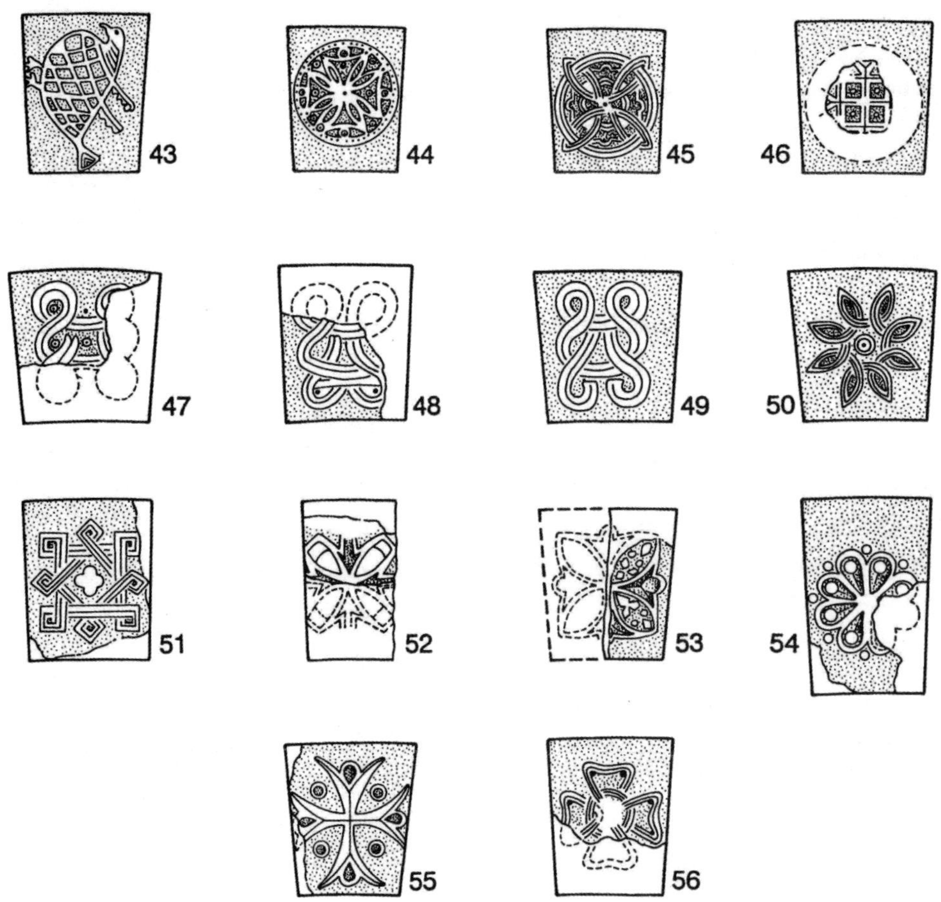

48. *Voussoir* stone 21 cms high, 18 cms wide tapering to 17 cms, and now 40 cms long, in yellow sandstone (Figure 43 No 48).

49. *Voussoir* stone 20 cms high, 20 cms wide tapering to 17.5 cms, and now 32 cms long, in yellow sandstone (Figure 43 No 49; *QI 78/C18; GP 361,* and Plate 194).

50. *Voussoir* stone 20 cms high, 20 cms wide tapering to 16 cms, and now 30 cms long, in white sandstone (Figure 43 No 50; *QI 78/C127; GP 200,* and Plate 193).

Plate 193: Group 4 voussoirs *Nos 42, 50 and 54 (EES Photo GP 200).*

51. *Voussoir* stone 21 cms high, 17 cms wide tapering to 16.5 cms, and now 32cms long, in purple sandstone (Figure 43 No 51; *QI 78/C128; GP 201,* and Plate 195).

Plates 194 and 195: Group 4 voussoirs *Nos 49 and 51 (EES GP 361 and 201).*

52. *Voussoir* stone 21 cms high, 13 cms wide tapering to 12 cms, and now 38 cms long, in yellow sandstone (Figure 43 No 52; *QI 78/C35*).

53. Part of a *voussoir* stone 20 cms high, but now only 10 cms wide and 11 cms long, in yellow sandstone (Figure 43 No 53; *QI 78/C129*).

54. Possible *voussoir* stone 26 cms high, 17 cms wide tapering to 15 cms, and now 20 cms long, in brown sandstone (Figure 43 No 54).

55. *Voussoir* stone 20 cms high, 17.5 cms wide tapering to 14 cms, and now 32 cms long, in yellow sandstone (Figure 43 No 55; *QI 78/C17*).

56. *Voussoir* stone 20 cms high, 17 cms wide tapering to 15 cms, and now 32 cms long, in yellow sandstone (Figure 43 No; *QI 178/C30; GP 354,* and Plate 196).

Plate 196: Group 4 voussoir *No 56 (EES Photo GP 354).*

Group 5: Large *Voussoirs* with Interlace Decoration

This is a group of four pieces with interlace decoration, some of which are painted (Figure 44 Nos 57-60). Only one piece is complete (No 57), and this is 60 cms long and undecorated at the other end, whilst the others are all broken. When re-assembled these form an arch of large radius and probably derive from an opening across the full width of the nave of the Cathedral Church, in front of the Phase 2 apse or its counterpart at the west end of the church. They have radii of about 240-250 cms and 227 cms respectively.

57. *Voussoir* stone 21.5 cms high, 16.5 cms wide tapering to 15 cms, and 60 cms long of grey sandstone (Figure 44 No 57; *QI 78/C29; GP 354,* and Plate 197). It is decorated at one end, with traces of red paint in the recesses, and plain at the other.

Plate 197: Group 5 voussoir *No 57 (EES Photo GP 199).*

58. Part of a *voussoir* stone, originally about 19 cms wide tapering to 18 cms, of grey sandstone with some red paint (Figure 44 No 58; *QI 78/C126; GP 199,* and Plate 198).

59. *Voussoir* stone 21.5 cms high, 19 cms wide tapering to 17 cms. Of grey sandstone with black, red and white paint (Figure 44 No 59; QI 78/C123; GP 199, and Plate 198).

Plate 198: Group 5 voussoir*s Nos 58 and 59 (EES Photos GP 199 and 354).*

Group 6: Large *Voussoir*s with Greek Fret Decoration

A group of eleven pieces, all made from white sandstone and decorated with Greek fret decoration, some of which are painted (Figure 44 and Plates 197-200). The two complete examples (Nos 61 and 63) are 63 cms long and undecorated at the other end. The remainder are all broken. When re-assembled they form an arch of large radius and probably derive from an opening across the full width of the nave of the Cathedral Church, in front of the Phase 2 apse or its counterpart at the west end of the *naos*, which each have a radius of about 240-250 cms and 227 cms respectively.

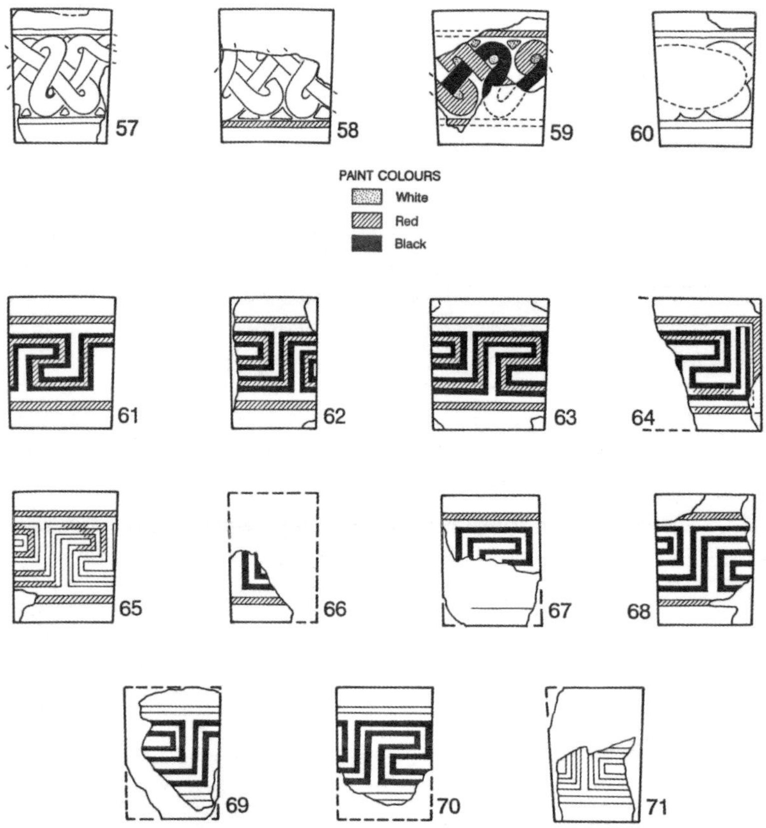

Figure 44: Voussoir*s of Group 5.*

Plate 199: Group 6 voussoir*s (EES Photo GP 188).*

60. *Voussoir* stone 21.5 cms high, 17 cms wide tapering to 15 cms. Of grey sandstone with much of the decoration defaced by a pilgrim scrape (Figure 44 No 60; *QI 78/C36*).

61. *Voussoir* stone, 21 cms high, 18 cms wide tapering to 17 cms, and 63 cms long, with red and black paint (Figure 44 No 61 ; *QI 76/C6; GPs 192, 193 and 486*; and Plate 200).

62. *Voussoir* stone, 21 cms high, 14.5 cms wide tapering to 14 cms, and now 57 cms long with red and black paint (Figure 44 No 62; *QI78/C8; GPs 192, 193 and 486*, and Plate 200).

63. *Voussoir* stone, 21 cms high, 19.5 cms wide tapering to 18 cms, and 63 cms long, with red and black paint (Figure 44 No 63; *QI 78/C7; GPs 192, 193 and 486*, and Plate 200).

64. *Voussoir* stone, 21 cms high, 18 cms wide and now 10 cms long, with red and black paint (Figure 44 No 64; *QI 78/C119; GPs 192, 193 and 198*; and Plate 201).

65. *Voussoir* stone, 21.5 cms high, 17 cms wide tapering to 16.5 cms, and now 30 cms long with traces of red paint (Figure 44 No 65; *QI 78/C117; GPs 192, 193 and 198*; and Plate 201).

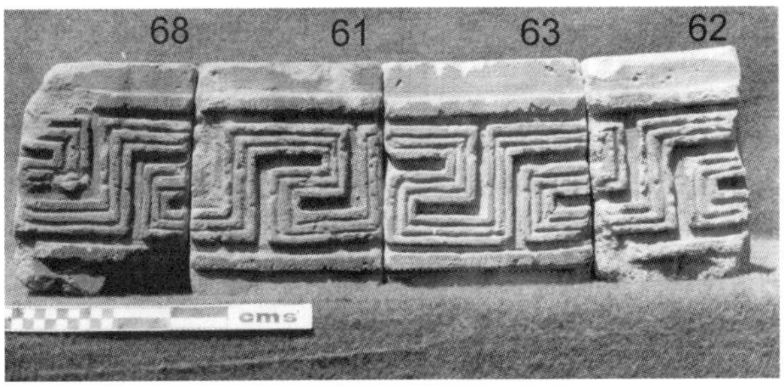

Plate 200: Group 6 voussoirs *Nos 61-63 and 68 (EES Photo GP 486).*

Plate 201: Group 6 voussoirs *Nos 64-67 and 71 (EES Photo GP 198).*

66. Part of *voussoir* stone, now 10 cms long, with red and black paint (Figure 41 No 66; *QI 78/C120; GPs 192, 193 and 198*; and Plate 201).

67. *Voussoir* stone, 21 cms high, 16 cms wide and now 16 cms long with red and black paint (Figure 44 No 65; *QI 78/C118; GPs 192, 193 and 198*; and Plate 201).

68. *Voussoir* stone, 21 cms high, 16.5 cms wide tapering to 15.5 cms, and now 27 cms long with red and black paint (Figure 44 No 68; *QI 78/C5; GPs 192, 193 and 486*; and Plate 200).

69. *Voussoir* stone, 21 cms high, 16 cms wide and now 23 cms long with black paint (Figure 44 No 69; *QI 78/C10; GPs 192 and 193*).

70. *Voussoir* stone, 21.5 cms high, 16 cms wide tapering to 15.5 cms, and now 25 cms long, with black paint (Figure 44 No 70; *QI 78/C9; GPs 192 and 193*).

71. Part of *voussoir* stone, tapering to about 14 cms wide and now 34 cms long, with no surviving paint (Figure 44 No 71; *QI 78/C122; GPs 192, 193 and 198* and Plate 210).

ARCADE MOULDINGS

Amongst the excavated material lying at the west end of the Cathedral in 1992 were six pieces of decorated stone which throw light on the form of the openings in the outer arcade in its reconstructed (Phase 2) form, prior to the Phase 3 reconstruction (Figure 45 Nos 72-77).

Four of them are imposts (Nos 72-75), designed to cap square pillars and carry the arches, whilst the other two formed parts of a decorative hood mould above the openings (Nos 76 and 77).

The four imposts each carry an identical profile, with a half-round moulding surmounted by a concave section finishing with a flat band, about 25mm wide, at the top. Similar pieces are incorporated in the existing arcade (Figure 30WW and Plates 139, 142 and 144-147). All the pieces show signs of being defaced on the flat band and there is a strong likelihood that they were originally decorated along this edge, perhaps with a chevron pattern like that surviving on the section of hood mould (No 76 - Figure 45 and Plate 204).

72. Impost, 70 cms long, with defaced flat band (Figure 45 No 72).

73. Impost, 49 cms long, with defaced flat band and rectangular panel, 22 cms long (Figure 45 No 73; *GP 24,* and Plate 202).

74. Impost, now broken, but perhaps about 60 cms long originally, with defaced flat band and square panel, 11 cms long (Figure 45 No 74).

75. Impost fragment, now 46 cms long, with mouldings which may indicate the original form of the interface between imposts and hood moulding (Figure 45 No 75; *GP 22,* and Plate 203).

Plates 202 and 203: Arcade mouldings Nos 73 and 75 (EES Photos GP 22 and 24).

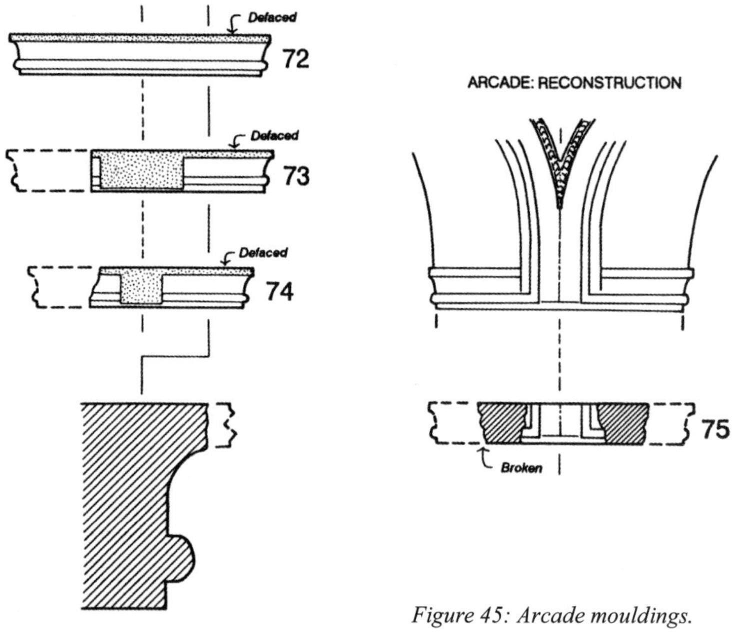

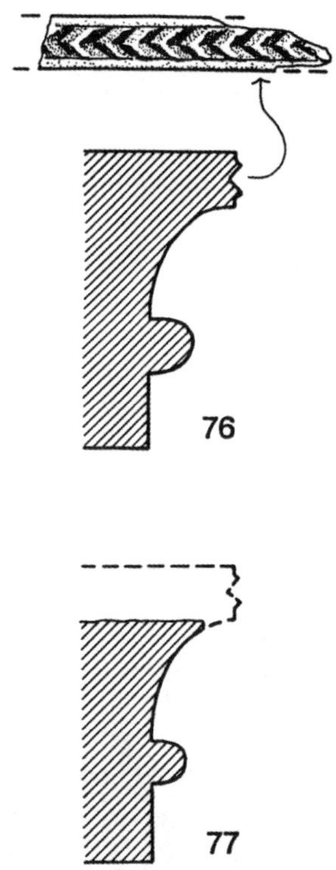

Figure 45: Arcade mouldings.

There were numerous pieces of hood mould either incorporated in the south arcade (Figure 30WW and Plates 139, 142 and 144-147) or lying at the west end of the Cathedral in 1992. One fragment (No 76) has a flat band decorated with a chevron pattern but on all the other pieces this detail is absent, although otherwise the profiles are very similar. There are indications that the decorated band may have been removed from the pieces that were re-used, but there is no obvious reason why this would have proved necessary or desirable.

The radius of the openings represented by the surviving hood mould fragments is difficult to assess, but from those where measurement could be attempted it may have been as small as 55 cms, indicating perhaps that, along with the imposts (Nos 72-75), they may have been designed for the original (Phase 1) outer arcades.

76. Fragment of hood mould, now only 13 cms long and 13.5 cms high, with chevron ornament (Figure 45 No 76; *QI 78/C139;* and Plate 204).

77. Hood mould, numerous pieces of varying length and now 11 cms high, without flat band decorated with chevron design, but evidence of having been defaced (Figure 45 No 77).

Plate 204: Fragment of hood mould No 76, with surviving chevron decoration (Photograph by Fred Aldsworth).

WINDOW GRILLE

A single fragment of window grille lay at the west end of the Cathedral in 1992.

78. Stone window grille fragment, of yellow sandstone, with triangular openings (Figure 46 No 78). The repeating pattern of decoration suggests that it was originally either 50 cms square or, more likely, rectangular measuring externally 50 cms by 96 cms. This would fit the existing Phase 2 window openings.

78

Figure 46: Fragment of a window grille.

Other stone capitals

The following capitals have been associated in the past either with the Cathedral Church or with the remains at Qasr Ibrim generally, although there is no direct evidence to indicate they were employed in the construction of the Cathedral Church.

Nos 1 and 2

A photograph from the 1963 season depicts an inverted stone capital resting on a ground surface, with fragments of a stone base or capital sitting on it (Plate 205). The pieces appear to be located within a building constructed of stone and mud bricks, and the arrangement of walls and what little detail is visible in the background suggests that this structure was most likely the interior of the Church on the Point.

Plate 205: Stone capitals Nos 1 and 2 in 1963 (EES Photo 63-508).

The same two pieces are also recorded in the same arrangement, but sitting on the paved floor of the nave of the Cathedral Church, in several photographs taken after the completion of excavations within the building, presumably in 1964 (Plate 206). They are not included in the 1964 record drawing (Figure 36) and must have been repositioned there.

Plate 206: Stone capitals Nos 1 and 2, repositioned in the nave in 1964 (Unreferenced EES photo).

These two pieces, which are probably of a light-coloured sandstone, are unlike any of the capitals and capital fragments from the Cathedral Church and derive from the Church on the Point (Kjølbye-Biddle 1994 and see below No 3).

Nos 3-6

Four stone capitals are attributed to Qasr Ibrim by Monneret de Villard (*1935* Plate LX). One of them (No 3) appears to have been associated with a structure, but the other three are noted as being in the Cairo Museum (Plate 207).

Plate 207: Stone capitals Nos 3-6.

No 3 is probably of a light-coloured sandstone and is similar in design to those photographed at Ibrim in 1963 and 1964 (Nos 1 & 2 above). The accompanying caption gives the derivation of this piece as being from the tomb of Sheikh Ali, which can be identified as the Church on the Point at Ibrim (*Monneret de Villard 1935*: 116).

The second piece (No 4) also appears to be of a light-coloured stone, but is unlike any others known from the site (Plates 207 and 208). The caption under the photograph gives the Cairo accession number - 20.2.26.4, which is probably a date followed by an inventory number.

Plate 208: Stone capital No 4.

The remaining two pieces (Nos 5 and 6) are the two granite capitals now held in the Nubia Museum in Aswan (NM1 and NM2) and are described below.

Nos NM1-NM5

Five stone capitals, described as coming from Qasr Ibrim, are currently on display in the garden of the Nubia Museum, Aswan. They were measured and photographed by Fred Aldsworth in February 1998.

NM1 Complete granite capital, probably of Gartkiewicz's Type II, approximately 59 cms square at the top, 39 cms across at the bottom, and 55 cms high, carrying the Cairo Museum *Accession Number J 40276* (Figure 47 NM1 and Plates 209 and 210).

Plates 209 and 210: Granite capital NM1, from a 1930s photograph and as displayed at the Nubia Museum, Aswan in 1992 (EES Photo QI 63-803d and photograph by Fred Aldsworth).

NM2 Complete granite capital, probably of Gartkiewicz's Type II, approximately 63 cms square at the top, 40 cms across at the bottom, and 60 cms high, carrying the Cairo Museum *Accession Number J 40275* (Figure 44 NM2 and Plates 211 and 212).

Plates 211 and 212: Granite capital NM2, from a 1930s photograph and as displayed at the Nubia Museum, Aswan in 1992 (EES Photo QI 63-803c and photograph by Fred Aldsworth).

There can be little doubt but that the two granite capitals (NM1 and NM2) are of a similar design to the three found at Qasr Ibrim and indeed encountered elsewhere in Christian Nubia (*Gartkiewicz 1990*: 189-197). However, neither of them are depicted in the photographs taken during the excavations at Qasr Ibrim in the 1960s. They appear to have found their way to the Cairo Museum sometime before 1935, and were transferred to the Nubia Museum at Aswan in the 1990s.

If they are from Qasr Ibrim, they must have been removed from the site before 1935, and this would imply that they were not buried with the other three examples beneath the substantial deposits which overlay the floor of the Cathedral Church, but lay elsewhere on the site.

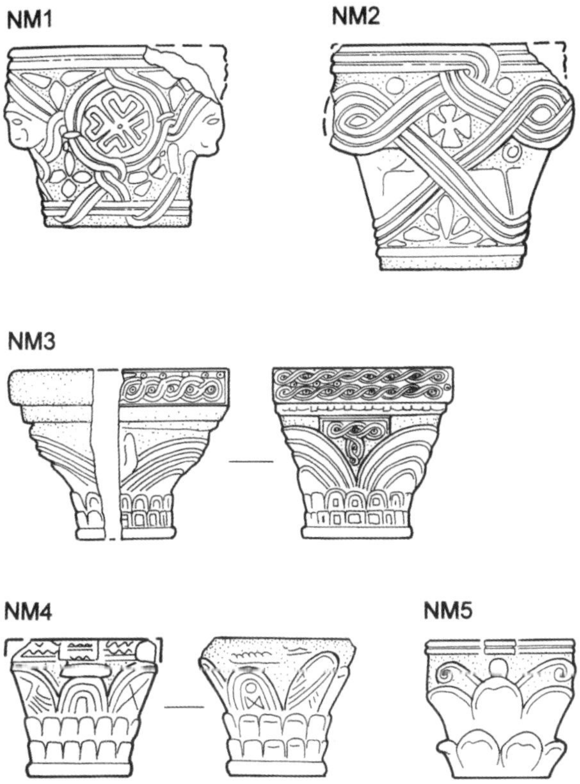

Figure 47: Stone capitals in the Nubia Museum, Aswan

NM3 A complete capital in grey sandstone, approximately 49 cms by 60 cms at the top, 28 cms across at the base, and 36 cms high, bearing the *Accession Number 10371* (Figure 47 NM3 and Plates 213 and 214). It has vertical slots, 6 cms wide and up to 12 cms deep in either side.

This capital (NM3) has not been identified on any of the photographs taken during the investigations of the Cathedral at Qasr Ibrim. If it does derive from the Cathedral Church it may have been removed from the site before 1963. The only obvious location for it would be on the column in the baptistry, the base of which also had slots on either side which are thought to have been to support a screen.

NM4 A complete capital in grey sandstone, approximately 39 cms square at the top, 28 cms across the base and 36 cms high, bearing the *Accession Number 10371* (Figure 47 NM4 and Plates 215 and 216).

Plates 215 and 216: Sandstone capital NM4 (Photographs by Fred Aldsworth).

Plates 213 and 214: Sandstone capital NM3 (Photographs by Fred Aldsworth).

NM5 A complete capital in grey sandstone, approximately 40 cms square at the top, 34 cms across the base and 37 cms high, and bearing the *Accession Number 10366 or 10368* (Figure 47 NM5 and Plates 217 and 218).

There is no certain evidence to indicate that any of these three sandstone capitals (NM3, NM4 and NM5) derive either from Qasr Ibrim or the Cathedral Church in particular. The first of them (NM3) may be Christian in origin and could possibly come from the baptistry in the Cathedral. The other two (NM4 and NM5) are unlike any of the Christian capitals or capital fragments from the Cathedral Church, although NM5 is similar to the three pieces associated with the Church on the Point (Nos 1-3 above).

Plates 217 and 218: Sandstone capital NM5 (Photographs by Fred Aldsworth).

Chapter 6: THE BISHOP MIEL OR MIELKUDA INSCRIPTIONS

In the discussion of his third period of construction of the Cathedral Church, Przemyslaw Gartkiewicz refers to the occurrence of a series of commemorative inscriptions incised on the flagstones of the floor near the southern and western rows of piers and on the corresponding walls of the *naos*. He mentions ten inscriptions containing the name of Bishop Miel (or Mielk) – thought to be an abbreviated form of Mielkud*a*, and illustrated three of them (*Gartkiewicz 1982a*: Figures 7A, 7B and 8). He suggested that the name may commemorate the initiator of the restoration of the Cathedral after it had been damaged during an attack.

Since Gartkiewicz wrote his paper, investigations at the Church on the Point at Qasr Ibrim, in 1992, revealed a further Miel(kuda) inscription on wall plaster (*Kjølbye-Biddle 1994*: 31-32 and here Plate 219).

Plate 219: The Miel or Mielkuda inscription on the Church on the Point (Photograph by Fred Aldsworth).

In Kjølbye-Biddle's interim report she refers to eighteen inscriptions on the stones in the Cathedral with the name Miel or Mielkuda.

As regards the date of the Miel(kuda) inscriptions, Kjølbye-Biddle notes :

> "Since this name is not known in the twelfth century at Qasr Ibrim (*Plumley 1978*), the destruction is unlikely to be that of 1172-3 (the invasion of Shams ed-Dawla). Gartkiewicz (*1982a*, 91 n.10) suggests (and notes that Plumley has agreed with this suggestion) that the destruction and reconstruction could as well be tenth century in date and associated with destruction known to have happened in 956 when the Arabs captured Qasr Ibrim. This would agree with the pottery dating the destruction layers in the Church on the Point and its domestic buildings, the reconstructions of both churches being tied together by the name of Bishop Miel or Mielkuda inscribed in plaster high on the west jamb of the door opened in Period VI (that is after the initial rehabilitation of the Church on the Point) from Room 3 into Room 8.
>
> 'The inscription on the Church on the Point reads -
>
> +]ABMI EΛ^{K}EΠI C^{K}
>
> It has been translated as 'Father Mielk Episkopos' i.e. Father Mielk Bishop.
>
> 'In the Cathedral, of the eighteen inscriptions mentioning him in this way, three are reproduced by Gartkiewicz (*1982a*: Figs 7A, 7B and 8). One is on the stone floor, and one on a stone of the northern jamb of the door leading up from the staircase to the inner narthex (see below No 3). This latter reads –
>
> MI EΛ^{K}EΠI C^{K}
>
> 'It is almost identical to the inscription on the west jamb of the door between Rooms 3 and 8 of the Church on the Point. These inscriptions are crucial for dating the reconstruction of both the Cathedral and the Church on the Point."

In January 1995, a concerted effort was made by Shelley White and Fred Aldsworth to locate and record as many of the Miel or Mielkuda inscriptions as possible in the Cathedral, and eight were found (see below Nos 1-8). In the following list they are illustrated and their locations are described in the context of their relationship with the phases of construction of the building.

A drawing by Gartkiewicz includes a large number of carved stones and inscriptions from the Cathedral. Amongst them are ten showing Miel or Mielkuda inscriptions, presumably the ten referred to in his 1982 article. Five of them duplicate inscriptions recorded in 1995 (Nos 1-4 and 8) but five (Nos 9-13) are new additions, giving the number of Miel or Mielkuda inscriptions certainly recorded in the Cathedral to thirteen.

The captions to Gartkiewicz's drawings give reference numbers and some locational information, and these are included in the listings below.

The captions are each in three parts (eg 11/VII/S WALL), the first evidently being a unique number ascribed to each inscription, whilst the other two parts appear to be locational information. Similar information is provided for his photographs. The initial numerals for the ten inscriptions are 1-6, 11, 12, 15 and 17 and this may imply that he recorded at least seventeen inscriptions, although nothing is known of the remainder.

No 1 This is located on the north face of the south wall of the Cathedral, to the west of the *mihrab,* on a large block of stone which forms part of the second course of masonry above present floor level (Figures 48, 49 and 50 No 1 and Plates 220 and 221). The inscription, which is illustrated by Gartkiewicz (*1982a* Figure 8), seems to be defaced at the end. The caption on his site drawing reads '11/VII/ S WALL'. To the right, but on the same block of stone, are two Christian symbols in the form of a bird and a cross, which may form part of the same inscription.

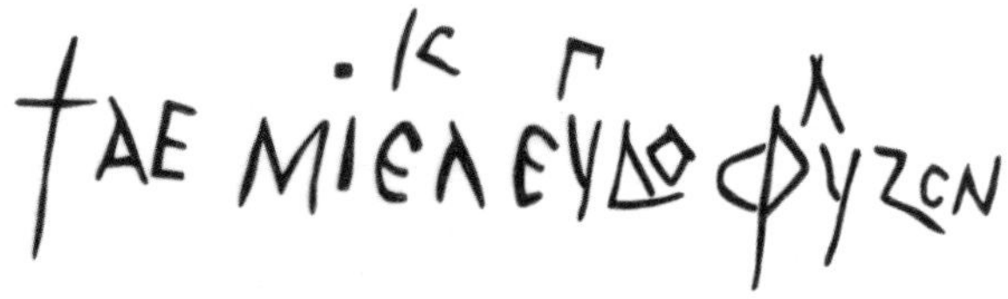

Figure 48: Inscription No 1.

Figure 49: The Christian symbols perhaps associated with inscription No 1.

The block of stone on which the No 1 inscription was carved formed part of the first phase of construction of the Cathedral (Phase 1). In this position it might appear to represent a commemorative inscription on the original structure, but it was probably added at a later date when the building was restored.

Plate 220: The Miel or Mielkuda inscription No 1 (EES Photo GP 83).

Plate 221: The Christian symbols associated with Miel or Mielkuda inscription No 1 (EES Photo GP 152).

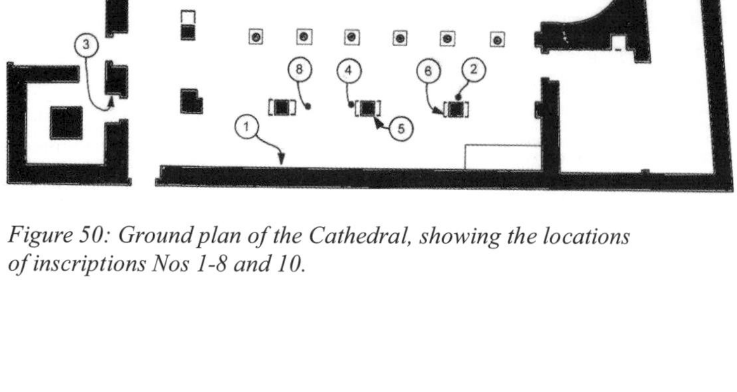

Figure 50: Ground plan of the Cathedral, showing the locations of inscriptions Nos 1-8 and 10.

No 2 This is located on a small paving slab which butts up against the north side of the most easterly pier forming the south arcade (Figures 50 No 2, Figure 51 and Plate 222). It is illustrated by Gartkiewicz (*1982a* Figure 7A) but he shows it as less complete than it is. The caption on his site drawing reads ' 1/I/S'.

Figure 51: Inscription No 2.

Plate 222: Inscription No 2 (EES Photo GP 47).

The stone on which the No 2 inscription is cut is a small floor slab laid either after the pier was first constructed in its square form (Phase 2) or after it was extended to its rectangular form (Phase 3).

No 3 This is on the north jamb of the door which leads from the west tower into the west ambulatory (Figures 50 No 3, Figure 52 and Plate 223). It is illustrated by Gartkiewicz (*1982a* Figure 7B) but, again, he appears to show it less complete than it is since there appears to be a group of letters further to the right (east). The caption on his site drawing reads '15/VII/STAIR SE'.

Plate 223: Inscription No 3 (Photograph by Fred Aldsworth).

Figure 52: Inscription No 3.

The positioning of the No 3 inscription seems to be a particularly important as it appears to commemorate the repair or reconstruction of the west end of the Cathedral Church, which is currently assigned to the second phase of construction (Phase 2), although the inscription could have been added at a later date.

No 4 This inscription is on a broken paving slab immediately west of the second pier from the east end of the south arcade (Figures 50 No 4, Figure 53 and Plate 224). The caption for the photograph taken by Gartkeiwicz reads 'on a paving slab westwards to the western face of the 2nd from the east pier of the southern range' whilst the caption on his drawing reads '2/II/S'.

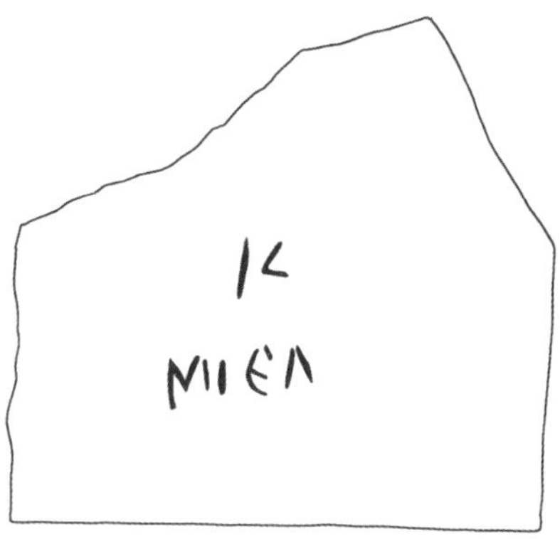

Figure 53: Inscription No 4.

Plate 224: Inscription No 4 (EES Photo GP 46).

Inscription No 4 is incomplete and its occurrence on a paving slab, which was probably laid either after the pier was first constructed in its square form (Phase 2) or later after it was extended to its rectangular form (Phase 3), suggests that it may have been re-used.

No 5 This is located on a stone which forms part of the south face of the second pier from the east end of the south arcade, and was not recorded by Gartkiewicz (Figure 50 No 5, and here Figure 54).

Figure 54: Inscription No 5.

The stone on which inscription No 4 is cut forms the second course above floor level at the south-east corner of the pier as reconstructed in its rectangular form (Phase 3).

No 6 This is located on a stone which forms part of the face of the first pier from the east end of the south arcade, and was not recorded by Gartkiewicz (Figure 50 No 6 and Figure 55).

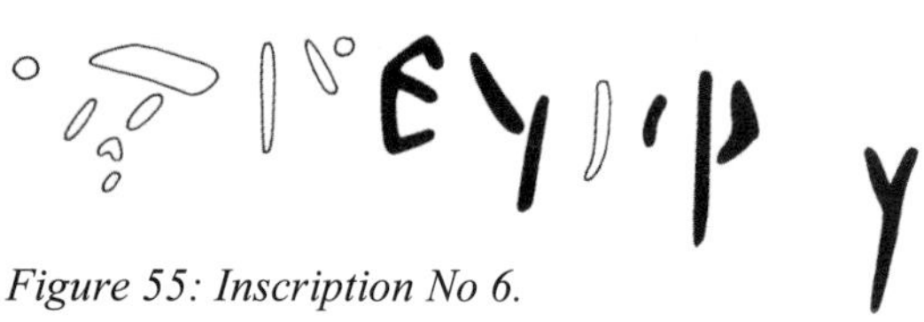

Figure 55: Inscription No 6.

The stone on which inscription No 6 is cut forms the first course of stonework at the south-west corner of the pier as reconstructed in its rectangular form (Phase 3).

No 7 This is located on a stone which forms part of the north jamb of the northernmost door in the west side of the west ambulatory, but was not recorded by Gartkiewicz (Figure 50 No 7 and Figure 56). It occurs at the top edge of the second block of stone up from the floor level, which is rebated for a door.

Figure 56: Inscription No 7.

As with inscription No 3, No 7 appears to be an important inscription as it seems to commemorate the repair or reconstruction of the west end of the Cathedral, which is currently assigned to Phase 2.

No 8 This inscription is on a paving slab to the east of the third pier from the east end of the south aisle and has presumably been re-used (Figure 50 No 8, Figure 57 and Plate 225). The caption on Gartkiewicz's site drawing reads '3/II/SW'.

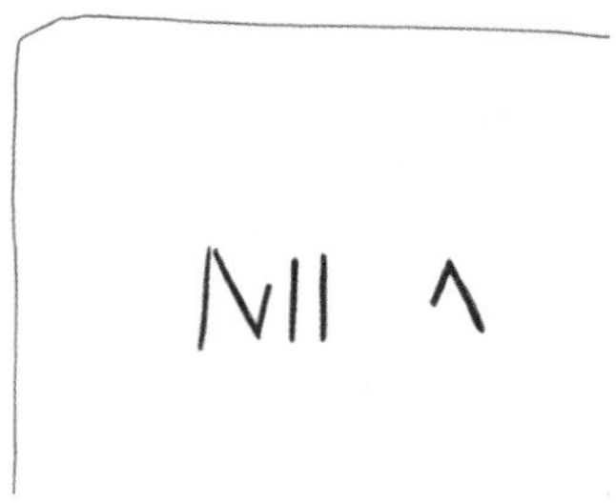

Figure 57: Inscription No 8.

Plate 225: Inscription No 8 (EES Photo GP 107).

The other five inscriptions noted by Gartkiewicz in the 1970s were not recorded in 1992, and their precise locations have not been confirmed on the ground.

No. 9 Gartkiewicz's drawing (Figure 58) suggests that the inscription was on a paving slab, but the location has not been identified. The caption on his drawing reads '12/IX/NEAR TRE S'.

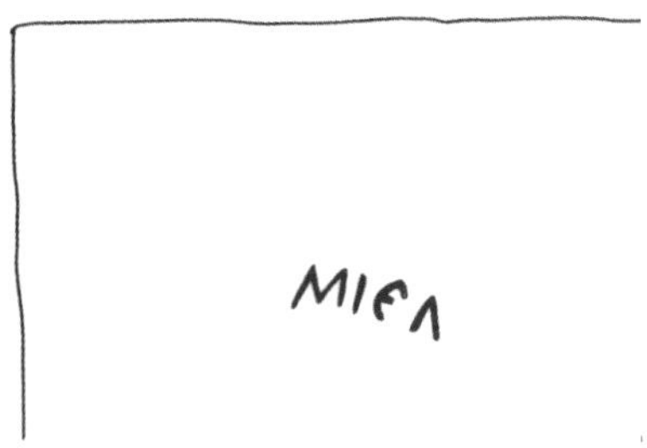

Figure 58: Inscription No 9.

No.10 Gartkiewicz's photograph shows two inscriptions on one large broken paving slab alongside a pier base (Figure 59 and Plate 226). Its caption reads '.. on the paving slab eastwards to the eastern face of the north-western corner pier ', but its precise position has not been confirmed on the ground. The caption on his drawing reads '6/VI/WN'.

No.11 Gartkiewicz's drawing and photograph indicate that this inscription was on the corner of a paving slab (Figure 60 and Plate 227). The caption for his photograph reads '.. on a paving slab westwards to the western face of the south-western corner pier ..', but its precise position has not been confirmed on the ground. The caption on his drawing reads '4/IV/SW1'.

Plate 227: Inscription No 11 (EES Photo GP 48).

Figure 59: Inscription No.10.

Plate 226: Inscription No 10 (EES Photo GP 45).

Figure 60: Inscription No 11.

Penny Wilson has informed the author that she noted the first part of this inscription during her study on the site which included the inscribed Meroitic blocks reused in the construction of the Cathedral (*Wilson 2007*: 112-115). It was located on the paving slab butting up against the eastern side of the most westerly pier in the northern arcade (Figure 50 No 10). It was subsequently destroyed by vandalism before 1995.

No 12 Gartkiewicz's drawing and photograph indicate that this was on the corner of a paving slab alongside a pier base (Figure 61 and Plate 228). The caption for the photograph reads '.. on a paving slab southwards to the southern face of the pier 2nd from the north in the western range', but its precise position has not been confirmed. The caption on his drawings reads '5/V/W'.

Figure 61: Inscription No 12.

Plate 228: Inscription No 12 (EES Photo GP 50).

No 13 Gartkiewicz's drawing and photograph indicate that the inscription was on the corner of a paving slab (Figure 62 and Plate 229). The caption for the photograph reads '..in front of the threshold of the entrance from the naos to the staircase/south-western corner room …', but its precise postion has not been confirmed on the ground. The caption on his drawing reads '17/X/W WALL'.

Figure 62: Inscription No 13.

The evidence from their positions suggests that the Bishop Miel or Mielkuda inscriptions on the Cathedral Church relate to works undertaken on the building, particularly at its west end and south side.

Of the thirteen inscriptions, eight (Nos 2, 4, and 8-13) are on paving slabs. These may have been laid in the first (Phase 2) rebuilding of the Cathedral Church, or they could have been re-laid later (Phase 3) and the inscriptions could have been added at either stage. The remaining five pieces (Nos 1, 3, 5, 6, and 7) are all cut on walls. No.1 is on a large stone which forms part of the original (Phase 1) structure and the inscription could have been added to it at a later date. Nos 3 and 7 are on walls forming part of the first (Phase 2) rebuilding, but again the inscriptions could have been added later.

The final two inscriptions (Nos 5 and 6) are both located on piers of the south arcade, which are known to have been rebuilt in the later (Phase 3) reconstruction. The two inscribed stones could have been re-used from the first (Phase 2) reconstruction, and it may be significant that the south arcade was rebuilt almost entirely from re-used (Phase 2) material. In the case of the undecorated blocks, only the face, or in some cases two faces, were carefully tooled in the original arrangement and it is usually these that were placed externally on the rebuilt piers. If the inscriptions belonged to the first (Phase 2) reconstruction this might explain why the inscriptions remained on view.

Plate 229: Inscription No 13 (EES Photo GP 49).

However, the absence of inscriptions in other parts of the Cathedral Church, for example in the apse, the baptistry, and the sacristy, might indicate that the inscriptions do not relate to the Phase 2 reconstruction of the entire building, but to specific works on the south arcade and the west ambulatory (Phase 3), although their relative absence from the north side of the *naos* could reflect the fact that very little survives of the standing masonry in that area.

On balance, it seems most likely that the Bishop Miel or Mielkuda inscriptions relate not to the major (Phase 2) reconstruction works that affected the entire building, but to lesser works undertaken at the west end and on the south side of the building at a later (Phase 3) date.

The Miel or Mielkuda inscription found at the Church on the Point is cut into the pink or purplish-grey plaster employed for repairs in the church phase of the building. Closely similar plaster was used for one of the plaster phases of repair or refurbishment of the Taharqo temple church complex on the Qasr Ibrim site. This plaster surface could be traced around a series of elements of the structure, including the narthex, suggesting that they were all repaired at the same time. The similarity in the plaster used to repair this building and the Church on the Point may suggest that the works were undertaken at the same time.

Traces of a purplish-grey lime plaster were also noted on the walls of the sacristy, the baptistry, and the north and south walls of the *naos* of the Cathedral Church (see Chapter 4).

The employment of similar plasters in at least two, and possibly three, of the buildings and the occurrence of identical, dedication inscriptions in two of them, would appear to suggest that all these three buildings at Qasr Ibrim – the Cathedral Church, the Church on the Point, and the late church phase of the Taharqa temple church complex - were repaired by Bishop Miel or Mielkuda. Kjølbye-Biddle has suggested that this may have been following an attack on the site in AD 956, when the Arabs captured Qasr Ibrim (*Kjølbye-Biddle 1994*: 31). For further discussion concerning the date for the works undertaken by Bishop Miel or Mielkuda see Chapter 8.

PART TWO: THE INTERPRETATION

Chapter 7: PRE-CATHEDRAL CHURCH OCCUPATION

The promontory of sandstone on which the remains of Qasr Ibrim stand had been occupied for at least fifteen hundred years when the Cathedral Church was first erected in the late sixth or seventh century AD. It is not surprising, therefore, to find quantities of re-used building material from earlier temples in its fabric.

Without extensive excavations beneath the Cathedral Church it is not possible to be precise about its foundations and what underlies them. However, on the south side of the building, the surface of the natural sandstone bedrock, which had been modified by quarrying during earlier building operations, can be seen immediately under the paved floor and under the external wall of the building for a distance of about 7.5 metres commencing about 2.4 metres from its west end. The south door of the Cathedral Church is positioned on the highest point of the bedrock at Qasr Ibrim, at about 183.6 metres above sea level (Figure 24 CC), and to the west of the door the bedrock is cut in the form of a vertical cliff or bluff, about three metres high, into which a series of rock-cut chambers were cut and used for burials (Figures 24 CC, 25 EE, Plate 93 and Appendix 2 Figure 85).

The quarrying activity and tombs cannot be dated but are certainly Meroitic or earlier in date, since Plumley noted in 1966 that X-Group pottery was found at the lowest level of fill, where the vertical face joined the level of the Podium floor. He further suggested that the tombs were cut into the face of the cliff during the eleventh or twelfth century AD (see Appendix 2).

In 2004 Hans Barnard identified all the exposures of bedrock on the site and prepared a contour survey, which demonstrates the likely profile of the bedrock prior to the commencement of quarrying and building (Figure 63).

Along the south wall of the Cathedral Church, to the east of the vertical cliff, the surface of the bedrock then falls away in a series of shallow steps, interrupted by what appears to be a large pit or cutting, some 3 metres wide and commencing about 3.6 metres east of the south door (Figure 24). At the east end of the south wall the bedrock is about 3.2 metres below the level of the paved floor in the main body of the building, approximately 180.3 metres above sea level. Its surface can thus be seen to have fallen away by a height of about 3.3 metres over most of the length of the south wall of the Cathedral Church.

Figure 63: Topography of the bedrock prior to the commencement of quarrying and building (after Hans Barnard). The walls of the remains of the Cathedral Church are shown black.

The top of the bedrock forms the floor of the north and south crypts at that same lower level (about 180.3 metres above sea level) over the entire width of the building, which measures 17.3 metres internally. It forms the foundations for the east wall of the building, the west wall of the crypts and the dividing wall between them, and the walls of the two antechambers. It extends westwards under the antechambers for a distance of a little over 6.0 metres to the foot of the north and south steps (Figures 26 GG & HH, 27 JJ, KK, LL & MM, 28 NN, PP, QQ & RR, 29 SS, TT, UU & VV, 31YY, and Figures 64-66). A series of graves were cut into the bedrock within the crypts (Chapter 2 Graves N1, N2 and S1 to S4).

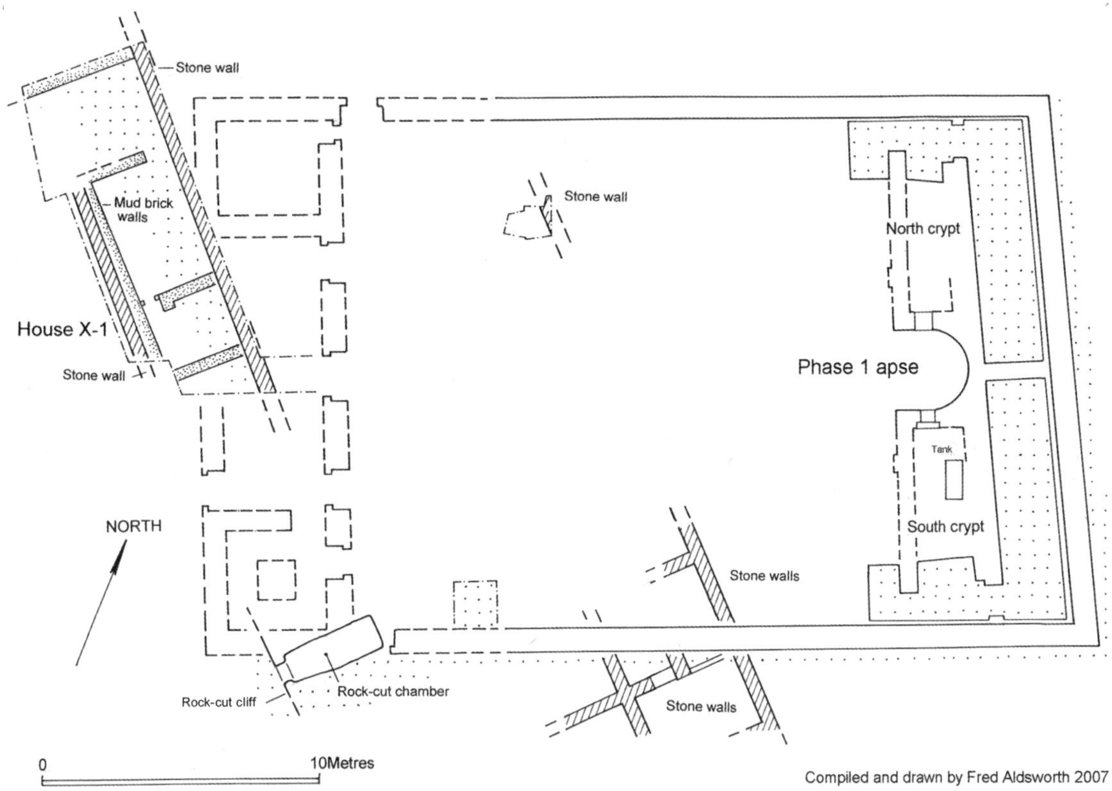

Figure 64: The extent of bedrock (shown stippled) and of features exposed beneath the Cathedral Church.

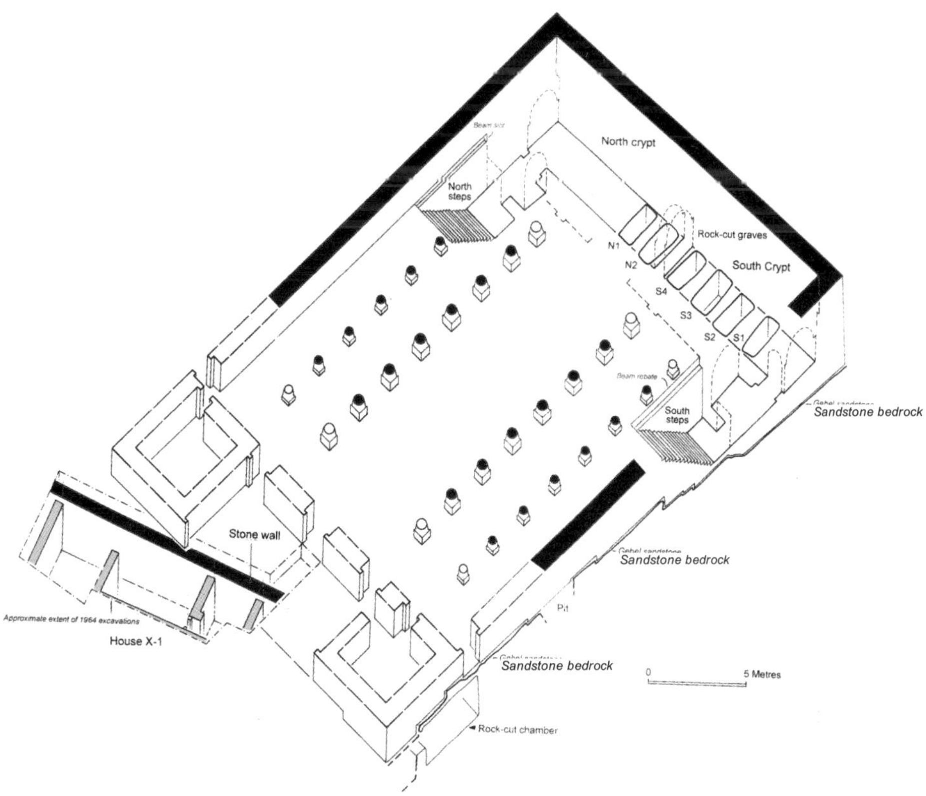

Figure 65: The relationship between the house (X-1), the stone wall, the exposures of bedrock, and the original (Phase 1) arrangement of the Cathedral Church.

The relatively flat surface of the floors in the crypts may have been an artificial creation at the time that the Cathedral Church was erected. The footings on the outside of the east and south walls of the building were cut through older, Meroitic or X-Group, buildings (see Chapter One Trench F Houses M-2 and X-2 and *Adams 1996*: 73-78).

The areas under the paved floor have not been investigated in the main body of the Cathedral Church, except in small areas, but the cliff-like natural bedrock formation under the south-west corner of the Cathedral Church, was encountered during the investigations outside the west end of the surviving building in 1964. Here a stone wall was found which was thought at the time (1964) to have formed part of a retaining wall for an earth and rubble platform upon which the western and northern parts of the Cathedral Church had been built, but is now seen as part of an extensive masonry structure or structures of Meroitic date (Chapter 4 Figures 15, 64 & 65). A mud brick building of X-Group date had been built against the wall, and into this a small structure was inserted in the Early Christian period (Chapter 4 Houses X-1 and EC1-8).

The excavations undertaken in 1964 indicate that a bedrock surface was encountered at a depth of 3.05 metres below the level of the paving at the west end of the Cathedral Church, i.e. at about 180.45 metres above sea level. This would equate approximately with the level of the bedrock visible at the bottom of the small cliff at the south-west corner of the Cathedral Church and the floor of one of the rock-cut chambers cut into it (Figure 66).

This evidence suggests that prior to the construction of the Cathedral Church, the surface of the bedrock included a small cliff or bluff, about three metres high, extending across the area which was to accommodate the west end of the building, extending northwards from the entrance to the rock-cut chamber under its south-west corner, in an irregular alignment.

The immediate predecessors of the Cathedral Church were clearly a series of Meroitic stone structures on a different alignment to the later church, successively altered and colonised during the X-Group and Early Christian periods, and the cliff was clearly part of this arrangement.

All these features conform to an alignment which differs markedly from that adopted by the Cathedral Church (Figure 64), but is very similar to that of Meroitic structures to the north (Temple 6 and Structure 1000) and to that of the Meroitic temple complex and podium to the south (*Rose 2007*: 1 and Figure 1.2).

It does appear from this evidence that no monumental structure stood on the site of the Cathedral Church immediately prior to its construction, whether the 18th dynasty temple of Tuthmosis III or anything else, which is surprising since the south-west corner of the Cathedral Church was to occupy the highest point on the rock outcrop.

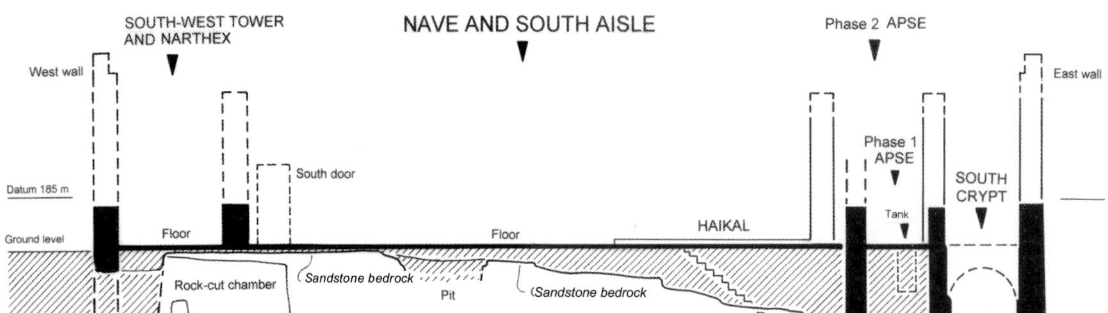

Figure 66: A generalised section through the south side of the Cathedral Church, looking north, showing the surface of the bedrock and the made ground between it and the paved floor of the building (shown hatched).

At least one large house (X-1) had been built against or close to the cliff and prior to the construction of the west end of the Cathedral Church and this was infilled in order to raise the ground level to that of the surface of the bedrock to the east. The surface of the bedrock then falls away, and the space between it and the paved floor of the Cathedral Church is made ground, except where it has been removed by the north and south steps, gradually increasing in depth until close to the east end of the building.

The made ground extends under the two apses and parts of the baptistry and sacristy, where it is a little over three metres deep.

Like the made ground to the west, that at the east end may also contain evidence of earlier occupation.

The south wall, the east wall, the east end of the north wall, and the east wall of the *naos* of the Cathedral Church are all built on the bedrock, and all stand to something close to their original height. The west end of the north wall, the north-west tower, and the west wall of the building appear to have been built on made ground, and all have either collapsed or have been demolished. The south-west tower was also founded on made ground and it is, perhaps, not surprising that it too eventually fell in 2006-2007.

Chapter 8: PERIOD 1 – THE CATHEDRAL CHURCH

Phase 1: THE 'GREAT OR OLD' CHURCH - *circa AD* 600.

The masonry of the standing structure falls into two distinct elements. The first consists of the surviving lower parts of all four external walls; the wall separating the *naos* from the western rooms; the north wall of the south-west tower; and the walls supporting the apse, the baptistry and the sacristy. These are all of massive ashlar blocks, many re-used from earlier buildings. The second consists of the upper parts of these walls and those forming the later (Phase 2) apse and the rooms adjoining it on its north and south sides. These are faced externally and, in important areas, also internally, with tightly jointed and smaller rectangular blocks, with a very distinctive tooling (see Chapter 4).

Discontinuities of plan between the upper and lower structures, especially in the two apses, and the fact that, for example, the present east nave wall abuts the lower element of the north and south walls but bonds with the upper, make it quite clear that the break in the masonry implies two distinct phases of construction (i.e. Phases 1 and 2), rather than a change in the supply of building materials or a short hiatus in the building work.

The coursing in the south wall, which changes at a point some 4 metres east of the south door, and the employment of smaller stones on the internal face (see Chapter 4) may indicate a rebuilding of the west end of the original (Phase 1) building (the significance and implications of these changes of fabric are discussed further below).

Much of the masonry of the original (Phase 1) building is clearly derived from a monumental temple structure or structures of Meroitic date (*Rose 2007*: 6, 70-72 and 112-115). The blocks retain evidence of whitewashing, painted decoration, and graffiti, including the characteristic 'Pilgrim' carvings of hands and feet (Plate 230).

Plate 230: Typical pilgrim carvings on a re-used stone block in the Cathedral Church (Wilson 2007: 113 CTH 10 Figure 18.26 – Photograph by Fred Aldsworth).

The much rougher nature of the walling below ground level, not intended to be seen, is clear from the east elevation. No precise dates are available for the construction of the earliest walls. Gartkiewicz investigated the footings of some of them, but no dating evidence appears to have been found (Chapter 3 Area 10).

Those parts of the structure built of large blocks of sandstone comprise the three surviving external walls of the building, as well as those forming the west end of the *naos*, the south-west tower, and the rear of the apse, baptistry, and sacristy. They all survive consistently throughout the building to heights of 1.1 to 1.4 metres above the paved floor level (Figures 24 AA, BB, CC; 25 DD, EE, FF; 26 GG, HH; 27 LL; 28 NN, PP, QQ, RR; 31 YY).

They support evidence for an original ground plan comprising a *naos*, with to the east an apse, baptistry, sacristy, a north crypt and antechamber, and a south crypt and antechamber, and, to the west, a south-west tower. Evidence from excavations undertaken in the 1960s and 1970s and observations of the standing structure indicate that there was also a room at the north-west corner, presumed to have been a tower, and a *narthex* to the south of it (Figures 67 and 68).

However, the changes in fabric noted some 4 metres to the east of the south door may suggest alternative scenarios.

On the external elevation, the regular courses of sandstone blocks, which survive for a distance of 21.0 metres from the south-east corner of the structure, change at the level of the internal paved floor at a distance of 4.1 metres from the east side of the south door (Figure 24 CC). The four courses above floor level are stepped towards the east end and against them is laid an irregular arrangement of small blocks. The wall then continues to the west and beyond the door opening as one course of small blocks and three courses of large blocks. The horizontal joints are not at the same levels as those further east, and the general impression is that the lower part of the south wall of the building, and perhaps, by inference, the whole of the west end of the lower part of the building may have been rebuilt.

However, the change in fabric on the external elevation is not seen as conclusive evidence for a reconstruction of the west end of the south wall and the west end of the Cathedral Church, as it might equally well represent a change in building technique, perhaps reflecting availability of materials or problems associated with bridging over the substantial pit which underlies this part of the building.

On the internal elevation, the regular courses seen to the east are again interrupted for a short distance, and then the wall is built or rebuilt with small pieces of stone, rather like those in the reconstructed (Phase 2) wall above it. This is probably best seen as a repair or replacement of the lower part of the wall in Phase 2.

The change in fabric is difficult to interpret for a number of reasons, not the least of which is the fact that on both faces of the wall, to the east of the change, the lowest two courses of masonry above the floor level terminate at precisely the same point, and in both cases the upper of the two courses is rebated to taken another stone butted up against the stone forming the third course (Figures 24CC and 26HH). It is possible that an architectural detail or feature of some form may have been present at this point, which passed through the full thickness of the wall, although its form and function is difficult to determine.[1]

Gartkiewicz excavated a small trench adjacent to the interior face of the wall at this point and revealed the surface of the natural sandstone bedrock immediately under the paving of the south ambulatory (Chapter 3 Area 12 and Plate 92). The surface appeared to be flat and this may indicate either the former existence of a threshold for a door at this point or the preparation of the surface to serve as a footing for the wall.

If the change of fabric represents a reconstruction of the lowest part of the wall, it is difficult to understand why the original coursing was not maintained and why the smaller pieces of stone were employed for a short distance in the lower courses on both elevations.

Three alternative scenarios are proposed:

1. The change of fabric observed on the external face of the wall is of little significance and represents no more than a change of building technique. The west end of the original (Phase 1) building is represented by all the courses of stonework comprising large blocks of sandstone.
2. The change of fabric <u>is</u> significant and represents a reconstruction of the west end of the Cathedral Church at an intermediate date between its original (Phase 1) construction and the major reconstruction works undertaken at a later (Phase 2) date (provisionally assigned to a Phase 1a).
3. The change of fabric <u>is</u> significant and represents a complete reconstruction of the west end of the Cathedral Church at the time that the major reconstruction works were undertaken at a later (Phase 2) date. These works were mostly undertaken using smaller, carefully tooled and tightly fitting blocks of sandstone on the external faces, as elsewhere in the structure, but usually replicate the existing courses of stonework in the remainder of the building, with large blocks of stone for the first few courses on both the external and the internal faces of the new walls.

The implications of the last two scenarios are that the walls at the west end of the original Cathedral Church were replaced, either because an alternative arrangement was desirable or because they became unstable and had to be rebuilt from the level of their footings.

The employment of large blocks of stone for the lowest courses of the walling was not confined to the original (Phase 1) construction of the building, as the same technique was employed when the east wall of the *naos* and the apse were rebuilt in Phase 2, and this could have been the case with the west end of the building.

Despite extensive investigations in the 1960s and 1970s no alternative arrangement to that represented by the courses of large stonework at the base of the existing walls forming the west end of the building has been found and the existence of eight pairs of large (Type A) columns and at least seven pairs of the small (Type C) columns indicate that the building must have been about the length of the existing one, if not longer.

In the absence of any other information, it is assumed, therefore, that the surviving arrangement of walls loosely represents that of the original building, and that it was completed at its west end either by a full *narthex* extending across the full width of the building or that it was already in its latest arrangement of three rooms (Figures 67 and 68). Other interpretations of the evidence are also possible.

[1] The reconstructions of both phases of the Church of the Stone Pavement at Dongola, interpreted by the Polish Centre of Mediterranean Archaeology, Warsaw University, as Cathedrals (ECI and ECII), have a door in approximately this position (*Godlewski 2006*).

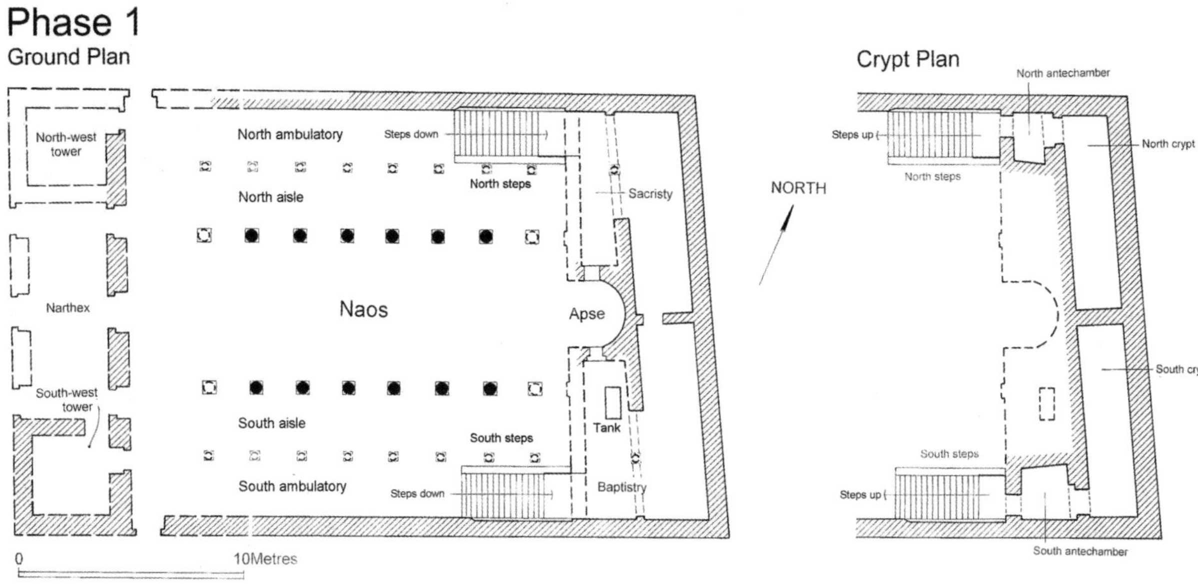

Figure 67: Simplified plan of the original (Phase 1) Cathedral Church.

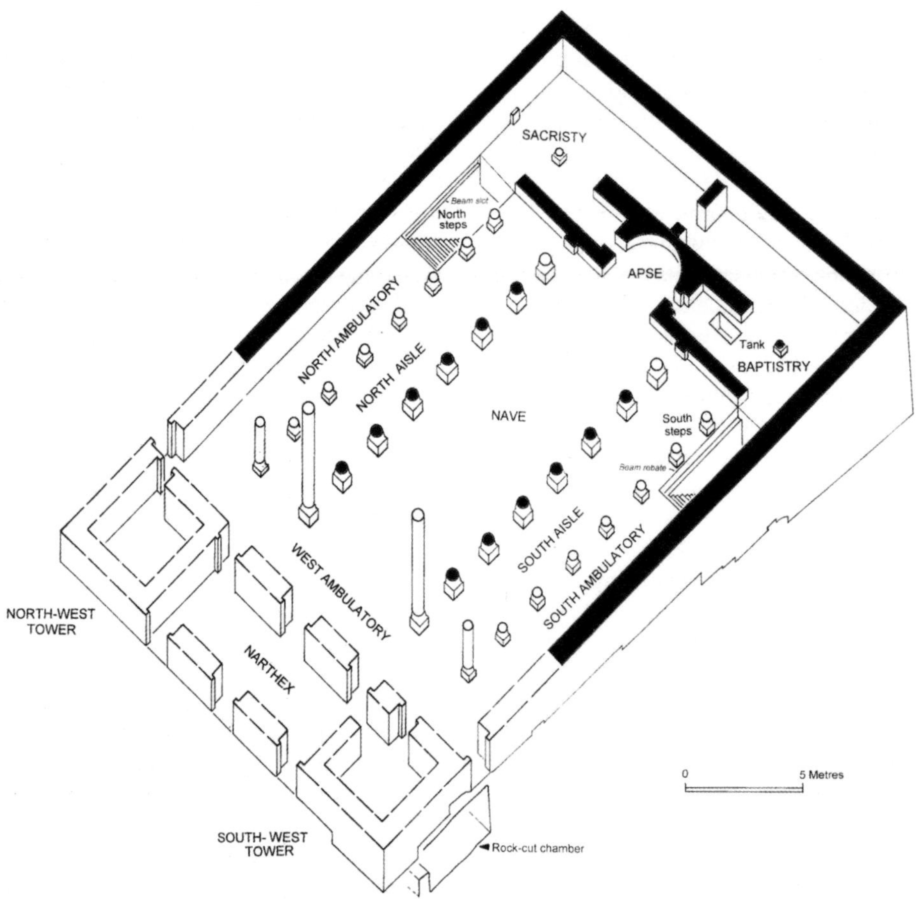

Figure 68: Part reconstruction drawing of the original Cathedral Church.

Returning to the remainder of the building, the walls forming the west sides of the two crypts, and their western returns through the antechambers to form the inner walls of the stairwells, were built up from a single thickness of massive sandstone blocks, placed within a much larger cut through earlier levels. The cut was extended westwards to encompass the line of the east wall of the *naos* but within it the position of the apse was approximately defined and the baptismal tank was formed. The cut was then packed with sandstone boulders, from which 'raft' the walls of the sanctuary area were carried up in the usual way. The raft was exposed by Gartkiewicz within the late (Phase 2) apse and baptistry, and partly in the sacristy (Chapter 3, Areas 1 and 2).

On the raft the bottom course of a narrow and somewhat irregular stilted apse survives below the later one, with the worn thresholds of narrow doorways in the north and south walls (Chapter 3, Area 1 and Chapter 4, Figures 22 and 32, Plates 118-120). That on the south has a door rebate on the south side. Some fragmentary paving slabs of reddish sandstone survive in the eastern apex of the apse. The position of the eastern wall of the *naos* is closely fixed from the surviving return of the foundation as the north side of the apse, and more precisely from the base course surviving below the later sacristy floor, exposed by Gartkiewicz (Chapter 3, Area 2).

There is a distinction between the finished level of the blocks forming the head of the wall separating the north stairwell from the antechamber and that to the south, which is cut down lower and roughly tooled, and this suggests that there were arched openings beyond the two stairwells at church floor level. Direct communication from the *naos* to the baptistry and the sacristy may have been provided by these openings when wooden floors had been inserted over the stairwells.

Further south, the edge of the stone raft gives a line for the west side of the baptistry wall, which agrees with that established with certainty on the opposite side of the apse. This also agrees with the position of an offset in the south wall, plastered and clasped by the later (Phase 2) eastern *naos* wall. The absence of wall scars on the north and south walls at the surviving level confirms the suggestion that there were openings in the *naos* wall adjacent to them.

It is evident that the wall between the chambers behind the sanctuary is bonded both to the east wall of the crypt and to the back wall of the sanctuary.

In the baptistry, the rectangular tank is formed of large re-used sandstone blocks sunk into the stone rubble raft, constructed integrally with the west wall of the south crypt and the stone raft. Its walls retaining 5-10 mm of the distinctive coarse off-white plaster used in the south crypt (Chapter 4, Plaster B), with the inner corners rounded off.

The outer south arcade line is fixed by the north wall of the stairwell, which survives to full height and is in part plastered on its upper surface, suggesting its expression, here at least, as a stylobate. The plaster continues downwards around an offset.

The north outer arcade, standing between the north aisle and the north ambulatory, was shown in a small investigation, conducted by Paul Drury in the north aisle in 1990, to have been robbed between later pier bases. Gartkiewicz records finding part of the foundation of the western return of the arcades, again underlying their successor, and of a rubble foundation approximately under the inner north arcade, very irregular but perhaps displaced slightly to the south of its predecessor (Chapter 3, Area 8).

Excavation in the north aisle in 1990 also revealed a substantial base of re-used sandstone blocks, 17-21 cm thick, standing on X-Group levels and tooled off *in situ*. The northernmost block was cut to fit around the projection of the foundation course. Its east side lined up with the face of the *haikal*. Between it and the top step of the stair, finished about 15 cms above this, was stone paving of re-used blocks, rough but serviceable, which probably formed the primary paving of the church. They were partly cut around something which stood on the underlying block. Answering the foundation in the south aisle is a roughly cut hole in the wall face, about 1.0 metres wide, its base about 0.8 metres above floor level. These features seem to be related to the closing of the outer aisles before the heads of the steps and could, perhaps, be related to the creation of vestibules.

Phase 1: Reconstruction

The original (Phase 1) building, complete with two western towers and *narthex*, would have been 32.0 metres long and 19.6 metres wide and was laid out as a parallelogram (Figures 67 and 68).

The setting out of the east end is even more irregular than the external envelope might suggest. The crypts naturally follow the alignment of the east wall, but it seems that at this stage the intention was to adjust the lengths of the antechambers to produce an east wall to the *naos* approximately at right angles to its north and south walls.

The doorways from the apse would have opened into the corners of the rooms to the north and south. However, the final decision was clearly to cause the east wall of the baptistry to veer eastwards at its south end, and was obviously taken after the construction of the retaining structure for the raft but before its construction. The reason for the decision could well have been to allow greater space around the baptismal tank. There is no sign of bonding of the eastern *naos* walls to the north and south walls at the surviving level, confirming the suggestion that the outer aisles terminated in archways over the stairwells, opening into the baptistry and sacristy. Evidence for the paved threshold of that into the sacristy was recorded in the 1970s (Chapter 3, Area 2 Plate 64). Slots in the outer walls and rebates on the opposing sides of the steps appear to have been designed to take temporary wooden floors when access to the crypts was not required, and would have given access to the rooms to the east.

Such evidence as exists suggests that the *naos* of the original (Phase 1) Cathedral Church, like its successor, took the form of a five aisle basilica, with the north ambulatory, north aisle, nave, south aisle, and south ambulatory all terminating short of the west wall, to form a west ambulatory.

There is no direct, *in situ*, evidence for the form of the outer arcades, but there is much circumstantial evidence to suggest that the shorter (Type C) granite columns, one of which was later re-used in the rock-cut chamber under the south-west corner of the Cathedral, were in fact intended for the original building.

The three types of column shaft are the only significant occurrence of red granite on the site, beyond offering tables and other small items of pre-Christian date. All are distinctive in that they were cut as square section blocks and roughly rounded to a sub-circular section, rather than turned in classical fashion. They are specifically Christian, since the large Type A shafts have crosses worked in relief high on them.

The examination of all the pieces of shaft concluded that they probably comprised the remains of sixteen shafts of the large Type A, only twelve of which could be accommodated on the surviving bases flanking the nave; two shafts of the intermediate-sized Type B; and at least fourteen shafts of the smallest Type C (Chapter 5 Figure 35).

It seems reasonable to conclude that the columns were brought to Ibrim for a major early Christian building, and that some were later released.

It is highly likely, in the absence of any other church at Ibrim of comparable scale, that they were imported for, and used in, the primary (Phase 1) Cathedral Church, and that the redundant columns were removed at the time of the later (Phase 2) reconstruction of the Cathedral Church.

How these columns were used is more problematic.

The sixteen large (Type A) shafts must be from the inner arcades flanking the nave, and the remains of twelve of them were found alongside the bases on which they stood in the later (Phase 2) reconstruction of the building. The greater length of the *naos* at its east end in the original arrangement allows for the use of fourteen columns, and it can only be assumed that the other two were originally accommodated at the west end of the *naos*, and were replaced during the later (Phase 2) reconstruction by stone piers (Figures 67 and 68). When complete with their bases and capitals they would have reached a height of about 5.10 metres.

The two intermediate-size shafts (Type B), one of which was found in the 1960s in the baptistry alongside the base of which it originally stood, seem to have been employed to support small arcades, perhaps carrying screens, dividing the sacristy and the baptistry each into two parts. When complete with their bases and capitals they would have reached a height of about 3.50 metres

The most likely use for the fourteen, or more, smaller (Type C) shafts is, therefore, in the outer arcades. The assumption is that they mirrored those in the inner arcades, and that they were replaced during the later (Phase 2) reconstruction of the building by piers. They vary in height, but when complete with their bases and capitals they would probably have reached a height of up to about 2.30 metres.

It is unlikely that they carried a flat entablature or lintel; rather an arcade seems essential (Figure 69). This would relate well to the arched openings of the east ends of the outer aisles, and would support a flat roof on timber joists at the same level as joists carried on a beam spanning over the Type B columns in the sacristy and baptistry.

In the reconstructions, the roofs are assumed to be flat, supported on timber joists, since that was clearly the case in the later building. A mud brick vault would have been feasible over the outer ambulatories, as indeed would be mud brick walls above the surviving masonry. The latter would certainly account for the relatively finished appearance of the wall tops, with a course of large stones thinner than those below.

Phase 1 Reconstruction

Alternative cross-sections looking east

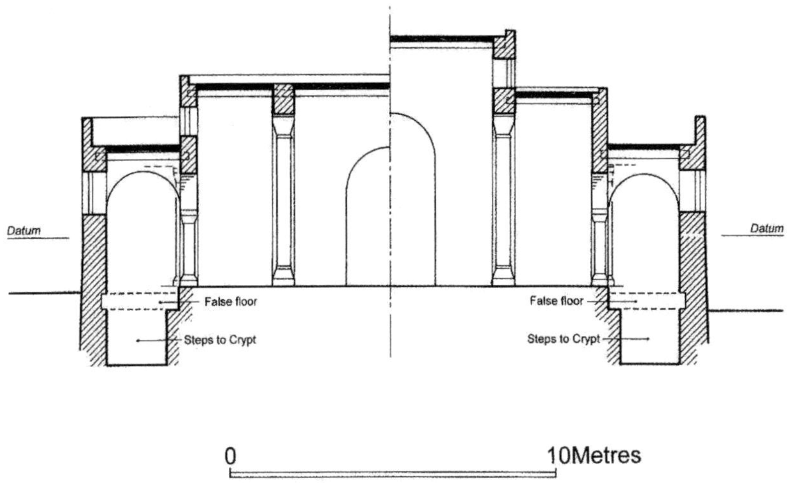

Figure 69: Alternative cross-sections of the Phase 1 naos, *looking east (prepared by Paul Drury).*

It would also account for the later (Phase 2) reconstruction above that level in masonry, since it is clear that the arrangement would have allowed much more of the earlier superstructure to be incorporated.

In the later (Phase 2) building, it is the outer arcade which returns to unite the west end of the *naos* and form a *narthex*, and there is no reason to think that the same did not apply to its predecessor. The use of a single large arch in the nave does, however, seem improbable; breaking it down into a three-bay arcade seems more likely. This can reasonably account for a minimum of fourteen Type C columns, even allowing for piers at the corners to increase stability. Alternatively 16 could equally well be fitted in, and other variations could be suggested to accommodate more.

The section of the central parts of the *naos* presents greater problems of reconstruction. The drawing (Figure 69) suggests two alternatives for the height of the apsidal opening into the sanctuary. The lower has the springing height roughly equal to the width of the opening; the higher puts its apex at the top of the inner arcade capitals, producing a rather attenuated opening. These may represent the limits of probability.

Two alternative reconstructions are put forward here for the nave and inner aisles. Both propose an entablature over the inner columns, since an arcade would raise the building to a height out of all proportion to the outer aisle arcades, and on both structural and aesthetic grounds this can reasonably be eliminated.

The first alternative (to the left) puts a small clerestory over the outer arcade and a flat roof at a common level over the inner aisles and nave; the second alternative (to the right) places the clerestory above the inner arcade and thus steps the *naos* roof up above the aisles. A cogent argument can be put forward for either version: the first unites the central space distinct from the outer aisles, which seem to have been functionally different, and would thus allow for a less attenuated sanctuary opening; the second represents a smaller scale version of the most probable reconstruction of the later (Phase 2) building.

A problem with the reconstruction plan and drawing (Figures 68 and 69) is that, if a west ambulatory had existed at this time, then the treatment of the west ambulatory/*naos* arcade should perhaps have included at least two more columns in line with the north and south walls of the apse. The real problem here is to contain the westward thrust of the outer arcade arches beyond the last column, and it would not work out as drawn unless there were wide arches springing to the west wall (Paul Drury *pers comm*).

No embellishments survive *in situ* from the original building, but it is likely to have included the three decorated granite capitals found in the building in 1964 (Chapter 5, Figure 35 Nos 1, 2 and 3), and the two granite capitals now in the Nubia Museum, Aswan (Chapter 5, Figure 47 Nos NM1 and NM2). It may have included some of the sandstone capitals or fragments of them found on the site, or in the Nubia Museum in Aswan (Chapter 5, Figure 38 Nos 13-22, Plate 207 No 4, and Figure 47 NM 3 – NM5).

In view of the extent of uncertainty, it does not seem worthwhile to develop reconstruction drawings of the original Cathedral Church further. However, one major point does emerge from the known elements of the plan: the visual prominence of the entrances to the crypts. The southern crypt has a grave or graves virtually *ab initio*, and the two elements together suggest that the Cathedral Church could have been intended to be a pilgrimage centre, as Ibrim had been in pre-Christian times (*Rose 2007*: 1-3), the southern crypt holding the body of a saint.

The lack of success of this enterprise might be reflected in their much reduced prominence in the (Phase 2) reconstruction, and their later (Phase 3) infilling; but their importance in the original scheme cannot be denied.

However, against this argument for the use and prominence of the crypts must be set the lack of any connection between them, making circulation impossible at the lower level.

Phase 1: Primary dating evidence

Dating-evidence is extremely limited. The building stands on truncated X-Group deposits, and the building levels associated with the construction of the mud brick vaults of the crypts contained only residual X-Group and Meroitic material. The artificial platform through which the east end of the Cathedral Church was built included X-Group and Early Christian pottery, tentatively dated by Adams to perhaps *circa* AD 600, and his view was that the building of the first church took place early in the Christian period, but not actually at the beginning of it (see Chapter 1). Meroitic and X-Group structures at the west end of the Cathedral seem to have been modified in the Early Christian period, prior to being filled to form a foundation for the Cathedral Church (see Chapter 2).

There are no architectural details *in situ* in the original fabric; only the granite columns and capitals can reasonably be associated with it. The primary graves in the south crypt were robbed, and whilst the third produced a later X-Group goblet almost intact, this was in the fill about the burial, and sufficiently small to have been introduced with general filling material.

Phase 1: Discussion

In the absence of any other independent dating evidence for the construction of the original building, it can only be otherwise ascribed on a comparative basis.

The first synthetic study which attempted to establish a chronological typology of Nubian church architecture was published by William Adams (*1965*), although earlier classifications had been devised by Mileham (*1910*), Somers Clarke (*1912*), and Monneret de Villard (*1935* and *1957*). Adams' work was based on his first hand knowledge of the area and the buildings contained within it, gained whilst working on behalf of UNESCO in the 1960s in the threatened parts of Egypt and Sudan. He identified four common, and fairly distinct, combinations of architectural elements that formed the basis of his four principal types (Types 1, 2, 3 and 4). To these he added two more at the beginning (Types ?0 and T) and one at the end of the sequence (Type ?5).

Adams' typology has recently been described and illustrated by Birthe Kjølbye-Biddle (*1994* : 37-41 and Figure 16 – reproduced here as Figure 70).

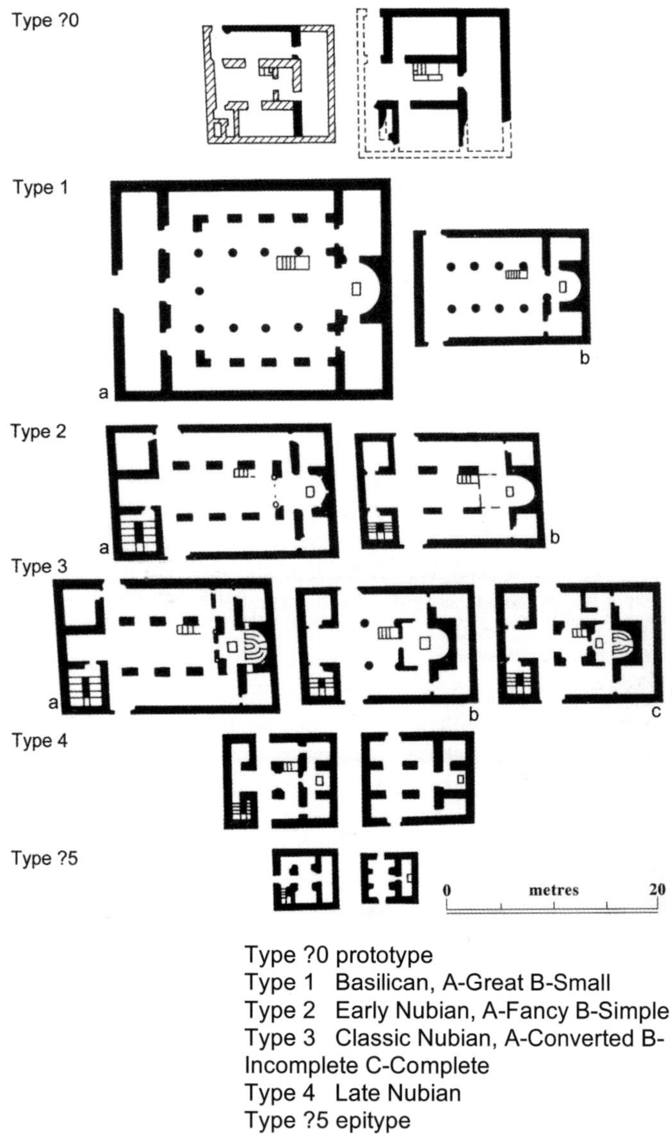

Figure 70: Adams' architectural evolution of the Nubian church (after Adams 1965 Figure 4: Gartkiewicz 1990 Figure 144: and Kjølbye-Biddle 1994 Figure 16).

Adams noted that 'In its internal plan, the Nubian church, like many other elements in Nubian culture, seems almost to have followed a circular course of development.' (*Adams 1965*:119-120). At this point some might question the validity of the typology proposed, not least because the types constantly overlap in date, distribution, and attributes.

Przemyslaw Gartkiewicz presented his own 'new outline' of the development of Nubian church architecture (*Gartkiewicz 1980*: 144 and Figure 71), though this has been challenged by Peter Grossman particularly concerning the cruciform church (*Grossman 1985*).

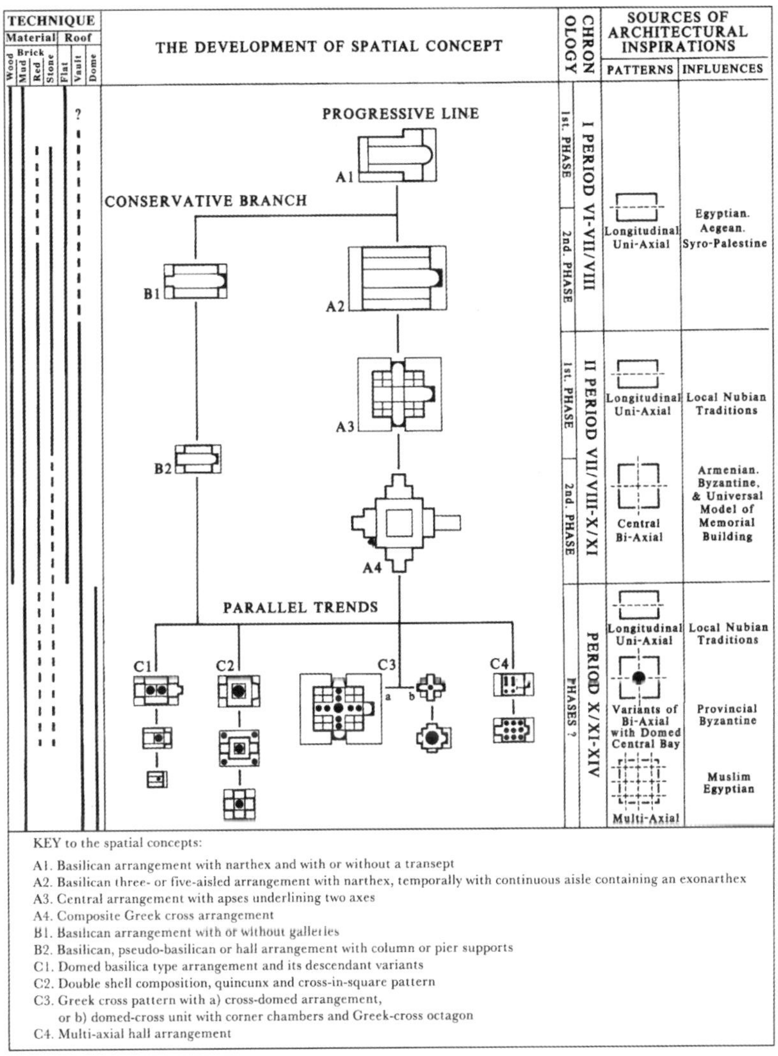

Figure 71: Gartkiewicz's outline of Nubian church architecture, with plans drawn to approximately the same scale (after Gartkiewicz 1980, Figure 23 and Kjølbye-Biddle 1994, Figure 17).

In the absence of any alternative scheme which is definitive, Adams' typology is that generally now adopted.

Despite reservations about its validity, Adams' typology is that which is also most frequently cited and, given that the Cathedral Church at Qasr Ibrim is the largest known church in Nubia and was adopted as his classic Great Basilica Type site 1a, his comments and conclusions are included here and in the discussion concerning the later (Phase 2) alterations (see below).

Adams recognised that the *external plan* of the Nubian church was almost invariably in the form of a single rectangle, having its largest axis aligned east-west. The overall size of the building and the proportion of the length to the width diminished during the Christian period, with the earliest churches being consistently large, long, and narrow, having an average length to width ration of about 1.67 to 1. The largest example is that at Qasr Ibrim measuring 32.0 metres by 19.5 metres in its later (Phase 2) form and, with a length to width ration of 1.64 to 1, it covered an area of 620 square metres.

A peculiarity of some of the earliest churches is the skewed plan, with corners deviating as much as 10% from a right angle. This is seen in the east wall of the Cathedral Church at Qasr Ibrim which is about 5° off a right angle. Adams suggests that such deviations are not found after the eighth century AD (*1965*: 91).

The first Nubian churches, whose plan included a *narthex,* were entered from the west, either by a single door in the centre of the west wall or by doors at the extreme western ends of the north and south walls, or both. The *narthex* is thought rapidly to have gone out of fashion, and the mode of entry was altered. According to Adams all Nubian churches from the seventh century onwards were entered by doors in the north and south wall, located slightly to the west of the centre of the building, and corresponding with the western end of the aisles.

The internal plan, with the exception of some of the very earliest and very latest examples, embody a common design comprising some nine compartments, with the division between rooms being either structural or symbolic (Figures 72 and 73).

It had three basic functional or liturgical divisions. The east end of the building, which may be collectively known as the *bema,* was reserved for the clergy, and consisted of the *haikal* or sanctuary in which divine service was reformed, and the corner rooms, or sacristies (sometimes a sacristy and a baptistry), on either side in which elements of the service were prepared.

The remainder of the church or *naos,* comprising a nave and aisles, was occupied by the congregation and was divided between male and female worshippers. In the earliest churches there may also have been a *narthex,* probably reserved for penitents and those under discipline.

The sanctuary chamber comprised all or part of the *haikal* (Figure 72 No 1). The internal form of this room, except in the very early and very late churches, was in the form of an apse, enclosed within a rectangular masonry shell, as at the Cathedral Church of Qasr Ibrim. In its original (Phase 1) form, there were doors into the apse at Qasr Ibrim from the rooms to the north and south. It was not screened from the congregation, but was identified symbolically by an arch resting on stone columns or piers. The altar originally stood near the back of the sanctuary, with direct access from one or both of the adjoining sacristies, as originally at Qasr Ibrim.

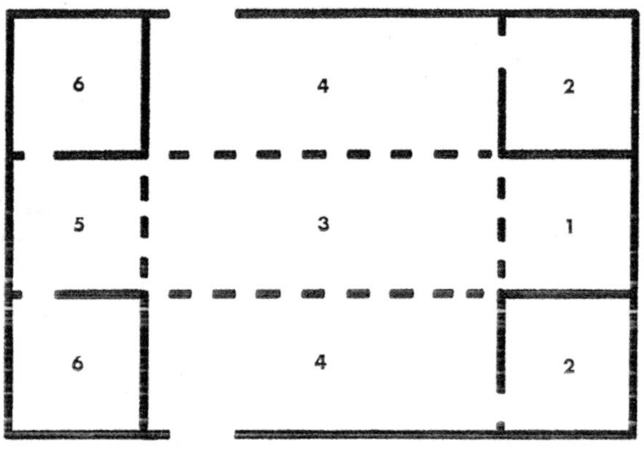

1. Sanctuary
2. Eastern Corner Rooms
3. The Nave
4. The Aisles
5. The Western Bay or *Narthex*
6. The Western Corner Rooms

Figure 72: The common elements in the internal plan of Nubian churches, showing structural (solid) and symbolic (dashed) divisions (after Adams 1965: Figure 2).

A wooden *haikal* screen or *higab* was subsequently adopted some time in the seventh century, and in later years, particularly after the tribune was introduced, it became necessary to move the altar to a position further to the west and enlarge the *haikal* so that it included part of the nave, as well as the sanctuary chamber, as in the later (Phase 2) rebuild at Qasr Ibrim. The added area, the *presbyterium,* was always completely screened from the nave, and was frequently raised above it by a step or two. The first *haikal* screens were made of wood, but after the eighth century mud brick became the rule in Nubia (*Adams 1965*: 99).

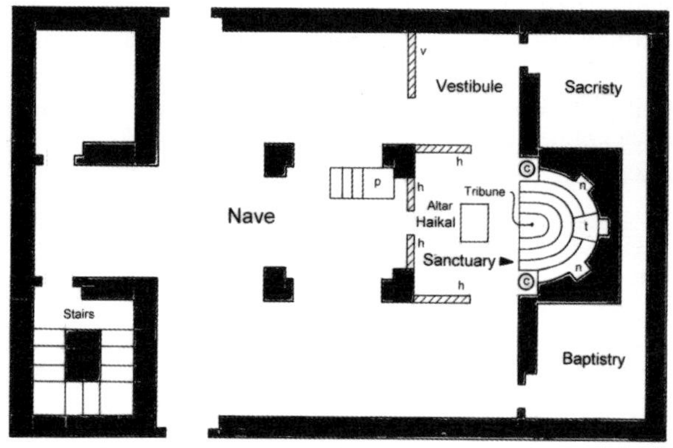

c – column
h – haikal screen
n – niche
p-pulpit
t – throne
v – vestibule screen

Figure 73: The functional uses of spaces in Nubian churches (after Adams 1965: Figure 3).

The building of a tribune, surmounted by a throne or bishop's seat occupied by the highest clergy during services, made it impossible to gain direct access to the sacristies and a portion of the north aisle was often screened off as a vestibule in order to provide passage from the *haikal* to the north sacristy. According to Adams (*1965*: 98-99), the tribune is not found in any of the earliest Nubian churches, and was apparently introduced in the eighth or ninth centuries and evidently became a standard feature.

Thus the total area of the *bema,* originally fairly small, was gradually enlarged at the expense of the *naos* until it included a portion of the nave, or *presbyterium,* and parts of one or both the aisles as a vestibule or two vestibules.

The two eastern corner rooms, or sacristies (Figure 72 No 2), were intimately connected with the divine service, and were reserved for the clergy. The north sacristy may have been used for the preparation of the sacred element which preceded the liturgy, and often contained benches along the walls. These are perhaps represented at Qasr Ibrim by the slots and scars on the east wall (Figure 28 NN). The south sacristy was usually devoid of furniture, although it occasionally contained a baptismal tank or font, as at Qasr Ibrim. In the 'Classic Christian' period (*circa* AD 800-1200) the two rooms were sometimes linked by a narrow passage behind the sanctuary chamber, as at Qasr Ibrim.

The central nave was separated from all the adjoining spaces only by archways (Figure 73 No 3) and was occupied by the congregation during services. During the Classic Christian period the east end of the nave always included the *haikal,* and was segregated from the remainder of the nave by a screen or *higab* (*Adams 1965*: 95).

The *aisles* flanking the nave to the north and south were also occupied by the congregation (Figure 72 No 4). The archways separating them from the nave supported the roof and did not signify a functional division, although in later churches one aisle may have been reserved for women.

The western bay or *narthex* was a western extension of the nave and, although separated from it by an archway, it appears to have had no special liturgical significance (Figure 72 No 5).

One of the western corner rooms usually contained stairs leading to overhead galleries, found above the aisles in some large early churches, or to the roof, but the function of the other is obscure (Figure 72 No 6). In the early churches the rooms were often entered from the aisles, but in the Classic Christian church they were always entered from the western bay (*Adams 1965*: 94).

The *narthex,* a single, rather narrow, antechamber running across the western end of the church is found, according to Adams (*1965*: 94), only in the very earliest Nubian churches.

The pulpit or *ambo,* with the altar, was the most consistent secondary feature of the Nubian church. It was always located along the north side of the nave and immediately to the west of the *haikal,* often alongside the easternmost pier or column separating the nave from the north aisle (*Adams 1965*: 99). The earliest pulpits were made of wood, but these were frequently replaced by mud brick structures in later churches, as at Qasr Ibrim (see below).

Adams identified four basic types of Nubian churches (Types 1-4), which fell quite readily into chronological order.

In addition he identified two hypothetical types (Types ?0 and ?5) and a group of churches built into former Pharaonic temples (Type T).

The chronological ordering of the types was based on direct dating from inscriptions or documents, indirect dating by association or dated pottery types or other remains, relative dating from stratigraphy, and what Adams referred to as 'guess dating advanced by the original excavator, usually without explanation' (*1965*: 101).

The Cathedral Church at Qasr Ibrim was classified as the type example in his Type 1a or Great Basilican church (Figures 70 and 74). This type has an estimated date range of 550-750 AD (*Adams 1965:* Figure 4; *Gartkiewicz 1990*: 248; and *Kjølbye-Biddle 1994*: 38-39). The type consists of the largest churches in Nubia. Diagnostic features are two aisles on either side of the nave, a *narthex* at the west end, a rectangular or apsidal *haikal,* and an external length between 20 and 30 metres. They are found between the First and Second Cataracts.

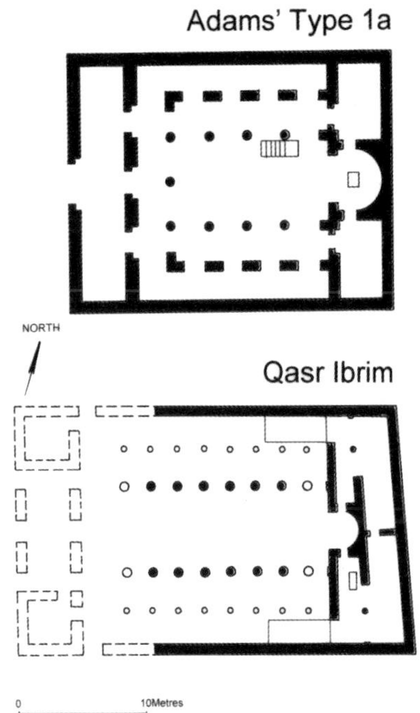

Figure 74: Adams' Type 1a, based on the Cathedral Church at Qasr Ibrim (top), and the actual plan of the building in its original (Phase 1) form (bottom).

All the members of the Type 1a group were, or became, Cathedrals but the Qasr Ibrim example differs from the others in having a passage behind the apse in its Phase 1 form. This feature was absent from the earliest cathedrals at Faras and Old Dongola, and elsewhere in Nubia it did not make its appearance until the middle of the eighth century or later. The passage behind the apse is seen in a number of Nubian churches, not all of which belong to this type (see *Gartkiewicz 1990:* Figure 127 reproduced here as Figure 75).

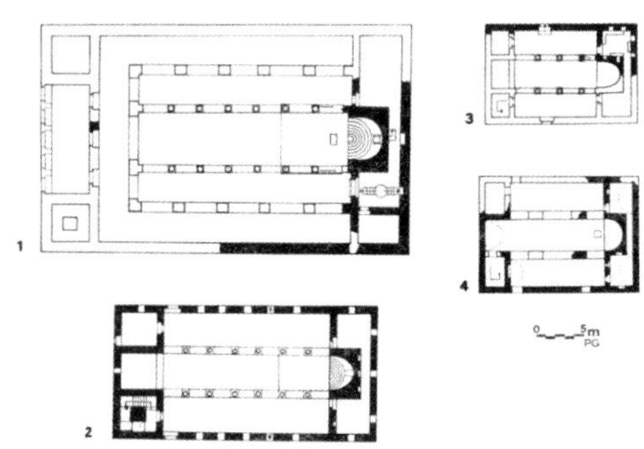

1. Church of the Stone Pavement at Dongola.
2. Monastery church at el-Ghazali.
3. Church of the Southern Slope of the Kom in Faras.
4. Monastery church at Kageras.

Figure 75: Other Nubian churches with a passage behind the apse (after Gartkiewicz 1990: Figure 127).

On the present evidence, the first phase of the construction of the Cathedral Church at Qasr Ibrim can only be ascribed to an approximate date of *circa* AD 600. However, the official arrival of Christianity in this part of Nubia in AD 543, the apparently early conversion of the Taharko temple to a church, and the absence of early Christian occupation associated with buildings under and cut by the footings of the Cathedral Church raises the possibility of an earlier date in the second half of the sixth century AD.

Given that that the site does not appear to have been elevated to the status of a Bishopric until the seventh century, it seems likely that original building was constructed as a church, sometimes referred to in the past as the 'Old Church' or, because of its considerable size, the 'Great Church' of Qasr Ibrim.

Phase 1: Context

William Adams has already placed the Cathedral Church within the context of the town plan of Qasr Ibrim in his 'Late Christian 1', 'Late Christian 2', and 'Terminal Christian' periods of occupation on the site (*Adams 1996*: 31-34 Figures 3, 4, and 5), and there is a proposal to place it in the context of his 'Early Medieval' period (*Adams 2010*).

The overall plan suggests that the church stood in a space already defined by buildings and, where there were changes in level, lanes, with most space located to the liturgical south where an open space or 'plaza' was established. A critical, but as yet unanswered, question is whether this wider space existed in the settlement plan before the Cathedral Church was erected, in which case the Meroitic stone buildings may have been the remains of a high status residence, or whether it arose from acquisition and clearance of the kinds of 'ordinary' buildings evident elsewhere on the site.

Whatever the origins of the precinct, the Cathedral Church was in many ways a tight fit. Its axis was seemingly shifted round as far as the site would reasonably allow and certainly different enough to make a statement. The extreme skew alignment of its east wall looks very much as though it was constrained by an existing building or boundary. This raises not just physical but political questions as the site was presumably granted to the church by some sort of secular authority, in the midst of an existing settlement in which the neighbours had property rights, rather than land being there for the taking. This, of course, has implications for the nature of what occupied the precinct before the Cathedral Church and, indeed, the status of the small church on its south side.

The other awkwardness is at the west end, where the *narthex* and towers overhang a rock-cut cliff, but were founded on fill against the cliff and earlier walls when it was built. This may suggest that the Cathedral Church expanded westwards from an earlier core – the 'nest of churches' model – yet there is no definite evidence for this in the remaining structure.

However, Paul Drury has suggested (*pers comm*) that the walls revealed by Gartkiewicz in Areas 8 and 11 may indicate the existence of an earlier (hypothetical Phase 0) church occupying, approximately, the area within the ambulatory of the later Cathedral Church, although its eastern end is unclear. This suggestion is based on the walls in Area 8 being earlier than the Phase 1 Cathedral Church and those in Area 11, abutting the Meroitic stone wall, suggesting that the levelling of the latter was part of the same operation of building the first church.

This first church need not have been elaborate nor need it have lasted long, but rather established a presence. A church of this plan would have fitted in with the obvious constraints of the site, whilst that of Phases 1 and 2 would have pushed it to its limits. It might explain the break in the Phase 1 masonry east of the south doorway, as a construction joint, demarcating successive rebuilding, first east and then west of the west wall of the earliest (Phase 0) church. The construction is too similar to either side, and different from Phase 0, for this to suggest any physical remnant of the original church. The small size of the apse in the Phase 1 Cathedral Church could be another memory of the earliest structure.

Phase 2: THE CATHEDRAL CHURCH – *circa* AD 700

At a subsequent date the original building was extensively reconstructed, essentially as a refinement, rationalisation, and scaling up of the original scheme. The east end was remodelled; the outer and western arcades were replaced on a larger scale; and the outer walls, the wall forming the west end of the *naos*, and the two western towers were mostly rebuilt with smaller blocks of carefully tooled stones with narrow joints (Figures 76 and 77). The west end may have been remodelled or replaced at this time (see above).

The crypts and antechambers remained unchanged from Phase 1, and there is no evidence even for any redecoration after the original work. It is, however, possible that some of the burials which were not primary to the building took place at this time.

However, the widths of the staircases accessing the crypts were significantly reduced, by means of the insertion of blocking walls. These contained a number of deep recesses, plastered out and some clearly fitted with wooden shelves (Chapter 4, Figures 23, 27 KK and MM, and Plates 116 and 117).

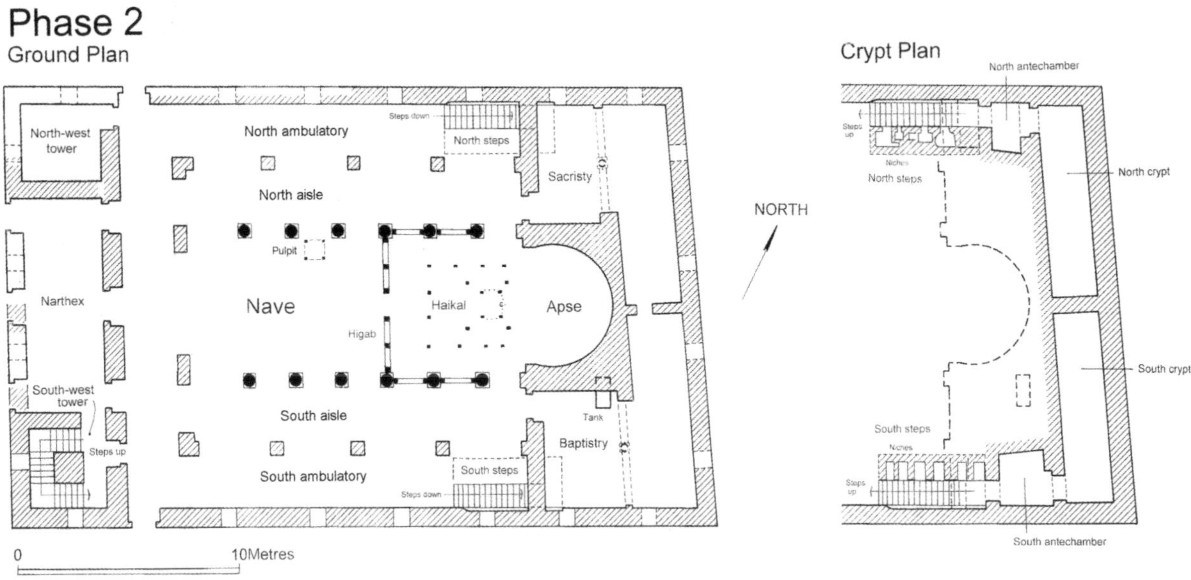

Figure 76: Simplified plan of the reconstructed (Phase 2) Cathedral.

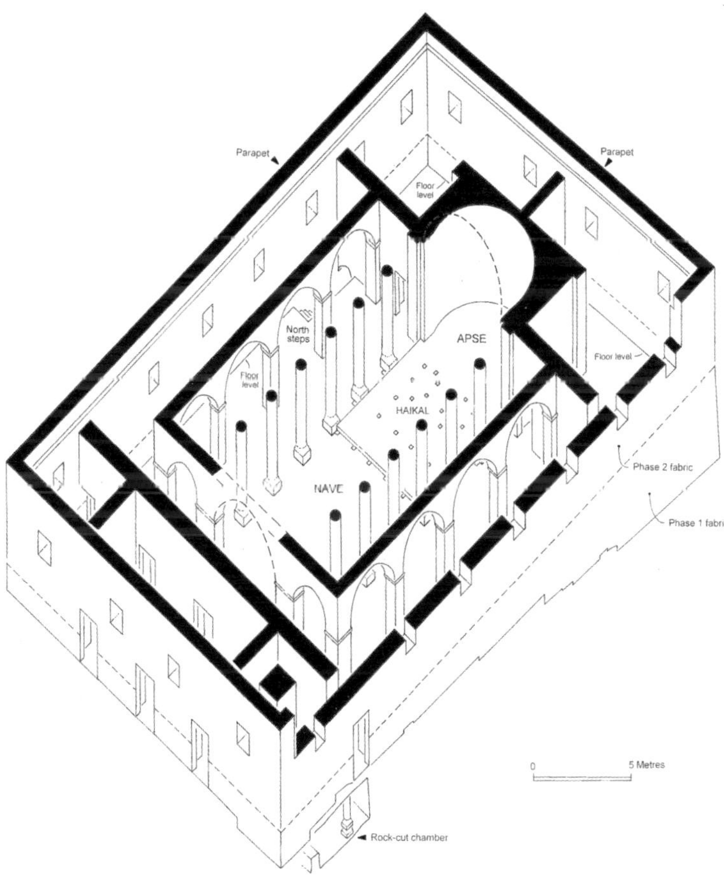

Figure 77: Part reconstruction drawing of the rebuilt (Phase 2) Cathedral, cut-away in the foreground and with the columns in the baptistry and sacristy omitted for clarity.

Most of the original walls of the building, presumably either of similar large stones to the surviving lower courses or, more likely, of mud brick, were demolished down to a consistent level of about 1.1 to 1.4 metres above the paved floor at this time and rebuilt either with small dressed ashlars, or squared or random rubble, all evidently newly quarried.

The ashlars were used consistently externally, and also in significant parts of the interior, suggesting that they were intended to be left exposed rather than plastered over. These areas are the east and west walls of the *naos* including the apse; the outer *naos* arcades; the *narthex*; and the solid newel of the stair in the south-west tower. By contrast, the eastern rooms and the north and south walls of the *naos* were clearly intended to be plastered, and some of this remains. It is a fine purplish grey lime plaster on a mud dubbing-out layer. On the south *naos* wall slight traces of painted decoration are said to have been visible in the 1970s.

The external batter of the enclosing external walls was continued upwards to the base of the windows. Here, pairs of wooden bracing frames or ring beams were incorporated, set on the inner and outer faces, with lap-dovetailed ties at frequent internals.

The remains of six window openings survive in the south wall, although there may have originally have been seven. None of these retain traces of stone grilles although a fragment of one was found on the site (Chapter 5, Figure 46 No 78). These openings were probably mirrored by seven in the north wall and there may have been four in each of the east and west walls, of which only part of one survives in the west side of the south-west tower.

Above the windows in the south wall, the outer face of the wall is vertical. At a height of 5.5 metres above the paved floor it reduces in thickness to form a parapet 60 cms high, above the beam slots for the roof timbers. It can reasonably be assumed that this continued around all four sides of the building. There are no remains of any provision for its drainage.

The eastern *naos* wall was moved westwards in the rebuilding and set at right angles to the north and south walls. The new arrangement provided for a larger apse of more than a half circle in plan, and its construction necessitated encroaching southwards onto the baptismal tank, with the new wall being carried on an arch over its northern end.

The arrangement of columns and pilaster buttresses supporting the roofs of the baptistry and the sacristy appears to have been maintained, the base of that in the baptistry being found *in situ* in 1964 (Chapter 2, Plates 126 and 127 and Chapter 5, Figure 35 No 10 and Plate 174). However, the structure carried by the columns probably changed.

Two pairs of granite bases, and the shafts and capitals which they supported, were removed from the inner arcades. Their structural roles were transferred to pilaster buttresses on the new east wall of the *naos* and a new set of piers at the west end of the nave. The remaining twelve bases of the granite columns of the inner arcades remained *in situ* on either side of the nave.

The granite columns of the two outer arcades were removed at this time and both were replaced by arcades of four round-headed openings. These were supported on a pilaster buttress at the east end, three intermediate piers each about 70 cms square, and an L-shaped pier at the west end where it abutted the west ambulatory (Chapter 4). The south arcade and its supporting piers was rebuilt at a later date (Phase 3). The corner piers to the west show that this structure returned within the main west wall of the nave.

The steps in the south-west tower have monolithic treads, with solid fill to the two lower flights. Above this level the treads appear originally to have been supported by palm logs set directly beneath them; the present brick vault is a later (Phase 3) insertion.

The evidence for the remainder of the west end of the building is fragmentary, but it is assumed that the components that are now missing, such as the *narthex* and the north-west tower, mirrored those that survive elsewhere in the structure. A projecting jamb on the corner of the stair enclosure, implies an arrangement exactly analogous to that to the east, at its junction with the west wall of the main body of the church, that is a door. It is therefore likely that the west wall had three doorways exactly answering those immediately to the east.

The surviving paving in the church, although much damaged and probably repaired, appears to belong essentially to this phase of reconstruction (Chapter 4). The layout of the raised *haikal* and the timber *higab* that enclosed it, which were probably introduced at this time, as well as the structures erected on it is clear from mortices for timber uprights cut in the stone paving and kerbs. These included placements for an altar, several screens, and a *ciborium* or similar structure over the altar.

Phase 2: Reconstruction (Figures 78-80)

Part of the south wall survives to its full height, including the parapet, of 6.2 metres above the paved floor level and this shows that the south outer aisle had a flat roof. This was presumably of palm fronds, matting and mud, laid on joists about 30cms deep at centred at intervals of about 1.1 metres, and supported in beam pockets located 5.2 metres above the paved floor level. Above this, the wall was carried up as a parapet of diminished thickness.

Within the enclosed space, the highest surviving wall is the south end of the west wall of the *naos*, which rises to 5.3 metres above floor level, but has been rebuilt at a later date to a height of 6.2 metres where it forms the interior wall of the tower, and the south side of the apse, which rises to 5.1 metres above the paved floor level of the nave. The south arcade appears to survive at one point at its east end to a height of 5.65 metres, but is more commonly 5.1 metres above the paved floor.

The apse is more than half a circle, so that the opening into it, which is 5.2 metres wide, is slightly smaller than the apse diameter of 5.26 metres. This makes the soffit lower on the centre line. It seems likely that a clearly defined arch was used to span the opening into the apse, with a flat soffit on the centre line; it dies into the walls about one metre below the surviving top of the masonry. The topmost existing course on the south-west corner of the apse is at the same level as were the tops of the capitals of the south inner arcade, that is the springing level of the arches presumed to have been carried on the capitals.

Moreover, there is a projecting knob and a socket on this stone, facing west about 5.1 metres above the floor level of the nave, suggesting a primary fixing for some screen or hanging (Figure 24 JJ). It seems likely, therefore, that this stone carried the springing course of the apse arch, and the reconstruction is based on this assumption. It certainly cannot be lower. Given the quality of the stonework below, a masonry half dome is postulated over the apse (Figures 78-80).

At the east end of the nave, the heights of the doorways to the baptistry and the sacristy are given by the lintel remaining in the northern opening, that is a straight joint extending through three courses (Figure 27 JJ). At some later date, a lintel at a lower level was substituted, perhaps because of the serious structural settlement of the inner arcade abutment. The jambs of the upper opening to the sacristy, presumed to have been a window and mirrored by another in the baptistry, also survive and it is suggested that the lintel height was probably related to the height of the capitals of the inner arcades.

It seems likely that the corner piers of the outer nave arcade carried a continuous impost at one level. If this is assumed to apply also to the central piers, to produce a coherent structure, arches can be struck across all the openings which appear visually and structurally acceptable. Moreover, the central arch would allow the roof of the space between it and the main west wall to be carried across at the same level as that of the south and north outer aisles. A west clerestorey window has been assumed above the western arch; a more elaborate arrangement would of course be possible. There is nothing in the more fragmentary remains on the north side of the nave which adds to or contradicts this reconstruction.

Beyond, to the west, the height of the five doorways is taken from the surviving evidence for internal and external lintels, especially for the central doorway.

In the baptistry, the column base found *in situ* was centred between the projecting pier at the south-east corner of the apse structure, and a pilaster retained from the original (Phase 1) structure and extended upwards in the (Phase 2) reconstruction in the rebuilding of the south wall. A fallen (Type B) column was found here, and suggests a two-bay arcade, supporting roof joints spanning east-west. The wall above this arcade could not have been more than about 45 cm thick, that is the same width as the base, so could not have been carried up very far. In fact, to carry a roof at the same height as that of the south outer arcade it need not have risen substantially higher than the keystones.

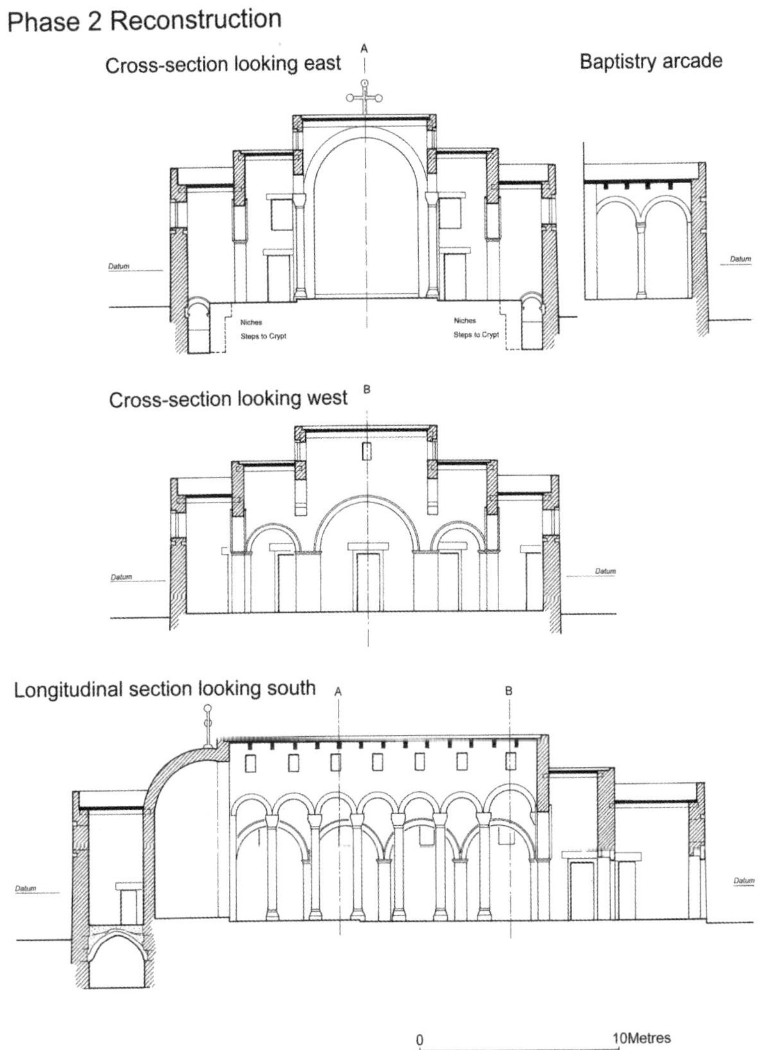

Figure 78: Hypothetical reconstruction of the interior of the Phase 2 building (prepared by Paul Drury).

Turning to the elevations, the height, the batter to the first timber bonding course, and the sill and head heights of the windows are known from the standing south wall (Figure 79).

On the south elevation, the door position is known, and its height is assumed to have matched those on the west front. The windows shown from west to east all survive in whole or part except the easternmost one. This window is placed to answer that to the extreme west, and fits the internal layout. It is possible that there was a further window above the south door.

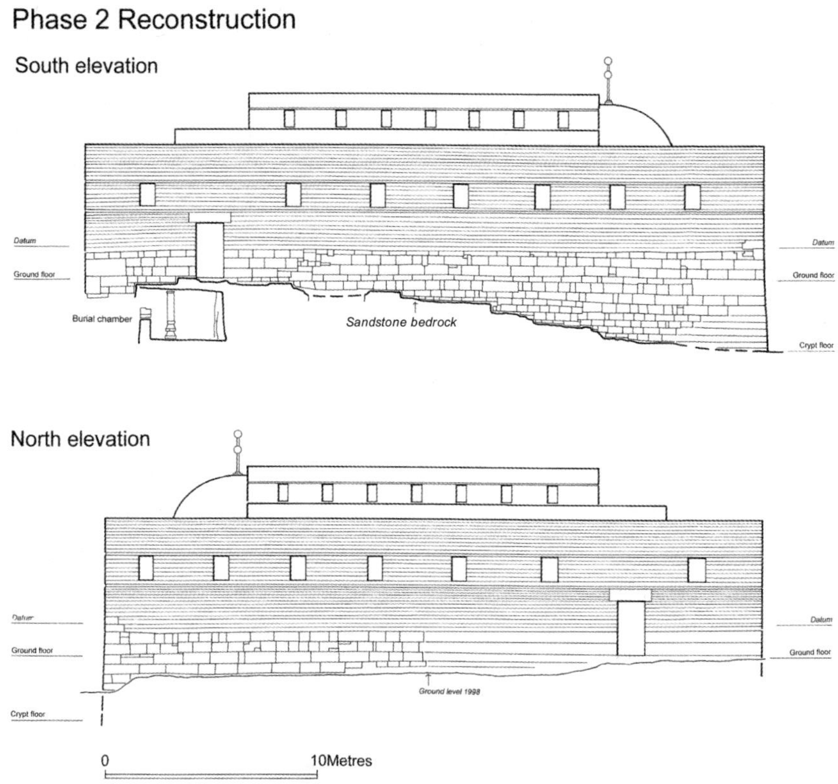

Figure 79 : Reconstruction drawings of the Phase 2 building (prepared by Paul Drury and Fred Aldsworth).

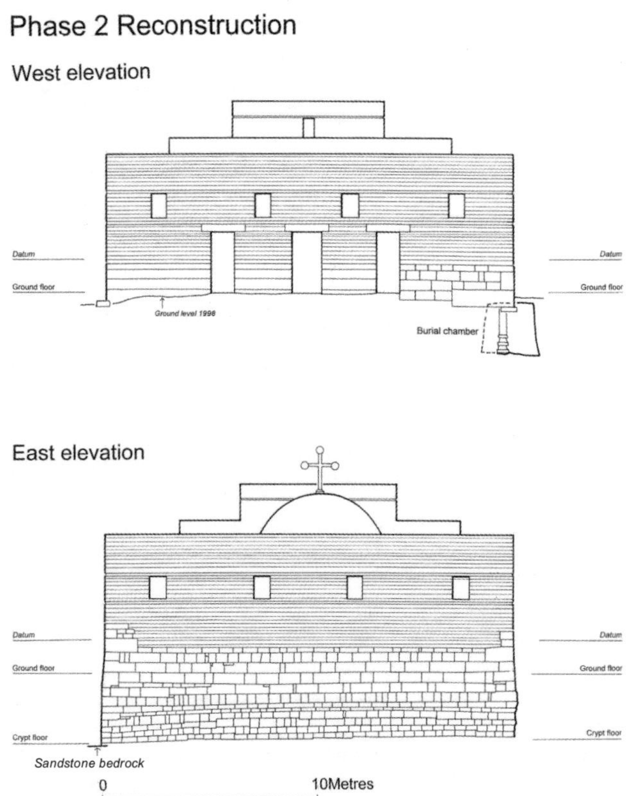

Figure 80: Reconstruction drawings of the Phase 2 building (prepared by Paul Drury and Fred Aldsworth).

On the north elevation, the door position is known and its height is assumed, to match that on the south. The fourth and fifth windows from the east survive in part; the remainder are disposed essentially to resemble the south elevation.

On the west front, the argument for the layout of doorways has already been given. That their height conformed to that of the layout of doorways within is confirmed by the bearing of the lintel of the south doorway which survives in recognisable form, indicated by a vertical straight joint. The south window exists in the tower and the north window is suggested as answering it. The other two windows are suggested as being centred in the piers between the doors, thus giving a balanced elevation.

On the east elevation, the windows are hypothetical, based loosely on the west front.

The dome of the apse is assumed to have projected visibly, rather than being encased in any superincumbent structure. It appears to have been described by Abu al-Makarim, formerly attributed to Abu Salah 'the Armenian'. in *circa* AD 1200 (*Vantini 1975*: 327, *Adams 1996*: 77 and *Van der Vliet 1999*). The cross is added in response to that description of the building, and its form follows those depicted in murals at Faras (*Gartkiewicz 1982*: Fig 20)

Phase 2: Architectural enrichments

The masonry structure was characteristically plain. Externally there seems to have been no enrichment whatsoever, save presumably for window grilles (Chapter 5, Figure 46 No 78).

Internally, the principal enrichment would have been from the red granite shafts, the capitals, and the bases, re-used from the original (Phase 1) building and considered in detail above.

The small arches leading into the crypt, and over the baptismal tank, have square drip moulds and, in the case of the former, decorated keystones (Chapter 5, Group 1 Figure 39 Nos 26 and 27, Plates 185 and 186). There are a few other decorated *voussoirs* from the Cathedral which appear to derive from small openings, about 36 cms and 58 cms in radius, but it is not clear where these were located (Chapter 5, Groups 2 and 3 Figure 40 Nos 28-32, Plates 187, 188 and Figure 41 Nos 33-37, Plates 189, 190).

The outer arcades have moulded imposts and drip moulds, on both sides, the latter rising from a common springing related to the former. Below, the keystones and some *voussoirs*, dressed in the standard way, have Christian symbols which were originally on both on the ends.

Whilst the arches survive only in re-built form, it seems clear that they follow the original arrangement with some *voussoirs* and the keystone ornamented in each bay. Large quantities of *voussoirs* (including decorated examples), as well as drip moulds and imposts were recovered in the clearance of the interior, but unfortunately their locations were not recorded (Chapter 5, Group 4 Figure 42 Nos 38-42, Plates 191 & 192, Figure 43 Nos 43-56, Plates 191-196 and Figure 45 Nos 72-77, Plates 202, 203).

Voussoirs with interlace or Greek key ornament from large arches may have been *in situ* when the Cathedral was abandoned. Their scale is consistent with the openings at the east end of the nave into the apse and at the west end of the nave into the west ambulatory (Chapter 5, Groups 5 and 6 Figure 44 Nos 57 – 71 and Plates 197-201).

No direct evidence for the form of the inner arcade arches, if they were indeed arches, survives, but it is probable that they resembled the smaller arches elsewhere.

Phase 2: Dating Evidence

The second phase of refurbishment produced virtually nothing but residual pottery brought in with filling material. Adams' notes on the 1963 season show that the material behind the tribune was similar to that found to the south of the Cathedral Church, in 'Tavern Street', perhaps derived the partial dismantling of Meroitic and X-Group houses, and including X-Group and very early Christian wares (Chapter 1).

The change to the arrangement of the *bema* would appear to conform to the general development of liturgical practice of the period, with an extended *haikal* enclosed by a wooden *higab*. According to Adams (*1965*: 99), the latter was introduced in the seventh century as a wooden screen and was often replaced in mud brick in the eighth century.

If, has been suggested, the subsequent (Phase 3) restoration works to the south arcade and west ambulatory can been seen as a response to damage during to the Arab attack in AD 956, then the major (Phase 2) rebuilding of the Cathedral must have been before this date, but the Phase 3 works could have been as late as the end of the thirteenth century (see below).

Thus, there is no evidence from which to closely date the Phase 2 reconstruction, but its features conform broadly to Adams' datings. A date for the reconstruction of the 'Great' or 'Old' Church at Qasr Ibrim early in the eighth century is possible.

Phase 2: Discussion and Dedication

The circumstances which brought about the extensive reconstruction of the building at this time are difficult to comprehend, since they involved not only the re-arrangement and enlargement of the *bema,* including the building of a larger apse, and the creation of a larger *haikal* that encroached on the east end of the nave, but also the rebuilding of all the existing walls, perhaps originally of mud brick, in stone above a level about 1.4 metres above the paved floor, and, perhaps, the creation of a new west end all using carefully marginally tooled and freshly-quarried sandstone blocks.

If the west end was a new creation at this stage, it implies that the previous arrangement was either completely destroyed or completely demolished to make way for the new one, evidently without leaving any trace of the original layout. One possible explanation for this radical rebuilding may be that it followed the elevation of the site to a Bishopric some time in the seventh century.

The dedication of the Cathedral Church at Qasr Ibrim has, until recently, remained a mystery. A late twelfth or early thirteenth century handbook of Coptic *topographica sacra* (*Zanetti 1995* and *Adams 1996*: 66), includes an account by Abu al-Makarim which states that in the town of Ibrim "is a large and beautiful church, finely planned and named after Our Lady the Pure Virgin Mary. Above it is a high dome upon which rises a large cross" (*Vantini 1975*: 327).

Adams concluded that this was not a reference to the Cathedral Church since 'There is nothing in the surviving fabric of columns and piers that could possibly have supported a dome, even of wood' (*Adams 1996*: 77). The reconstruction proposed above for the Phase 2 building, in fact, permits the presence of a half dome over the apse, answering Adams' concerns, and it is also clear that the only church at Qasr Ibrim that could possible be described as 'large and beautiful' is the Cathedral.

However, in the consecration scrolls of Bishop Timotheos, written in the late fourteenth century (see Chapter 2), Timotheos is named as bishop of a double diocese of Faras and Ibrim. From this Van der Vliet has recently suggested that, since it is known that the Cathedral Church at Faras was dedicated to the Virgin Mary, it is likely that the church he served at Ibrim was the other building referred to in the Arabic scroll, dedicated to the Holy Apostles (*Van der Vliet 1999*). How this can be reconciled with the Abu al-Makarim account is unclear: whether Abu al-Makarim himself confused the Faras and Ibrim churches in his account or whether the church was rededicated at some time, is unknown.

Phase 3: LATER ALTERATIONS

These appear to vary in date and are unlikely to represent a single remodelling of the building.

The most obvious evidence now remaining for later substantial, but ill-executed, structural work is the rebuilt south outer arcade. The original components were largely reassembled, but the piers were lengthened and, compared to the original work with its tightly-fitting joints, the stones are roughly coursed with very wide joints (Figure 81 and Chapter 4 Figure 30WW and Plates 142-152).

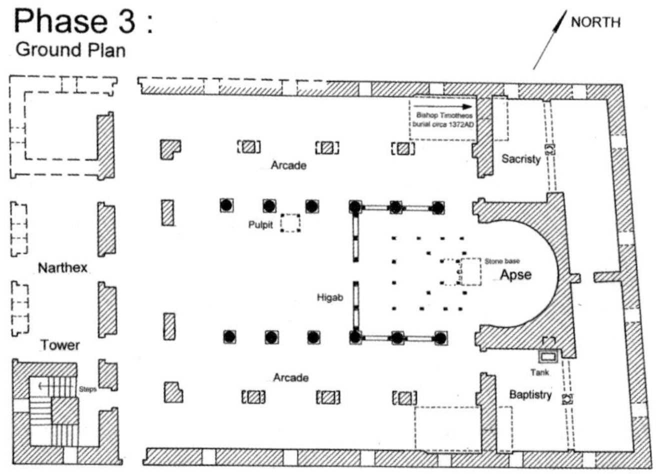

Figure 81: Simplified plan showing the later (Phase 3) alterations to the Cathedral.

The reconstruction included two bands of timber strapping, clearly intended to be visible, but the stonework may well have been plastered. The spans of the arches were reduced, clearly causing problems with the re-setting of the *voussoirs*.

A stone base and floor found in the opening to the apse at a relatively high level in 1963 might be the remains of a late altar (Chapter 1 Trench A1).

The timber pulpit was at some time replaced by one in rough rubble masonry, in the same position (*Adams 1996:* Figure 19). Its poor construction suggests that it too belongs to the final phase.

Late in the life of the Cathedral Church, the crypts were abandoned, filled, and paved over. At the east end of the south aisle, a pavement of 'large flat stones of irregular size and shape' was found in 1964 on a band of 'soft windblown debris, about 10 cms thick' (Chapter 2).

No plan was made of this pavement at the time, but it seems to have been set at the level of the *haikal* floor, about 15 cms above general floor level, and to have extended westwards as far as the west side of the *haikal*. Similar paving was found on the north side, again at *haikal* floor level, and included re-used stones, among them the Meroitic stele broken into two pieces and much worn (*Edwards and Rilly 2007*: 82-90). These works may, perhaps, be associated with the late creation of vestibules at the east end of the north and south aisles.

In both stairwells the material filling them appears to have been deliberate dumped therein, in the north antechamber on top of some 15 cms of grey silt on the antechamber floor (Chapter 2). The fill of the south antechamber and stair contained late Christian cup and saucer lamps, other late Christian pottery, and a bronze bowl. The entrances to the crypts proper were blocked by walls. On the north side it consisted of mortar-dressed blocks extending to within 18 cms of the roof, built on the silt deposit over the floor. Within the crypt, which was far from full, was brown earth and debris over the silt layer, and on this was an Arab manuscript dated to AD 1329, as well as a palm cross, a complete pot, and fragments of classic Christian and 'Islamic' pottery.

There are a number of other changes to the internal layout and fittings of the church, which generally show a high standard of workmanship, but which are demonstrably subsequent to the Phase 2 reconstruction. They are not stratigraphically related, but seem from links in materials and evident strategy to have formed part of a single campaign. Taken as a whole they probably reflect a major, if largely superficial, embellishment of the rebuilt structure, the principal component of which is likely to have been wall paintings, all of which are now lost. They included the construction of the tribune within the apse (described in Chapter 4 Plates 123 and 124); alterations to the baptistry; work to the north crypt; and repairs to the main steps in the south-west tower.

Investigations in the sacristy by Paul Drury in 1990 showed that a series of sandstone paving slabs bedded in sand were not primary to this phase of reconstruction. They overlay some surviving primary (Phase 2) paving blocks adjacent to the north apse wall, and were contemporary with the robbing of the west wall of the crypt to a low level. The evidence appears to indicate that the robbers broke into the east wall of the antechamber just below the crown of the vault. The hole was rapidly made good with distinctive purplish plaster, leaving part of the large block which it was intended to cut out *in situ*.

The repairs to the floor were associated with structural changes in this area.

The new paving covers the site of the putative granite column supporting the roof, which must have been removed at this time. No doubt it, and its probable arcade, were replaced by a single beam supporting the roof joists.

The baptistry was repaired in a similar fashion to the sacristy, but the original central column was retained. A new stone baptismal tank was set above the original, in part responding to the change of floor level (Chapter 2 Plate 58).

The south wall of the north antechamber to the north crypt below springing level was roughly re-plastered in the same distinctive material used for the repair. The rebate in the north wall at ground floor level, east of the *naos* wall, was filled with fired bricks, also set in the same distinctive plaster.

The third flight of the steps in the south-west tower was reinforced with a vault of fired brick set in the purplish plaster used elsewhere at this time. Other minor repairs were also undertaken, and the lower parts of the central stone newel plastered, probably for the first time.

Phase 3: Dating evidence for the later alterations

The positioning of the Bishop Miel or Mielkuda inscriptions suggest that they relate to the re-construction of the south arcade and other repairs in the vicinity of the west ambulatory following accidental or deliberate damage at this time (Chapter 6).

The Bishop's dates are unknown, but Włodzimierz Godlewski suggested (*1994*) that the work could have been undertaken at the end of the thirteenth century, following the Mamluk invasions and the large-scale destruction of churches in Nubia, since the compound ending with *-kuda* was very common at this time. Kjølbye-Biddle (*1994*: 31) suggested that the rebuilding of both the Church on the Point and the Cathedral, linked by the Miel inscriptions, was associated with damage that occurred in AD 956, when the Arabs captured Qasr Ibrim, and pottery from the destruction layers in the former building supports this. That the keystones with Christian symbols were reset in the arches and were not defaced suggests that the building work was Christian in date.

The pottery in the south crypt stair fill suggested to Adams a date bracket of *circa* 1200-1350 for the deposition of this material. An Arabic manuscript of AD 1329 provides a *terminus post quem* for the walling up of the north crypt proper. Taken together, a date in the middle of the fourteenth century seems likely for this work. There is, of course, no clear evidence to link the filling of the crypts and the reconstruction of the south arcade.

Bishop Timotheos was buried in the northern crypt antechamber, in a void of about 50 cms between the top of the filling and the soffit of the mud brick vault, in 1371-1372. He was, presumably, buried by cutting away the paving over the entrance to the crypt in the nave, which was subsequently made good.

This implies that whilst the crypts were filled before the interment, their existence was still remembered and is essentially consistent with the mid fourteenth century date suggested for the filling of the crypts.

Chapter 9: PERIOD 2 – THE POST-CATHEDRAL OCCUPATION AND COLLAPSE: *circa* AD 1480

The nature of the abandonment and destruction of the building was made clear by a burnt layer, 20-25 cms thick, over much of the area of the nave, and the fallen granite columns of the inner arcades lying on top of or amid the destruction layer (Chapters 1 and 2). The arrangement of the columns following the collapse of the building can be seen in the 1964 record drawing, save for that at the east-end of the south arcade, which remained standing (Figure 8). Four capitals, three of granite and one of red sandstone, were also found, two on their sides and two standing upright, one some distance from the other fallen debris in the south aisle (Figure 36).

By the time of this destruction, at least 20-30 cms of silt had already accumulated on the body of the church floor. In it, particularly in the area between the *haikal* and the late pulpit base, were a large number of fragments of liturgical manuscripts in Greek, Nubian and Coptic, all torn and some burnt, and in part 'protected by fallen granite columns'. This comment makes clear, despite contradictory references in some of the accounts of the clearance, that those fragments belong to the destruction phase, rather than with the phase of crypt infilling, which also included manuscript fragments. Yet by this time, at least in the nave and northern aisles of the church, there is clear evidence of decline. A layer of hard brown compact earth, 15-20 cms thick, was associated with a large hand-made pot standing on a bed of goat droppings. The general impression is that by the time the fabric of the Cathedral was largely destroyed by fire, its use as a church had dramatically declined if not totally ceased.

Among and over the fallen columns and other masonry from the destruction of the church, occupation debris and rubbish accumulated. In the outer south aisle, a succession of some twenty separate layers of 'barnyard debris, mainly straw, droppings and ash' lay on top of the church pavement (Chapter 2). Elsewhere in the nave 30 cms of deposits accumulated, made up of straw-matting separated by thin layers of wind blown dirt, and goat, donkey and sheep droppings.

The abandonment of the Cathedral was not matched by an abandonment of Qasr Ibrim itself; rather, the shell of the building was used to dump refuse and shelter animals, until the larger fallen debris, which was not readily removed, covered to a sufficient depth to provide an even level within the building. On top of these deposits was a layer of burning, perhaps representing the collapse of part of the roof which may still have been in place, at least in part, when it was occupied by squatters.

It was overlaid by a layer of sterile dark brown, sandy soil, between 20 and 25 cms thick, with traces of hearths. Some twenty-three fragments of Arabic texts were found in the latest squatter layers and these may provide a *terminus post quem* for the building overlying them.

A leather scroll written in Old Nubian from Gebel Adda, mentions that there was still a Christian bishop at Ibrim in 1484 (*Plumley Archive* Notes. *Adams 1977*: 533) and if this is the case then the squatter occupation must have occurred shortly after this.

Chapter 10: PERIOD 3 - THE PRE-MOSQUE BUILDING: *circa* AD 1570

This structure comprised only for the most part a single surviving course of walling approximately 0.8 – 1.0 metres above the level of the paved floor of the Cathedral (Chapters 1 and 2).

It included a series of pier bases and the one surviving standing column from the Cathedral Church, presumably helping to support roofs otherwise supported on parts of the shell of the building, the west wall of the *naos*, the apse and the south arcade (Figure 82).

The structure appears to have been a substantial house, entered at the north-west corner by a door, for which the pivot survived, and this gave access to a corridor linking a vestibule and three rooms on its south side (Rooms 1-3) and three further rooms on its north side (Rooms 4-6).

A space on the south side, partly contained by the south arcade of the Cathedral Church supporting some sort of roof, appears to have been associated with the preparation of food.

Similar structures were found between the apse and the east wall of the Cathedral and all appear to represent a short-lived phase of Bosnian occupation of the site, which commenced in *circa* AD 1570.

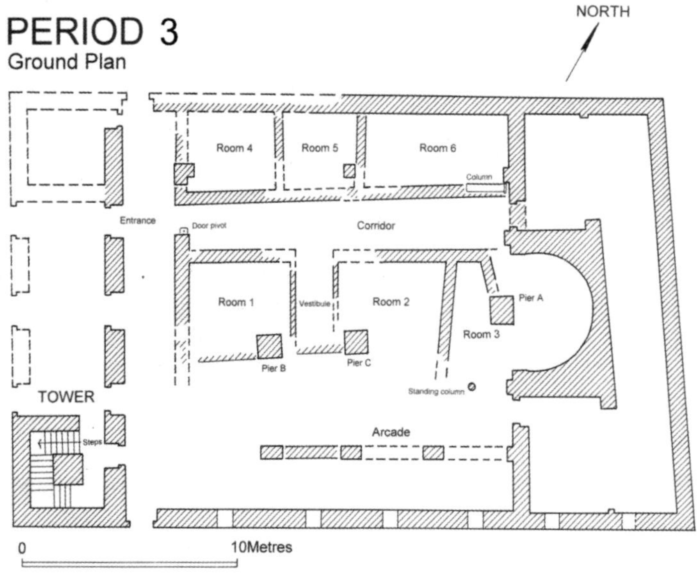

Figure 82: The pre-mosque building.

Chapter 11: PERIOD 4 - THE OTTOMAN MOSQUE: *circa* AD 1570-1811

The record plan and photographs from the 1963 season appear to show at least two phases of construction of the mosque, which lay within the space enclosed by the four walls containing the *naos* of the Cathedral Church. Part of the north wall was probably rebuilt at this time (Chapter 1 Figures 5 and 6, Plates 15-24).

Phase 1: The original mosque

The four existing walls of the Cathedral Church, which may by this time have lost its north-west tower and *narthex*, defined the outer shell of the new building, and the apse, the rooms to the north and south of it, three openings of the south arcade, and one standing column still survived (Figure 83). The south-west tower may have been used as a *minaret.*

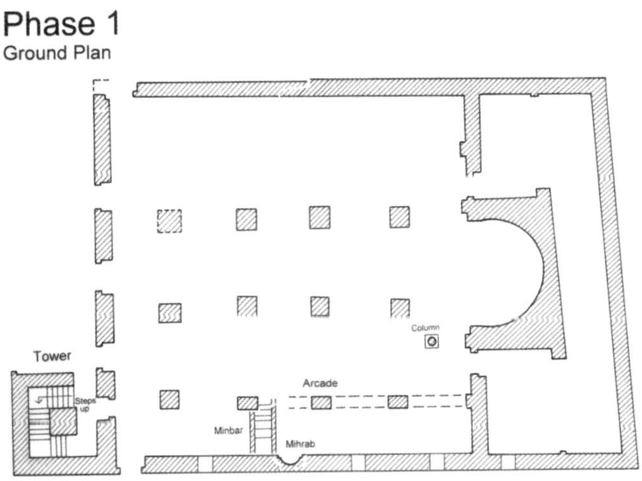

Figure 83: The first mosque.

The new building was constructed directly over the pre-mosque structure, with a floor level about 1.2 metres above that of the paved floor of the Cathedral. The existing walls of the former Cathedral enclosed a square space measuring 18 metres across, entered at the north-west and south-west corners.

It contained three openings of the south arcade, one surviving column, and a series of nine crudely-built piers, each up to a little over one metre across at the base and up to about four metres in height, which presumably supported a roof. The fourth opening at the west end of the south arcade must have been dismantled at or before this time, and the upper part of the west face of the pier that supported it on its east side was rebuilt.

A *mihrab* was built into the south wall and alongside it, on its west side, a stone *minbar* was constructed. These would have been centrally placed in relationship to the five bays forming the east-west axis of the mosque.

No independent dating evidence for the construction of the first mosque has been found, but it is likely to have been converted during the Ottoman occupation, but after the pre-mosque building had been demolished.

According to the Turkish traveller and writer, Evliya Çhelebi, who visited Ibrim in the later seventeenth century, a mosque was built in the middle of the fortress in the name of the Sultan Sulayman the Magnificent (AD 1520-1566), which was still in use for worship in his time. He noted that it possessed a 'minaret in the old style' (*Çhelebi 1671-72*: 841).

Phase 2: The later mosque

At some subsequent date, or dates, a series of linking walls, up to three metres in height, were constructed between some of the internal piers to create either one smaller space or a series of smaller spaces (Figure 84).

The principal open space on the south side was reduced in size to about 15 by 11 metres, with a large room to the north and a passage to the west linking the original north and south doors of the Cathedral. As a result the *mihrab* and *minbar* would no longer have been centrally placed within the four bays forming the east-west axis of the mosque.

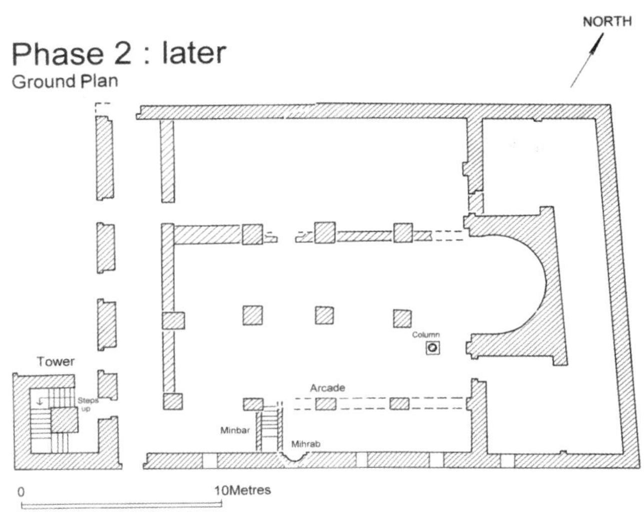

Figure 84: The later insertions to the first mosque.

There is an extended discussion of the early modern history of Ibrim based on Arabic documents (*Hinds and Sakkout 1986*: 1-4) and at least one of these appears to refer to the mosque. Most of the documents referred to were found in a pottery vessel buried in a house, including its title deeds dated May-June AD 1670 (*Hinds and Sakkout 1986*: 12-13).

The house was called 'the [well]-known house of *Tubshi Ibrahim.* The northern limit is at the lane, the southern limit is at the lane, the eastern is at *May Udabashi* and the western at the lane next to the mosque.'

It is assumed that the building continued to function as a mosque after these alterations had been made, until the site was abandoned by the Ottomans in 1811.

Chapter 12: LATER OCCUPATION: post 1811

At a very late stage in the occupation of the former Cathedral Church and mosque, a series of 'rough walls' were inserted into the building on its north and east sides (Chapter 1 Figure 5).

These may perhaps have been built whilst the remainder of the building was still in use as a mosque, for example to provide accommodation for the Imam, or after 1811 when for a short period the site was occupied by Mamluk refugees.

They may be responsible for the fact that wooden objects and architectural elements were almost entirely absent from the excavations (apart from beams in the Cathedral Church walls), although, given the likely abandonment of the fortress in favour of the valley well before the Mamluk incursion, these elements may have been removed for re-use at an earlier time.

However, by 1813, when Thomas Legh visited Qasr Ibrim, the fortress had been deserted.

Appendix 1: THE TOMBS AT THE WEST FRONT OF THE TOWER

by Fred Aldsworth

Two tombs located immediately adjacent to the west of the west wall of the tower were excavated during the 1964 season. They were referred to as Tombs 11 and 12 (see Appendix 2, Figure 85 and Plate 231).

The Egypt Exploration Society has typed and manuscript notes of the excavations, and several photographs, and the following description is based on those records (now in the Department of Ancient Egypt and Sudan at the British Museum).

Plate 231: The two tombs during excavation in 1964. That to the left is Tomb 11 and that to the right is Tomb12 (Unreferenced EES Photograph).

TOMB 11

The tomb to the north was constructed wholly of sun-dried mud brick (Plates 231 & 232). The east end abutted almost onto the footings of the west wall of the tower. In construction it consisted of three courses of bricks laid flat from end to end, forming a rough rectangle 3.10 metres long and 0.80 metre wide. From these three courses sprang the two ends of the vaulting which roofed over the tomb, rising to a height of 0.80 metres. The vaulting had been constructed in the usual Nubian manner, that is, a couple of courses of bricks laid on their sides, and rising up to about 20 cms on each side of the structure. Then successive semicircular courses of bricks were laid to lean out of the perpendicular towards the east end of the tomb. Thus the builders were able to achieve an elliptical vaulting which needed no centering. The west end of the tomb ended in a square chamber, about 90 cms across, from which access could be made into the main chamber of the tomb, and which could be sealed at the top, When found, the top of this chamber was open and a gap of about 60 cms had been made along the whole of the top of the burial chamber vaulting.

Both tombs had been buried under wind-blown debris, some of which had penetrated through the broken vaulting into the interior of this tomb. In this intrusive fill were a few pieces of broken pottery and, 30 cms down, several pieces of woollen cord, which were associated with the burials below.

Three burials had been made in the tomb, one body on top of another. Beneath these were the small remains of a coloured carpet, which lay on a bed of fine sand. For a reason which is not made clear in the original notes, the burials were numbered Burials 2, 3 and 4.

Plate 232: Tomb 11 during excavation (EES Photo Reference WF 3/3).

Burial 2

This was the uppermost body, and when found was seen to be headless. The body was in a surprisingly good state of preservation, the skin of the torso and the limbs being shrunken but complete. The only clothes worn by the dead man were two pairs of coarse white linen pantaloons, gathered at the waist and knees by draw strings. Part of an embroidered shawl had been wound about the upper portion of the body, which had also been wrapped in eight large sheets of linen, the whole being bound around with woollen cords. Those portions of the linen which covered the lower parts of the legs had been soaked in oil at the time of burial and had obtained the appearance and consistency of oil-skin. Similar treatment had been given to the wrappings of the other two burials.

Burial 3

This lay beneath Burial 2, towards the south wall of the tomb and was that of a man whose only clothing was a pair of coarse white pantaloons, similar in every respect to those found with Burial 2, but encircled at the waist by the remains of a leather belt. A cross woven out of long, very thin strips of leather had been suspended from the neck. The hands, which were placed on each side of the pubic region, were enclosed in white linen fingerless gloves, each tied at the wrist by a string. Within the gloves, three fingers on the right hand and two on the left were each wrapped individually in small white linen fingerstalls.

As was the case with Burial 2, this body was wrapped in a number of linen sheets being finally fastened with woollen cords. The innermost sheet was embroidered at both ends with a line of Kufic writing in red.

Burial 4

This lay beneath Burial 2, towards the north wall of the tomb. The body, which was that of a man, was in a remarkable state of preservation. The hair, brownish-grey and cut short, still clung to the head. The teeth were well preserved. Visible signs suggested that the body was that of a man in middle age. In contrast to the other two burials, it was noticeable that this body was dressed in a white linen shirt, embroidered with a line of Kufic writing, with a metal stud as ornament.

A cross, similar to that on Burial 3, hung from the neck. The hands, placed on each side of the pubic region, were enclosed in fingerless linen gloves. Unlike Burial 3, no attempt had been made to wrap the fingers individually.

The body had first been wrapped in a large sheet of white linen, fringed at one end, and worked in coloured threads. The outer wrappings consisted of three long sheets of white linen, doubled over at the feet and sewn up each side. At the end of each sheets was a line of Kufic writing in red thread.

The provision of these three sewn sheets at least postulates that this burial (Burial 4) was the original burial in the tomb and had been carried out in a less hurried manner than the two burials above it.

It is not impossible that this tomb, which originally was intended for one burial only, was opened up at a later date to receive the other two bodies, and it is within the bounds of possibility that these later burials may have been reburied after their removal from some other grave, possibly from the adjoining brick tomb (Tomb 12) if this was demolished to provide material for some other structure.

TOMB 12

This was separated from Tomb 11 by a distance of about 20 cms and was constructed of red fired brick and had been destroyed down to its third course of bricks, presumably as a result of robbing for some other much later building.

[For the inscriptions in the tombs see *Van der Vliet forthcoming*]

Appendix 2: HUMAN BURIALS IN AND AROUND THE CATHEDRAL CHURCH

by Fred Aldsworth and Hans Barnard

The Cathedral Church is built adjacent to and partly overlying a vertical cliff or bluff of natural sandstone, which is about three metres high and extends for about eighteen metres south from the south wall of the building (Plate 233). This feature was also encountered under the west end of the Cathedral in 1964 and it was recorded that a mud brick X-Group house, built below it, had to be filled before the Cathedral could be built over it (Chapter 2, Figure 13 and Chapter 7, Figures 65 & 66).

Plate 233: The sandstone cliff to the south of the Cathedral in 1992 (Photograph by Fred Aldsworth).

The cliff may in part be a natural feature, but it is evident that it has also been cut to extract sandstone before the Cathedral was erected. The flat surface below the cliff is clearly man-made and presumably designed, at least in part, to support buildings such as the X-Group house encountered in 1964.

In the vertical cliff face are six rock-cut openings behind which are larger chambers that have been used for burial (Figure 86 T1-T5 and T9). The chamber partially under the south-west corner of the Cathedral (T9) is about 2.5 metres wide, 4.0 metres long, and about 2.3 metres in height, and it is accessed via an opening, about 1.0 metres square, which is rock-cut and partially blocked by two slabs of sandstone (Figures 24CC and 25EE). Within the chamber are a re-used granite shaft and two re-used granite bases from the original Cathedral which are used to support to roof (Chapter 5, Figure 35 Nos 8, 11and 12, Plate 173).

The other chambers vary in size from the largest (T9) down to the smallest at the south end of the cliff (T5), which is about 0.8 metres wide and 2.0 metres long. It is not known when these chambers were cut or when they were first used for burial, but it is conceivable that they pre date the Cathedral Church.

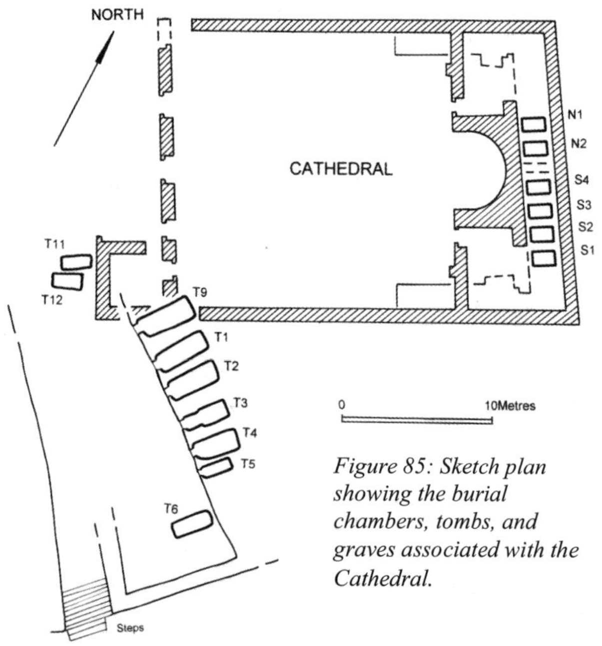

Figure 85: Sketch plan showing the burial chambers, tombs, and graves associated with the Cathedral.

In the 1964 and 1966 excavation seasons, the six rock-cut chambers, together with the six rock-cut graves in the Cathedral crypts and the two tombs outside the west front of the south-west tower, were all excavated.

The Bishop Timotheos burial in the fill of the north crypt was also excavated and removed in 1964.

Professor Plumley attributed the cutting of the vertical face in the sandstone to the Meroitic period (see Chapter 7) and in his interim notes for the 1966 season of excavations suggests that the rock-cut chambers, of which he refers to only four rather than six, were probably dug during the eleventh or twelfth centuries.

He noted that the largest one nearest the Cathedral (T9) had been examined in 1963 and revealed human remains and scraps of clothing, whilst the opening up of the three remaining tombs in 1964 had, 'like the first one, been violated in the past' (*Plumley Archives QI 1966*).

He noted, however, the tomb nearest the cathedral (T9) had yielded five complete funerary stelae and a great quantity of manuscripts in Greek, Coptic, Old Nubian, and Arabic. Three, and possibly four, were commemorative inscriptions of the Bishops of Ibrim in the eleventh and twelfth centuries, and included the place-name 'Phrim' for Ibrim.

Apart from these comments, no other records have as yet been found of the investigations of the rock-cut chambers in 1963 and 1964, but the results of the investigations of the Bishop Timotheos burial, the graves in the crypts, and the two tombs are known (Chapter 2, Graves N1 and N2, and S1-S4 and Appendix 1 Tombs 11 and 12).

It is not known where the bone material was deposited after the excavations in 1964 and 1966, but a large number of human bones were found in 1990 re-deposited in one of the graves in the south crypt (Grave S2), and these are believed to have derived from one or both of those two seasons of work. The bones were removed, cleaned, numbered, studied, placed in bags, and returned to the grave in which they were found.

The Egypt Exploration Society holds a copy of a detailed osteological report prepared by Dr Hans Barnard, who was assisted in his study of the material by a dentist, Hamish Robertson, and the following is an extract from his results and discussion.

During the 1964 and 1966 seasons it is understood that at least 25 skeletons are known to have been uncovered from investigations on three parts of the site – in the crypts of the Cathedral (Figure 14 N1 & N2 and S1-S4); from the rock-cut chambers to the south of the Cathedral and a rock-cut grave to the south of them (Figure 86 T1-T6 and T9); and the two tombs near the south-west tower (Appendix 1 Figure 86 T11 and T12).

The bones of at least thirteen individuals were identified in 1990, but none could be related to the burials from which they were derived. All were the remains of adults, some of which had female features. Minor variations in anatomy, such as a Caribelli's pit in two lower left second molars, the sacralisation of Co.1 in two sacrums, and the presence of a supracondylary foramen in three humeri, suggests a close family relationship between at least some of the skeletons.

Apart from some traumatic remnants, and one collapsed vertebra, no pathological changes were seen but no microsopical or biochemical methods were used to look for them.

The condition of the teeth points in the direction of a mildly gritty diet without, or with very little, sugar.

Average height was estimated to be between 173 and 175 cms (5ft 8inches and 5ft 9inches).

BIBLIOGRAPHY

Adams, W.Y. (1965). 'Architectural evolution of the Nubian Church, 500-1400 A.D.' in *The Journal of the American Research Center in Egypt* 4 : 87-139.

Adams, W.Y. (1996). *Qasr Ibrim: The Late Medieval Period* (Egypt Exploration Society Fifty-Ninth Excavation Memoir).

Adams, W.Y. (1977). *Nubia, Corridor to Africa.*

Adams, W.Y. (2010). *Qasr Ibrim: The Earlier Medieval Period* (Egypt Exploration Society Eighty-Ninth Excavation Memoir).

Betts, B.T.A. and Butler, A.J. (2002). *The Churches and Monasteries of Egypt and Some Neighbouring Countries – Attributed to Abu Salih, The Armenian.*

Browne, G.M. (1989). *Old Nubian texts from Qasr Ibrim* II (Egypt Exploration Society Texts from Excavations 10)

Browne, G.M. (1991). *Old Nubian texts from Qasr Ibrim* III (Egypt Exploration Society Texts from Excavations 12)

Çhelebi, E. (1671-72). *Seyahatname* X. (Quoted in Plumley's Notes. Evliya Çelebi's *Seyahatname* describes the author's travels through Europe between 1631 and 1670 and from Egypt via Nubia on his way to Ethiopia in 1671-72. Ten volumes originally printed in Istanbul in 1843.

Clarke, S. (1912). *Christian Antiquities of the Nile Valley.*

Crowfoot, E. (forthcoming). *Qasr Ibrim: the Textiles from the Cathedral Cemetery* (Egypt Exploration Society Ninety-Sixth Excavation Memoir)

Deichmann, F.W. and Grossman, P. (1988). *Nubische Forschungen* (Archäologische Forschungen 17)

Edwards, D.N. (2007). 'Meroitic Stelae from Qasr Ibrim' in *Rose 2007*: 76-92.

Edwards, D.N. and Rilly, C. (2007). 'The Amanish-akheto stele' in *Rose 2007*: 82-90.

Gartkiewicz, P.M. (1972). *Nubia, Récentes recherches. Actes du Colloque Nubiologique International au Musée National de Varsovie, 19-22 Juin, sons la redaction de K.Michalowski, Varsovie 1975.*

Gartkiewicz, P.M. (1980). 'New outline of the history of the Nubian church architecture' in *BAbesch* 55 Part 1: 137-160.

Gartkiewicz, P.M. (1982a). 'An introduction to the history of Nubian church architecture' in *Nubia Christiana* I: 43-105.

Gartkiewicz, P. M. (1982b). 'Remarks on the cathedral at Qasr Ibrim' in *Nubian Studies*: 87-94.

Gartkiewicz, P.M. (1990). *The Cathedral in Old Dongola and its antecedents* Nubia 1 Dongola 2.

Godlewski, W. (1994). 'Christian Nubia - After the Nubian Campaign: The Late Period in Nubian Art from the middle of the thirteenth to the end of the fourteenth Centuries', in *Nubia Thirty Years Later (Society for Nubian Studies Eighth International Conference) Arkamani – Sudan Electronic Journal of Archaeology and Anthropology*. No page numbers given in website version (consulted December 2009): www.arkamani.org/preliminary_reports/polish_exp_dongola/godlewski.htm. The website address no longer appears valid but the subject is covered by Wlodzimierz Godlewski in the following two published papers:

Godlewski, W. (1995). 'Christian Nubia – after the Nubian Campaign' *Cahiers de recherches de l'Institut de papyrologie et d'égyptogie de Lille* 17/1: 267-277.

Godlewski, W. (1996). 'The late period in Nubian art, from the middle of the 13th to the end of the 14th centuries' in Gundlach R., Kropp M. and A. Leibundgut, *Der Sudan in Vergangenheit und Gegenwart* [Sudan past and present – Papers presented at a conference in Mainz, Germany].

Godlewski, W. (2006). *Dongola, City of Kings and Bishops* (CD produced to accompany exhibition of the same name held at Warsaw University to mark the proceedings of the 11th International Conference of Nubian Studies).

Grossman, P. (1980). 'Typological problems of the Nubian four-pillar churches' in *Nubian Letters* 4: 23-25.

Hinds, M. and Sakkout, H, (1986). *Arabic Documents from the Ottoman Period from Qasr Ibrim* (Egypt Exploration Society Texts from Excavations 8)

Hinds, M. and Ménage, V. (1991). *Qasr Ibrim in the Ottoman Period; Turkish and further Arabic Documents* (Egypt Exploration Society texts from Excavations 11)

Holt, P.M. (1967). 'Sultan Selim 1 and the Sudan' in *Journal of African History* 8: 19-23.

James, T.G.H. (ed.) (1982). *Excavating in Egypt: The Egypt Exploration Society 1882-1982* (British Museum Publications).

Kjølbye-Biddle, B. (1994). 'The small early church in Nubia with reference to the Church on the Point at Qasr Ibrim' in Painter, K. (ed.) *Recent Studies in early Christian Archaeology*: 17-47.

Mileham, G.S. (1910). *Churches in Lower Nubia (Eckley B. Coxe Junior Expedition to Nubia* 2).

Monneret de Villard, U. (1935). *La Nubia Medioevale* (two volumes). Vol.I 1935; Vol II 1935.

Plumley, J.M. (1964). 'Qasr Ibrim 1963-64' in *Journal of Egyptian Archaeology* 50: 3-5.

Plumley, J.M. (1971). 'Pre-Christian Nubia (23BC-535 AD). Evidence from Qasr Ibrim' *Études et Travaux* 6: 7-24.

Plumley, J.M. (1975). *The scrolls of Bishop Timotheos.* (Egypt Exploration Society Texts from Excavations 1) .

Plumley, J.M. (1978). 'New light on the Kingdom of Dotawo' in *Études Nubiennes, Colloque de Chantilly*: 231-241.

Plumley, J.M. and Browne, G.M. (1988). *Old Nubian texts from Qasr Ibrim* I (Egypt Exploration Society Texts from Excavations 9)

Priese, K-H. (1984). 'Orte des mittleren Niltals in der Überlieferung bis zum Ende des Chistlichen Mittelalters' in Hintze, F. (ed.), *Meroitische Forschungen 1980 Meroitica* 7: 484-487.

Ray, J.D. (2005). *Demotic Papyri and Ostraca from Qasr Ibrim* (Egypt Exploration Society Texts from Excavations 13).

Rose, P. (1996) *Qasr Ibrim: The Hinterland Survey* (Egypt Exploration Society Sixty-Second Excavation Memoir).

Rose, P. (2007). *The Meroitic Temple Complex at Qasr Ibrim* (Egypt Exploration Society Eighty-Fourth Excavation Memoir).

Van der Vliet, J. (1999). 'Churches in Lower Nubia, Old and New' in *Bulletin de la Société d'Archéologie Copte* 38: 135-138.

Van der Vliet, J. (forthcoming). *The inscriptions in the tombs at the west front of the Cathedral at Qasr Ibrim.*

Vantini, Fr G. (1975). *Oriental Sources Concerning Nubia.*

Welsby, D.A. (2002). *The Medieval Kingdoms of Nubia: Pagans, Christians and Muslims along the Middle Nile* (British Museum Press).

Wilson, P. (2007). 'The Meroitic temple graffiti' in *Rose 2007*: 105-163.

Zanetti, U. (1995). 'Abu l-Makarim et Abu Salih' in *Bulletin de la Société d'Archéologie Copte* 34 135-138.